Standard Securities

Standard Securities

D J Cusine
Professor, Department of Conveyancing and
Professional Practice of Law, University of Aberdeen

Butterworths/Law Society of Scotland
Edinburgh
1991

Butterworths

United Kingdom	Butterworth & Co (Publishers) Ltd, 88 Kingsway, LONDON WC2B 6AB and 4 Hill Street, EDINBURGH EH2 3JZ
Australia	Butterworths Pty Ltd, SYDNEY, MELBOURNE, BRISBANE, ADELAIDE, PERTH, CANBERRA and HOBART
Canada	Butterworths Canada Ltd, TORONTO and VANCOUVER
Ireland	Butterworths (Ireland) Ltd, DUBLIN
Malaysia	Malayan Law Journal Sdn Bhd, KUALA LUMPUR
New Zealand	Butterworths of New Zealand Ltd, WELLINGTON and AUCKLAND
Puerto Rico	Equity de Puerto Rico, Inc, HATO REY
Singapore	Butterworth & Co (Asia) Pte Ltd, SINGAPORE
USA	Butterworth Legal Publishers, ST PAUL, Minnesota, SEATTLE, Washington, BOSTON, Massachusetts, AUSTIN, Texas and D & S Publishers, CLEARWATER, Florida

Law Society of Scotland
26 Drumsheugh Gardens, Edinburgh EH3 7YR

A CIP Catalogue record for this book is available from the British Library

ISBN 0 406 105871

Typeset by Phoenix Photosetting, Chatham, Kent
Printed by Mackays of Chatham PLC, Chatham, Kent

Preface

There is clearly a view in some government circles that conveyancing is simple or at least that it is not necessary to be legally-trained in order to be able to do it. It will presumably be puzzling for those who hold this view to see that yet another book on conveyancing is being published.

However, even those who have a more informed view may be surprised at the appearance of a book on standard securities, given the existence of Professor Halliday's commentary on the 1970 Act and, more recently, volume III of his excellent *Conveyancing Law and Practice*. It is not the author's intention to supplant either of these books, nor would he be likely to succeed, given the esteem in which Professor Halliday was and is held.

Rather the intention is to produce an introductory text for students and those who are in the early stages of practice. It attempts to set out the law, but introduces practical aspects which are commonly encountered. Given the intended readership, the book concentrates on the domestic transaction, but many of the issues which are dealt with are relevant to other transactions also.

I have benefited greatly from being a member of the Law Society of Scotland's Conveyancing Committee in that many of the practical issues which appear in the text have been raised with the Committee. Many of the members have tolerated questions about practice thinly disguised as casual conversation. To all of them, my thanks.

There are a number of people who deserve particular mention. In the first place, I am grateful to Alistair Rennie of the Keeper's office who kindly drew my attention to a number of problems which had been raised about standard securities. That was for a PQLE course, but he has been extremely helpful since I began writing this book in answering further points.

All of the building societies which have a branch in Scotland, the banks, Guardian Royal Exchange Insurance Company and Aberdeen District Council have given me permission to use their security documentation and I have been able through their kindness to reproduce some security documents in full, as styles. In that connection, I am particularly grateful to Mr C E Jowitt of Halifax Building, Tom Ewing of the Royal Bank of Scotland, Messrs Biggart Baillie & Gifford as agents for Guardian and Mr Towns of the City of Aberdeen District Council.

Last, but by no means least, I should like to mention three others who have made a considerable contribution to the book, viz: Colin Miller, Donald Reid and Robert Rennie. Despite the many other demands on their time, each of them read the text and made valuable suggestions for its improvement which I have been only too pleased to incorporate. I am extremely grateful to them for their help. However, it must be said that, without my help, they would not have managed to write the book. To Butterworths, the publishers, my thanks also. Some others are mentioned in the text.

I have attempted to state the law as at 1 January 1991.

Douglas J Cusine
Aberdeen
January 1991

Contents

Abbreviations

1970 Act	Conveyancing and Feudal Reform (Scotland) Act 1970, and, unless the context indicates otherwise, sections referred to are sections of the 1970 Act.
standard condition	Standard conditions contained in ibid, Sch 3.
Halliday *Commentary*	JM Halliday *The Conveyancing and Feudal Reform (Scotland) Act 1970* (2nd edn, 1977).
Halliday	JM Halliday *Conveyancing Law and Practice in Scotland* (3 vols, 1985, 1986, 1987).

Table of Statutes

References are to paragraph numbers; numbers in square brackets refer to material in the Appendix.

Table of Cases

CHAPTER 1

Introduction

1.01 Background information

Before entering into a loan transaction where the loan is to be secured over heritable property, there is some background information which the client may require, such as sources of finance, methods of repaying loans, the loan and the documentation, taxation, and surveys.

SOURCES OF FINANCE

1.02 General

While many clients will be aware of some sources of finance, the solicitor will frequently be consulted about this matter and he should know where to look for finance for a client. The main sources are (1) building societies; (2) 'high street' banks; (3) secondary banks, finance houses and mortgage corporations; (4) insurance companies; and (5) local authorities. In the following paragraphs, the term 'mortgage' may appear. While this is an English term, it is now commonly used in Scotland to mean a loan secured over heritable property. Purists may have a Canute-like repugnance to its use, but one has to recognise that it is a term used by lenders and borrowers alike and it is well understood.

1.03 Building societies

It is important to note that building societies usually lend only on domestic property and not commercial property and are normally restricted to lending money as a first charge, or a first-ranking security, but, in response to competition from other lenders, some societies are willing to lend on non-domestic property.

Building societies at one time had almost the whole of the mortgage market, but their position has been challenged, principally by the 'high street' banks. In 1986, the operation of building societies saw some far-reaching changes in the shape of the Building Societies Act 1986, much of which came into force on 1 January 1987. From that date, loans from these societies are either house finance loans or personal loans. House finance loans are the traditional mortgages by another name, and the other loans are what the 1986 Act calls regulated lending, where the loan does not exceed £15,000 and it is governed by the Consumer Credit Act 1974 as amended by the 1986 Act. For present purposes, the most important type of regulated loan is one used for re-mortgaging heritable property.

1.04 'High street' banks

At one time, banks usually lent only on an overdraft basis, sometimes to individuals, but more often to businesses. More recently, they have challenged the building societies in providing mortgages over domestic property and, of course, they also lend on commercial property. While building societies used to consider people for loans only if they were savers with them, they and the banks will now consider applications from the general public. While banks did not use to lend the same percentage of loan as building societies, this is also changing. Unlike building societies, banks will lend on a first charge, or postponed-charge basis.

1.05 Secondary banks; finance houses and mortgage corporations

Until relatively recently, secondary banks and finance houses were not involved in the mortgage market, but that is changing, and they and mortgage corporations are now offering loans on a basis which compares favourably with building societies and banks. They may also lend the additional amount required by the borrower where the principal lender is restricting the percentage of loan being offered. The additional loan or 'top up' from the secondary bank, finance house or mortgage corporation will be secured by way of a second charge.

1.06 Insurance companies

Although insurance companies will offer mortgages, they will normally be on an endowment basis. They were involved traditionally, and still are involved in providing a guarantee to the primary lender for the 'top-up' finance, for example, the 15 per cent above the initial 80 per cent being offered by a building society and that additional 15 per cent would be secured by an insurance policy, very often a single premium policy. The primary lender lends the full 95 per cent.

1.07 Local authorities

Under the Housing (Scotland) Act 1987, local authorities (district councils) will lend on heritable property and they will also lend money for improvements and repairs. Loan finance for initial purchases is usually on properties at the lower end of the market where neither a building society nor a bank is willing to lend. Because of budget restrictions, it is essential to check in advance that funds are available for lending. Local authorities will also lend to their tenants who wish to purchase their council houses.

1.08 Home loan scheme

This scheme, which was introduced in 1979, was designed to assist in the purchase of houses at the lower end of the market. The benefits of the scheme are that the borrower obtains a cash bonus of £110 and a loan of £600 which is usually added to the mortgage.

METHODS OF REPAYING THE LOAN

1.09 General

There are four methods for repaying loans: (1) capital and interest; (2) endowment; (3) pensions; and (4) unit trusts and personal equity plans (PEP).

1.10 Capital and interest

The capital and interest method of repayment is where there is neither an endowment policy, nor a pension plan, and, in essence, the monthly repayments go in part to repay capital and, in part, to repay the interest. Initially, the monthly payment will be applied more in payment of the interest than reduction of the capital, but the balance moves gradually as the repayment date approaches. It is advisable, where the loan is being repaid by this method, for the client to take out a mortgage protection policy, so that in the event of death, incapacity or redundancy, the loan will be repaid, or the instalments due during any period of incapacity or redundancy, will be paid.

1.11 Endowment

In the case of an endowment loan, the loan is linked with an endowment policy which is, or should be, assigned to the lender[1]. The borrower pays only the interest on the loan to the lender, because the capital sum is secured by the endowment policy. His monthly payments will therefore consist of the interest payable to the lender and the premium on the policy which is paid to the insurance company. When the loan period comes to an end, or on the earlier death of the borrower, the policy matures and the capital sum is repaid from the proceeds of the policy. In addition, there may be a profit on the policy which is paid to the borrower or forms part of his estate.

There are low-cost endowment policies which still secure the loan, but the profit at maturity, or on death, will not be as great as that under a 'full' endowment policy.

It is worth pointing out to a potential borrower that any endowment insurance may not live up to initial expectations. If in the end of the day, the proceeds of the policy prove insufficient the balance will be payable by the borrower or his executors.

1 Not all lenders require the policy to be assigned. For the implications of this, see para 2.07 below.

1.12 Pension plan

The pension plan method of repaying a mortgage is available to the self-employed, and to those who are not in pensionable employment[1]. It should be noted that a pension cannot be assigned and so the lender will require another life insurance policy which will be assigned in security, and the borrower will be asked to give an undertaking to use the proceeds of the pension plan to repay the loan. Some pension plans have 'built in' life cover.

1 for further details, see *Halliday* vol IV, para 54–153, 54–154.

1.13 Unit trusts and personal equity plans[1]

Instead of paying the loan directly to the lender, the borrower invests in either unit trusts, or a personal equity plan (PEP). As with the endowment method, the borrower pays interest to the lender and a monthly premium into a Personal Equity Plan or Unit Trust in the hope that the investment performance over the period of the loan will be such that the outstanding amount will be repaid. These methods of repaying loans currently enjoy the tax advantage that neither income nor capital growth is subject to income or capital gains tax respectively. While they are, at present, attractive for this reason, the tax regime may change but whether it does or not, investments in stocks and shares can be risky and the borrower should be advised to consider some additional investment to protect him against a possible shortfall.

1 I am grateful to Russell McIntyre, Financial Products Manager, Messrs Morton, Fraser and Milligan for his assistance.

THE LOAN AND THE LOAN DOCUMENTATION

1.14   The amount of the loan

Although the figure to be lent will be decided by the lender, it is usual to discuss the client's earnings and other income and his outlays, so that the solicitor can give the client some idea of the size of the loan which he might expect. The client should disclose all sources of income and earnings, as well as major outlays, eg hire purchase on a car. In many cases, the lender will give the solicitor a 'verbal', ie an indication over the telephone of the amount which the client will be given as a loan. In many cases, this is the only information which the solicitor will have before submitting an offer.

The amount which the borrower may borrow will depend on two factors: (1) the valuation of the property and (2) his income and other earnings. The maximum loan which the borrower may normally expect to receive will be 95 per cent of the valuation or a multiple of his earnings, whichever is the lesser figure. (Where mortgage funds are plentiful, 100 per cent mortgages are not uncommon.) Take the following example. A borrower wishes to purchase a house at £62,000 and it is valued at £60,000. The lender will give him a loan amounting to 2.5 times his salary of £28,000. The top amount which the borrower will receive is 95 per cent of the valuation, ie £57,000. His salary would justify a larger loan, up to £70,000, but the property is not valued at that figure. If the borrower's salary was £20,000, he would receive a maximum loan of £50,000 because that is the maximum amount based on his salary, even though the valuation is higher. In the normal case, therefore, the borrower will have to find the difference between the amount of the loan and the purchase price. In the first instance mentioned above, that would be £5,000, whereas in the second, it would be £12,000. If the borrower in the second instance is selling a house to finance the purchase of a new house, the differential may not be a problem. The situation might be quite different for a first-time buyer.

1.15 Deductions from the loan amount

The foregoing examples are an over-simplification in that there will be some deductions from the advance. The following will appear in the offer of loan/advance. There may be a premium to be paid on an insurance guarantee. Where building societies lend up to 95 per cent of the valuation, the excess above 80 per cent will be guaranteed by an insurance policy and the borrower pays a single premium in respect of that additional 15 per cent. If the lender is also insuring the property, there may be a deduction for the initial premium. Other possible deductions are the valuer's fee and where there is a retention, eg for repairs, or unfinished work that will be deducted also. It is always useful to draw the borrower's attention not only to the difference between the loan (less the deductions set out in the offer) and the purchase price, but additional outlays which will be involved in a house purchase, for example stamp duty if the price is above £30,000, the solicitor's fees and outlays, survey fees and the general costs involved in moving into a new house, for example re-decoration. (Only when the furniture has been removed, may the need for complete re-decoration become obvious and strategically-placed furniture may cover a multitude of sins).

1.16 Information for the solicitor

The client will receive the loan documentation at a later stage, not infrequently after there is a binding contract. The solicitor will also receive a copy with instructions to act for the lenders. That documentation will set out the amount of the loan, the period for repayment, the current interest rate, the address of the property over which the loan is being made, and any special conditions which have to be observed. Special conditions may include a retention, which might be made, for example, where major repairs or renovations have to be undertaken, or where the house is new and the roads have to be made up to local authority standard. Retentions in respect of roads are less common because builders are required to have road bonds to cover such works. It may be that there is no retention, but the borrower may be required, for example, to paint the exterior of the building. While many of the matters in the loan documentation are the responsibility of the borrower, they will be dealt with by the solicitor and hence are considered in chapter 2 below.

1.17 Percentage loans/top-ups

Under the Building Societies Act 1986, a society cannot lend more than 80 per cent of the valuation without additional security[1]. If a client wishes a 95 per cent loan, which is the maximum normally considered by building societies, the additional amount above the 80 per cent will usually be covered by an insurance company guarantee and the society usually takes out a single premium and deducts the premium from the initial advance. The additional amount may also be secured over another property, or over funds in the building society, or by assignation of stocks and shares, but the insurance method is by far the most common. The borrower will receive from the building society a Form 1 which will set out the amount of the initial advance and the amount of the excess together with particulars of the security for that excess. Before the loan cheque is released, the borrower must sign a duplicate Form 1 and return it to the society.

While it is still possible to obtain a 100 per cent mortgage, such a mortgage is not without its dangers. Many people purchased new houses from builders with 100 per cent mortgages where the purchase price included extras, such as a cooker, a refrigerator, washing machine, etc. When the purchaser came to sell, it was sometimes found that the valuation and, often too, the sale price was less than the original price, because the extras which had been included in the original price were worth very little on resale. Even if they were not going to be removed by the seller, the price of the house itself might be less. Sellers were therefore left with mortgages which were higher than the valuations and possibly higher than the selling prices.

1 Building Societies Act 1986, s 13.

1.18 Income tax

Interest which is payable on any sum borrowed will be an allowable deduction for income tax purposes if it is borrowed to finance the purchase of certain types of land or buildings. It will also be deductible if the money is borrowed to replace the loan which financed the original purchase. The land or buildings must be (1) used (or used within 12 months) as the only or main residence of the borrower, or a dependent relative, or a former or a separated spouse; or (2) let at a commercial rent for more than 26 weeks out of any period of 52 weeks, or available for letting, or used as indicated above at head (1). At present, the maximum amount of loan on which relief is allowable is £30,000[1].

1 Finance Act 1972, s 75, Sch 9 (amended by the Finance Act 1974, s 19, Sch 1, and the Finance Act 1985, s 37(1)).

1.19 The Mortgage Interest Relief at Source Scheme (MIRAS)

Under this scheme, the interest payable is under deduction of tax under the MIRAS (Mortgage Interest Relief at Source) Scheme. Thus, the borrower pays the monthly repayment figure under deduction of the tax relief which he is able to claim. The MIRAS Scheme is normally used only for loans of £30,000 or under, but loans in excess of £30,000 are sometimes dealt with under the MIRAS Scheme for the qualifying part (ie £30,000).

SURVEYS

1.20 General

It is outwith the scope of this book to deal in detail with the types of surveys which are available, or with the advantages and disadvantages and the legal implications arising, and what follows is a basic guide for the person advising an intending borrower/purchaser[1]. All institutional lenders will require a valuation of the property in almost every case. Others who may be contemplating lending on heritable property, for example trustees, should obtain a valuation also[2]. A lender will be concerned only with whether the value of the property is sufficient to justify the level of loan being sought. That is specifically provided for in the Building Societies Act 1986[3].

1 For further details, see Carolyn Slater 'House Valuations and Surveys' (1988) 33 JLSS 89.
2 See the Trusts (Scotland) Act 1921, s 30.
3 Building Societies Act 1986, s 13.

1.21 Types of survey

There are basically three types of survey which the potential borrower can have carried out, apart from various specialist surveys. These are (1) a mortgage valuation; (2) a house buyer's report; and (3) a full structural survey. Apart from surveys carried out by specialists, the surveyor will usually be a chartered surveyor and a member of the Royal Institution of Chartered Surveyors.

1.22 Mortgage valuation

The mortgage valuation type of 'survey' is the most common and it will be carried out by the surveyor, not on the instructions of the borrower, but on the instructions of the lender. The borrower, therefore, is not in a direct contractual relationship with the surveyor. However, a copy of the report will usually be supplied to the borrower, but perhaps only if he is subsequently offered and accepts a loan from that lender. The purpose of the report is to advise the lender on whether the valuation of the property is sufficiently high to justify the amount of loan which the borrower wishes.

That does not mean that the surveyor will not draw attention to defects, but the defects which he mentions will be those which are obvious and he will not inspect roof spaces or under floor boards, or any other part of the property to which access is not easily obtained. Furthermore, none of the services of water, gas or electricity will be checked or tested, and only if they are clearly defective or outmoded will the surveyor make a comment to that effect.

The surveyor may, in the light of obvious defects, suggest a retention, but the amount of the retention will be based on his estimate of the cost of any remedial work and it cannot be taken as a guarantee that the remedial work will not cost more than the amount retained. All of these factors should be drawn to the attention of the borrower and the solicitor should attempt to make clear to the client the limited protection which this type of valuation provides. When a property is older, or obviously in a deteriorated condition, the solicitor should consider recommending a house buyer's report.

1.23 House buyer's report

This is a survey which can either be instructed by the borrower direct or through the lending institution where there is a direct contractual relationship with the surveyor. If the borrower instructs the surveyor direct, he can ask the surveyor to look for particular problems, or give advice about matters which may have concerned the borrower on his inspection of the property. When the borrower is considering instructing a survey of this kind, he should, if possible, use a surveyor who is on the lender's panel of approved surveyors. That will usually result in a slight reduction in the cost of the combined survey fees, because the lender will still require a valuation. The major building societies also offer this type of survey and so that saves the borrower having to pay for both a valuation for the building society and a private survey.

The house buyer's report is usually a pre-printed form with questions and unless he is asked to do something else, the surveyor is required to answer only the questions on the form. The survey is a more detailed one than the mortgage valuation, but again, the surveyor will not inspect those parts of the property to which access is not readily obtained. He will, however, comment on the services, but will not test them. Any exclusion clauses in the loan application form which deal with the surveyor's liability should be considered.

1.24 Full structural survey

As its title suggests, this is a survey which looks at the structural condition of the property, and it will be carried out only on the specific instructions of the borrower. It will also usually follow an initial report by the surveyor where he has noticed something, for example settlement or subsidence, which, in his opinion, requires further investigation. The cost involved can be fairly high, because if there is doubt about the structure, inspection pits may have to be dug and 'tracers' inserted in cracks, etc. It would therefore only be in exceptional circumstances that this form of survey would be recommended.

1.25 Specialist reports

If, in the course of any of the above types of survey, the surveyor notices a defect (usually dry rot, wet rot, rising damp or woodworm) he may recommend a report from a specialist. Most older houses have woodworm and so it may be in the interests of the borrower to have such a survey carried out in any event. The specialist survey is usually free, but obviously the hope is that the borrower will instruct the specialist to carry out any remedial work. As remedial work can be expensive, especially where dry rot is discovered, it is wise to obtain at least two estimates of the cost of repairs. The remedial work normally carries a guarantee of 25 years or more, backed by an insurance company and the benefit of that guarantee can be transmitted to any subsequent purchaser without either a charge or a formal assignation. Some firms may request a fee for giving consent to the transmission of the guarantee to the purchaser.

Although timber specialists are the ones most commonly encountered, there are other specialists whose services may be required. These include specialists on water supplies and drainage (often required for rural properties), electrical wiring and gas appliances.

The quality of any guarantee which is to be given is only as good as the body granting it. Many such guarantees are backed by reputable insurance companies; in some cases, no such insurance backing exists.

CHAPTER 2

The role of the solicitor

2.01 General

The object of this chapter is to consider the parties for whom the solicitor may act and explain what he will do in a typical security transaction.

2.02 The parties for whom he acts

The solicitor may be involved in the security transaction in a number of different capacities. He may act as agent for the lender, or as agent for the borrower, or as agent for both. In many transactions, the borrower will be borrowing in order to finance a purchase and the solicitor can, and usually does, act for both him and the lender, provided that does not infringe the Solicitors (Scotland) Practice Rules 1986 on conflict of interest. The Rules recognise an exception to the general prohibition against acting in a situation where there is a conflict[1]. Rule 5(f) permits a solicitor to act for both the lender and the borrower if the loan arrangements have been agreed between the parties prior to the solicitor receiving instructions to act for the lender and the standard security is doing no more than giving effect to that agreement. In many instances, particularly in a domestic transaction, there will not be a conflict, but the general prohibition in rule 3 should be borne in mind because there are circumstances where a conflict does arise. It may be, for example, that the security subjects have been altered or extended, in contravention of a condition in the titles. The borrower may be willing to accept that (and run the risk of an action of irritancy), but the solicitor should draw attention to this in his report on title to the lender. If the lender is not prepared to accept the position, the solicitor would then have to sort the problem out at the expense of the borrower. However, if the borrower was not willing to incur the expense of that remedial work or cannot force the seller to do so, there would be a conflict of interest and the solicitor should cease to act for at least one of the parties, and preferably for both. Conflicts may be dealt with expressly in the lending institutions' instructions. Likewise, a solicitor cannot act for both the lender and the borrower if the security is being called up.

1 Solicitors (Scotland) Practice Rules 1986, r 3.

2.03   Finance

The solicitor may be consulted by the client/borrower before he approaches anyone for finance, or he may be asked to comment on a loan package which has already been arranged. (The source of finance and the methods of repayment of a loan are dealt with in chapter 1 above). The solicitor is obliged to give the client independent advice. Many of the building societies and banks are associated with insurance companies and, of course, earn considerable commissions on the insurance policies which they arrange. The solicitor should advise the client whether there is any need for an endowment policy, or whether a mortgage protection policy would suffice. It may be that the client has an existing policy and merely wants a 'top-up', for example, to build an extension on to his existing house. It is not unknown for a lending institution to try to persuade the borrower in such a case to encash his existing policy and take out another one for the total of the new borrowing. This process, known as 'churning', may not be in the client's best interests and the solicitor has an obligation to advise the client whether it is appropriate to cash-in the existing policy. It is almost certain that the client will lose out if there is an early surrender of the existing policy.

Some organisations which are involved in selling properties obviously earn commission from any policy arranged for a purchaser. It is not unknown for there to be pressure to ensure that a potential purchaser will not be successful unless he take out an insurance policy with the insurance company of the selling agent's choice. This type of conduct is unfair to both the seller and other potential purchasers. While it is easy enough to condemn it, it is more difficult to stop it happening. Nevertheless, the solicitor should draw this type of 'hidden agenda' to the attention of the borrower.

These are only a very basic points about the solicitor's role, but the need to give independent financial and legal advice cannot be overestimated.

2.04   A typical transaction

The most common transaction is a purchase coupled with a security where the solicitor is instructed to act for both the purchaser/borrower and the lender. That is the model used here to explain what the solicitor must do between the conclusion of missives and settlement, and after settlement[1]. Where the loan is linked with the purchase, it is necessary to ensure that the steps in the purchase transaction dovetail with those in the security transaction, particularly in connection with the date of entry and settlement. It will be essential to ensure that the date of entry and settlement is far enough ahead to ensure that the titles can be examined, a report given to the lender along with a request for the loan cheque and that the loan cheque will arrive slightly in advance of the settlement date. If it comes too early, it may have to be returned: if it comes too late, the borrower will have to find temporary funding for the purchase price. If the loan cheque comes early and the solicitor, contrary to his instructions, cashes it, the first monthly payment will be payable sooner than is necessary. That date may in some cases be one month after encashment of the loan cheque, but many institutions insist on monthly payments in advance.

All these matters have to be borne in mind in fixing the date of entry at the missives' stage. While the solicitor's convenience should not dictate the date of entry, the borrower has to be made aware of the dangers of fixing an entry date which is too close to the date of possible conclusion of the missives. If a realistic date is fixed, bearing in mind examination of title, preparation and revising of drafts etc, that should be sufficient to allow the loan documents to be prepared and the loan cheque requested. These documents should be prepared and ready for signature and signed before the loan cheque arrives. The loan cheque should never be encashed *before* the standard security is signed by the borrower.

1 For further details, see A McDonald *Conveyancing Manual* (4th edn) ch 34.

2.05 Between missives and settlement

The solicitor must obviously examine the title to ensure that the purchaser/borrower has a valid marketable title in respect of which he can grant a valid security in favour of the lender. He must also ensure that any special conditions in the lender's instructions can be complied with.

The solicitor will also draft and thereafter engross the standard security and any supporting documentation. For example, in a Form B standard security, there will be a personal bond or other similar document which contains the personal obligation. In more complicated transactions, for example a brewer's loan, there may be a standard security, a minute of agreement and also a pre-emption agreement. The Matrimonial Homes (Family Protection) (Scotland) Act 1981 with its requirement of consent affidavits, etc may have to be considered and an assignation of a life policy may be required.

2.06 Matrimonial Homes (Family Protection) (Scotland) Act 1981 Documentation

An affidavit, or consent, or renunciation under the Matrimonial Homes (Family Protection) (Scotland) Act 1981 will be required in the majority of cases, unless the title is in the 'joint' names of husband and wife. These documents should be prepared and ready for signature before the loan cheque arrives. It is not always possible to achieve this, but it is a desirable target. However, in terms of the 1981 Act in its amended form, the documentation prior to 1 January 1991 had to be produced *at or before* the granting of the security and that is the date of delivery of the deed[1]. If the solicitor is acting for both the lender and the borrower, there will not be any 'delivery', but good practice suggests that the documentation should be signed at the same time as the standard security, if not before it. If different solicitors are acting for the borrower and the lender, the lender's solicitors will wish to ensure that any documentation which is signed by the borrower under the 1981 Act is signed at or before the date of delivery of the standard security. Any affidavit, or renunciation which post-dates the date of delivery, and *a fortiori* one which post-dates the date of recording, does not comply with the 1981 Act. In a registered transaction where the loan is being called up, the Keeper will ask to see the documentation under the Act. That is when the non-statutory (or non-existent) affidavits, etc are discovered. The best practice is to comply with the Act and what the Keeper requires for land registration purposes so that any affidavits, etc given in a Sasine transaction will not be rejected when land registration comes along.

With effect from 1 January 1991 the 1981 Act has been amended by the Law Reform (Miscellaneous Provisions) (Scotland) Act 1990, Schedule 8, paragraph 31. The 1990 Act deletes the words 'at or before the time of the dealing' in section 6 and the words 'before the granting of the loan' in section 8. The effect of these changes are that the seller need no longer produce the affidavit at or before the time of dealing and may produce one after the dealing to the effect that the subjects were not at the time of the dealing a matrimonial home. Similarly where the interest of heritable creditors is concerned the affidavit need not be produced at or before the time of the granting of the security but may be produced afterwards and may be to the effect that a spouse of the granter has not, or had not, at the time of the granting of the security occupancy rights in the subjects. These changes apply also to renunciations.

---

1 Matrimonial Homes (Family Protection) (Scotland) Act 1981, s 8(2A).

2.07 Life policies

In many cases, the loan will be coupled with an endowment policy which may have to be assigned to the lender. In Scots law, the only valid method of creating a security over a life policy is by assignation followed by intimation to the insurance company. Despite that, many building societies require only notification that the policy exists and that it is related to the loan transaction. (That is all that is required under English law to complete what is called an equitable mortgage.) The Law Society of Scotland, through its Conveyancing Committee, has drawn the dangers of this practice to the attention of the Building Societies Association, but they seem to be prepared to take the risk. The risk which they face arises on the death or bankruptcy of the borrower prior to maturity of the loan and hence the policy. Without going into detail, the position there is that proceeds of the policy form part of the deceased's estate and are not automatically available to pay off the loan as they would have been had the policy been properly assigned. If for any reason, the proceeds of sale of the secured property are insufficient and there is insufficient in the estate to pay off the loan, the problems could be considerable. Similar problems could arise on bankruptcy. Some building societies have, however, been persuaded to revert to the use of assignations.

If the policy is to be assigned, the solicitor will draft and thereafter engross the assignation which should be signed along with the standard security. The assignation has to be intimated to the insurance company and that is best done by a letter of intimation in duplicate (both copies on the firm's notepaper or on forms provided by the lender) and the insurance company will be asked to acknowledge the intimation on the duplicate and return it to the solicitor. The following would serve the purpose:

The Uberrimae Fidei Insurance Company
Celestial House,
Wester Hailes Road,
Edinburgh.

Dear Sirs,

James Dalrymple: Policy No ABC 123 456 789
Failsafe Building Society

Please note that by assignation dated . . ., James Dalrymple, Author, residing 21 Erskine Street, Glasgow assigned to the Failsafe Building Society, Utopia Street, Glengarnock, Policy No ABC 123 456 789 on his life dated . . . We enclose a duplicate of this letter and should be obliged if you would acknowledge this intimation on the duplicate and return it to us as soon as possible.

Not all insurance companies will return the notice of intimation and so the solicitor should keep the evidence of intimation.

2.08 Report on title and request for advances

In addition to the conditions of the offer of loan which were mentioned in chapter 1, there are others which will be dealt with by the solicitor rather than the borrower. The solicitor will be required to certify to the lender that these conditions have been fulfilled, and this is done when he makes his report on the title and applies for the loan cheque.

These conditions include the following:

(1) that the borrower has a good and marketable title to the property;
(2) that the description of the property in the titles is in substantial conformity with that contained in the lender's instructions;
(3) that there are no other securities;
(4) that clear searches in the Property and Personal Registers will be exhibited at settlement, or, in the case of a transaction in an area subject to registration, a clear Form 10/11/12 report;
(5) that the borrower has or will be given vacant possession of the subjects;
(6) that there are no occupancy rights under the Matrimonial Homes (Family Protection) (Scotland) Act 1981;
(7) that any insurance policies [to be assigned] are in order [and will be assigned to the lender];

(8) that any allocated feu duty has been redeemed and that the redemption receipt will be put with the titles;

(9) that any cumulo feu duty is adequately secured;

(10) that the use of the property is permanent and conforms with the local authority development plans;

(11) that all consents to any developments to, or changes in, the property have been properly obtained and are in force;

(12) that there is no potential liability for road charges or that a road bond exists as security for such charges; and

(13) in the case of new properties, that the relevant warranties under the National House Builders Council (NHBC) Scheme are in operation, or there is some other form of warranty, such as a Certificate of Supervision from an architect.

2.09 Verb sap[1]

As has been said, some instructions to solicitors and reports on title expect more of the solicitor than what has just been described. For example, there are some lenders who wish the solicitor to give warranties which may be founded upon by someone lending to the lender or someone who may acquire the lender's rights in the standard security (a process known as 'securitisation') and the solicitor may be asked to warrant that the security is in order and that he owes a duty of care not only to the lender, but to the lender's successors. Any solicitor who contemplates signing a report on title to this effect should give the matter careful consideration, if he has not deleted the relevant part of the report.

The solicitor may also be asked to undertake to return the loan cheque if settlement of the transaction does not take place within 24 hours of the completion date, but he may be required to do this by telegraphic transfer and pay interest. He may be asked to record the deeds within two days of the date of completion of the transaction (for example Equity and Law Home Loans Limited). Quite how the latter is to be achieved particularly in a place (ie everywhere, except Edinburgh) with no local stamp office is not explained.

1 *Verbum sapienti sat est*—a word to the wise is enough.

2.10 Settlement and the aftermath

In terms of his instructions, the solicitor will not be able to encash the loan cheque unless he receives a valid disposition in favour of the purchaser/borrower. It is not therefore permissible to use the loan cheque to make payment of the purchase price, or a payment to account, nor to use it to put the purchase price on deposit receipt unless a signed deed is given in exchange. If the transaction is not to be finally settled, but is to be dealt with in this way, the purchaser will have to borrow other temporary funds (usually in the form of an overdraft from his bank) to pay the price, or the deposit and the loan cheque can be encashed only when the transaction is settled finally, ie the disposition is delivered. This is not recommended.

After settlement, the solicitor should immediately record (register) the disposition in favour of the purchaser/borrower or where appropriate record (register) it after it has been stamped. It is possible to send the deeds to the Stamp Office with the instructions to the Keeper and ask the Stamp Office to send them on to the Keeper after stamping. Some solicitors like to see that the deeds have been properly stamped and so will ask for their return and send the documents to the Keeper thereafter. The solicitor should also record/register the standard security at the same time, thus saving on recording/registration dues. If the selling solicitor delivers the executed discharge of his client's standard security, that should also be sent for recording (registration).

The solicitor acting for the borrower should also advise the lender of the date on which the loan cheque was encashed. Usually a form is provided for this. This allows the solicitor to advise the borrower of the date on which the first monthly instalment of the loan repayment will be due. Some lenders will require him to send any deeds delivered at settlement, any insurance policies which have been assigned, and any other relevant documents, for example the personal bond, or documentation under the Matrimonial Homes (Family Protection) (Scotland) Act 1981, feu duty redemption receipt, etc. In a Sasine transaction once the deeds are returned from the Registers, these should also be sent to the lender along with the search if that is to be delivered. Other lenders ask the solicitor to send all the documentation when the deeds are returned from the Registers. The solicitor will have aged a bit by then! In a land registration transaction, land and charge certificates are issued and these should be sent to the lender.

CHAPTER 3

The introduction of the standard security

3.01 General

Until the coming into force of the Conveyancing and Feudal Reform (Scotland) Act 1970, there were two main way of securing a loan over heritable property. One was the bond and disposition in security (sometimes in the form of a cash credit bond and disposition in security), while the other was the *ex facie* absolute disposition, with related qualifying documentation which was not usually recorded.

3.02 The bond and disposition in security

This was used as early as the seventeenth century and as its name suggests, the deed was *ex facie* a security deed. In the mid-nineteenth century, the bond and disposition in security was regulated by statute and these statutory provisions resulted in a loss of flexibility. There were detailed provisions, particularly in relation to enforcement, all of which had the laudable aim of protecting the debtor. Although initially, the bond and disposition in security could not be used to secure future advances, nor fluctuating advances, legislative changes, in the form of the Debts Securities (Scotland) Act 1856, made these possible. By that time, however, the *ex facie* absolute disposition had been introduced. It was not a creature of statute, but rather a device whereby lawyers acting for creditors could get round the strictures of the bond and disposition in security.

3.03 The *ex facie* absolute disposition

As the name indicates, this deed was not *ex facie* a security deed, but a disposition in favour of the creditor. The true nature of the transaction would be disclosed only by the separate documentation, in the form of a personal bond, back letter or minute of agreement. That separate documentation was rarely recorded and so, on the face of the record, the creditor was the proprietor. This could lead to abuse, and because of the bargaining position of the parties, the creditor was virtually unfettered in the terms which he was able to dictate. The enforcement procedures were not regulated by statute and the only guiding principle was that the creditor could not exercise his rights unreasonably, for example when he came to sell the security subjects on the debtor's default. For example, he had to obtain the best price which was reasonable in the circumstances. There were difficulties with postponed securities and completion of title on death where the debtor was not originally infeft. Furthermore, the discharge of the loan had to take the form of a reconveyance which was a lengthy disposition by the lender to the debtor.

3.04 Proposed reform

Because of the lack of flexibility in the bond and disposition in security on the one hand, and the fact that the *ex facie* absolute disposition was heavily slanted in favour of the creditor, a committee was set up in 1966 under the chairmanship of Professor Halliday to review the law and that committee proposed the introduction of a new form of security and it was that which was introduced in the Conveyancing and Feudal Reform (Scotland) Act 1970[1].

1 *Conveyancing Legislation and Practice* (1966) (Cmnd 3118).

3.05 The Conveyancing and Feudal Reform (Scotland) Act 1970

After the 1970 Act, bonds and dispositions in security and *ex facie* absolute dispositions could not be used to create a security. There were limited exceptions but these were and are of little practical consequence. These two forms of security are therefore virtually obsolete[1], but it is not uncommon to encounter them when they are redeemed, or have to be enforced. All new loans are, however, secured by the standard security, the topic of the remainder of this book.

1 For details of the pre-1970 securities, see Halliday *Commentary* ch 5; *Halliday* vol III, chs 33, 34; A McDonald *Conveyancing Manual* (4th edn) ch 21; W M Gordon *Scottish Land law* paras 20-03–20-102.

CHAPTER 4

Constitution and form

4.01 Introduction

Section 9 of the 1970 Act provides that, from 29 November 1970, the only valid method of creating a heritable security over an interest in land for securing a debt is by a standard security. Until the passing of the Tenants' Rights Etc (Scotland) Act 1980, the previous forms of security could still be used for heritable securities under the Small Dwellings Acquisition (Scotland) Acts 1899–1923. There is still one exception, which for all practical purposes can be ignored, and that is an entailed estate[1]. A heritable security over an entailed estate would have to be in the form on a bond and disposition in security or an *ex facie* absolute disposition. However, it has not been competent to create an entail since 1914 and if you come across an entailed estate, don't phone me, I'll phone you.

1 1970 Act, s 9(8)(b); App [8].

DEFINITIONS

4.02 General

Two of the terms which have been used above require explanation. The standard security is over an 'interest in land' and secures a 'debt'.

4.03 'Interest in land'

This term appears not only in the 1970 Act, but also in the Prescription and Limitation (Scotland) Act 1973, in the Land Registration (Scotland) Act 1979 and in the Requirements of Writing, Etc (Scotland) Bill. The definitions are not identical, but only the 1970 and 1979 Acts are relevant to determine what is an 'interest in land' for the purposes of a standard security. In the 1970 Act, an 'interest in land' means any estate or interest in land, other than an entailed estate, or any estate therein which is capable of being owned or held as a separate interest and to which a title may be recorded in the Register of Sasines[1]. It is clear, therefore, that only something which is capable of being so recorded can be an interest in land. The 1979 Act[2] requires a heritable security over an interest in land to be registered and the definition in that Act of an interest in land is virtually identical to that in the 1970 Act except that in the definition in the 1979 Act, an 'interest in land' means any 'estate, interest, servitude or other heritable right in or over land, including a heritable security but excluding a lease which is not a long lease'[3]. An interest in land therefore includes ownership of land held on feudal tenure, whether it is a superiority interest or an interest in the *dominium utile*, or both. It may, however, be a lesser right such as servitude or a lease, but, in each case, the servitude or lease must be recordable or registrable. It is unlikely that a standard security would be granted over the servitude right itself; it is more likely to be granted over the dominant tenement, one of the features of which would be the servitude. If a standard security has been granted over the *dominium utile* and the owner then acquires the superiority the standard security continues to attach to the *dominium utile* and would attach to the *dominium plenum* only if there was consolidation. If there was consolidation there would be no need to create a new standard security over the *dominium plenum*. If there was no consolidation, the standard security would remain effective over the *dominium utile*. If, however, the person owns the superiority over which there is a standard security and subsequently acquires the *dominium utile*, the standard security still attaches only to the superiority interest. It would attach to the *dominium utile* only if the estates were consolidated. If they were not consolidated, the heritable creditor could not demand a standard security over the *dominium utile* as well, but it would obviously be desirable to have such a security since the *dominium utile* would probably be more valuable than the superiority. A standard security itself is also an interest in land and so a standard security could be created over a standard security. Standard securities by companies, over leases, under the Consumer Credit Act 1974, and discount standard securities are dealt with in chapter 11 below.

1 1970 Act, s 9(8)(b); App [8].
2 Land Registration (Scotland) Act 1979, s 2(3).
3 Ibid, s 28(1).

4.04   'Debt'

The term 'debt' is defined in the 1970 Act as meaning 'any obligation due, or which will or may become due, to repay or pay money, including any such obligation arising from a transaction or part of a transaction in the course of any trade, business or profession and any obligation to pay an annuity or *ad factum praestandum*'[1]. The definition, however, specifically excludes 'an obligation to pay any feuduty, ground annual, rent or other periodical sum, payable in respect of land'[1]. Several points are worth noting about the definition. In the first place, the 'debt' need not be a debt of the granter(s) of the security. A, could therefore grant a security over his property in respect of a debt due by B. In the usual case, of course, it will be a debt due by the granter which is secured. The words 'due, or which will or may become due' clearly cover both future advances and fluctuating advances. The words 'transaction or part of a transaction in the course of any trade' etc are perhaps less obvious, but these are intended to deal with securities in respect of fluctuating sums in a current trading account such as may be operated by a business. If the business obtains overdraft facilities, the account may at times be in credit and at other times in debit. The words 'obligation to pay an annuity' clearly cover annual payments and it would appear that it is no longer competent to secure an annuity by way of reservation in a disposition. The last point is that the definition covers an obligation *ad factum praestandum*. This would not commonly be thought of as a 'debt' but such an obligation is capable of being secured by a standard security. Standard securities for obligations *ad factum praestandum* and nothing else are to my knowledge rare, but are nevertheless competent. The following is an example. A company acquires ground from a local authority in exchange for other ground owned by the company on condition that the company constructs a car park on the ground owned by it. It is suggested that the obligation to construct the car park could be secured by the grant of a standard security over the property which the company is acquiring. While a security could be granted at common law in respect of an obligation *ad factum praestandum*[2], it is not clear, should there be default, how the proceeds of the sale of the property are to be applied by the creditor in satisfaction of the obligation which has been breached. George Gretton speculates that they may be considered as damages in respect of the failure to perform[3], and it is difficult to see what else they could be. In many commercial transactions, the debtor will undertake a variety of obligations, some of which will consist of paying money, while others will be obligations *ad factum praestandum*.

1 1970 Act, s 9(8)(c); App [8].
2 *Edmonstone v Seton* (1888) 16 R 1.
3 'The Concept of a Security' in *A Scots Conveyancing Miscellany: Essays in Honour of Professor J M Halliday* at p 129.

THE PARTIES

4.05 Creditor, debtor

A standard security secures a debt and the 1970 Act provides that the terms 'creditor' and 'debtor' are to be construed by reference to the definition of 'debt'[1]. The original parties to the standard security would be the granter (debtor) and the grantee (creditor). However, the terms 'debtor' and 'creditor' also include successors in title, assignees and representatives, for example executors.

1 1970 Act s 9(8)(c); App [8].

4.06 Debtor, proprietor

The granter of a standard security will normally be infeft and will frequently become infeft at the same time as he grants the standard security. The debtor in the standard security will, in most instances, also be the proprietor of the subjects. In the common case, where the purchaser of a property grants a standard security in respect of his loan, the proprietor is also the debtor. However, the proprietor may be someone other than the debtor and the distinction can be seen clearly in many purchases of local authority houses by the sitting tenants. Many such tenants are older and so a relative may undertake the personal obligation to repay any loan. In that situation, the tenant would be the proprietor, but the relative would be the debtor in the standard security. The Act recognises this distinction by providing, for example, that the proprietor may redeem the security[1] and that the insolvency of the proprietor amounts to default[2].

1 1970 Act, s 18; App [32].
2 1970 Act, Sch 3, standard condition 9(1)(c); App [104].

4.07 Designation

As in any other deed, it is essential to design the granter accurately and to ensure that any designation in the standard security is the same as that which appears in the deed in his favour or that they are adequately linked. Thus the grantee in a disposition might be designed as 'John Smith, plumber, residing at Forty three Archimedes Avenue, Erewhon'. If, when he grants the standard security, he is residing elsewhere, the designation in the standard security would be something like 'John Smith, formerly plumber and now lecturer in sanitary engineering residing formerly at Forty-three Archimedes Terrace, Erewhon and now at Twenty-seven Eureka Crescent, Hudibras'.

4.08 Individuals as granters

An individual who is a granter of a standard security must have capacity. Apart from that, the only specialities are the uninfeft granter and a non-entitled spouse[1].

1 See paras 4.13 and 4.14 below respectively.

4.09 Partnerships

In dealing with partnerships, it is essential to distinguish the title from the beneficial interest. The latter is regulated by the partnership agreement. The title to partnership property may be held by the partners as individuals, or it may be held by trustees for the firm and the trustees are usually the partners, but need not be.

If the title to the partnership property is in the name of individuals, the infeft proprietors must grant the standard security, but only they need do so, whereas all of the partners would have to sign the personal obligation. If the title stands in the name of trustees for the firm, the trustees should grant the standard security and all of the partners should grant the personal obligation. Professor Halliday suggests that all the partners, whether infeft or not, should sign the standard security[1]. The reason which he gives lies in the fact that the title is a trust title. Under the Trusts (Scotland) Act 1961, a person dealing with the trustees for the firm needs to consider whether borrowing is at variance with the terms or purposes of the trust, and so it may be prudent to have all the partners sign the standard security.

If there is a change in the constitution of the firm by retiral or assumption, some thought will have to be given to the liability of a retiring partner in respect of any existing standard security and to the liability of any incoming partners. The fact that a partner retires does not of itself absolve him from liability under partnership obligations to third parties. Until the creditor in such an obligation becomes aware of the retiral, the retiring partner will be liable on the basis of holding out[2]. Where there is a new partner, he is not automatically liable under existing contracts[3], but he may become so if he has not paid in full for his share[4] and even then, he may be liable if he obtains the benefit of further borrowings under the standard security[5].

If a heritable creditor is considering taking a standard security from a firm where the title is held in the name of trustees, some of whom have retired as partners, it should be noted that changes in the partnership agreement do not affect the title and there may have to be a conveyance to the new trustees. If, however, the title stands in the name of A, B and C, as partners and trustees for the firm of ABC and Co, and any future partners thereof, the title position may be regulated by the appropriate deeds of assumption and conveyance and the present trustees could grant the necessary standard security provided the appropriate clause of deduction of title appears in the standard security in a sasine transaction and the appropriate links are exhibited to the Keeper where the subjects are in an area affected by registration of title.

1 Halliday *Commentary* para 7.44; *Halliday* vol III, paras 37-34, 37-35.
2 Partnership Act 1890, s 36.
3 Ibid, s 17(1).
4 *Thomson and Balfour v Boag and Son* 1936 SC 2; *Miller v John Finlay MacLeod and Parker* 1974 SLT 99. See also J B Miller *The Law of Partnership in Scotland* p 268.
5 See *Miller* pp 271–274.

4.10 Unincorporated associations

When dealing with unincorporated associations, it is necessary to check that the association has power in terms of its constitution to borrow or lend on heritable property. It is also necessary to ascertain who are the trustees and how deeds should be executed. The devolution of the title will be simpler in the case of an unincorporated body if the title is held by trustees *ex officis* because the title will automatically devolve on the successors to the various offices[1].

1 Conveyancing (Scotland) Act 1874, s 45.

4.11 Companies

Security transactions involving companies are dealt with in chapter 11 below and capacity and powers are dealt with there.

4.12 Other persons

The other special types of granters which may be encountered only occasionally are dealt with by Professor Halliday[1].

1 Halliday *Commentary* paras 7-36–7-45; *Halliday* vol III, paras 37-20–37-41.

4.13 Uninfeft granter

A standard security may be granted, varied, assigned or discharged by
someone who is not infeft[1], for example an executor, who may deduce
title. Anything which could be used for the purposes of deducing title
under the Conveyancing (Scotland) Act 1924 may also be used as a
mid-couple or link in a standard security[2]. This will most commonly
arise on death where the link will be the confirmation. It will also be
necessary in the discharge of a standard security if two lending institutions merge. If, for example, the X and Y Building Societies merge to
form the Z Building Society, the discharge would need to contain a
clause of deduction of title making reference to the deed constituting
the amalgamation. The 1970 Act specifically provides that when a
deed has been recorded with the correct clause of deduction of title
then the grantee and those deriving right from him will be in the same
position as a purchaser would be under the 1924 Act. However, once
an interest has been registered, an uninfeft granter does not use a
clause of deduction of title, but he must product the links to the
Keeper[3].

1 1970 Act, s 12(1); App [17]. For further details, see paras 6.02, 6.12 below.
2 1970 Act, s 12(3); App [19].
3 Land Registration (Scotland) Act 1979, s 15(3).

4.14 Non-entitled spouses

While the standard security will have to be granted by the person who
is infeft or who has a right to the subjects, in many instances, the
existence of a non-entitled spouse will have to be considered. Protection for such spouses against 'dealings' in the matrimonial home is
afforded by the Matrimonial Homes (Family Protection) (Scotland)
Act 1981 which came into force on 1 September 1982. Because of the
poor drafting of the original Act, it was amended by the Law Reform
(Miscellaneous Provisions) (Scotland) Act 1985 with effect from 30
December 1985[1]. It may therefore be important to determine whether
a security transaction was entered into prior to 1 September 1982,
between 1 September 1982 and 29 December 1985, or on or after 30
December 1985. We can ignore the position prior to 1 September 1982
in that occupancy rights are irrelevant, but it is essential to set out the
previous law (ie the 1981 Act in its original form) particularly when a
heritable creditor is seeking to exercise his remedies, usually the
power of sale, under a pre-1985 security.

1 Law Reform (Miscellaneous Provisions) (Scotland) Act 1985, s 13.

4.15 The previous law

Section 8(2) of the Matrimonial Homes (Family Protection) (Scotland) Act 1981 was intended to give a heritable creditor the same protection against occupancy rights as a purchaser. For the creditor to be protected, the granter had to produce either an affidavit that there was no non-entitled spouse, or alternatively a renunciation of occupancy rights by the non-entitled spouse, or the consent of the spouse to the granting of the security (unless that had been dispensed with under section 7). The 1981 Act required these things to be produced prior to the granting of the loan. The draftsman may have known what that meant, but no one else did. In practice, they were obtained at the time the security was executed, or at least before it was sent for recording. Between 30 December 1985 and 1 January 1991, an affidavit which post-dated the recording was not effective and that may also be so under the previous law[1].

1 See para 4.16 below.

4.16 The present law

Many of the drafting problems which were evident in the Matrimonial Homes (Family Protection) (Scotland) Act 1981 in its original form have been eliminated by the Law Reform (Miscellaneous Provisions) (Scotland) Act 1985. Section 13(b) of the 1985 Act inserts a new subsection (2A) into the original section 8. The granter of the security must now produce either (1) an affidavit that the subjects are not a matrimonial home in which a spouse of the granter has occupancy rights, or (2) a renunciation of these rights, or (3) the consent of the spouse (unless that had been dispensed with under section 7). A style of affidavit is as follows[1]:

> I, the Debtor designed in the foregoing Standard Security DO SOLEMNLY and SINCERELY swear/affirm as follows:—
>> As at the date hereof the Property described in the said Standard Security is not a matrimonial home in relation to which a spouse of mine has occupancy rights
> all within the meaning of the Matrimonial Homes (Family Protection) (Scotland) Act 1981 as amended SWORN/AFFIRMED by the said Debtor at   on the   day of   Nineteen hundred and
>
> before me

....

Notary Public
(and in the presence of these
witnesses)

....

Full Name ....
Address ....

....

Occupation ....
                                          (Signature of Debtor)

....

Full Name ....
Address ....

....

Occupation ....

Prior to 1 January 1991 whichever course was chosen, the documentation had to be produced at or before the granting, ie before delivery of the security deed[2]. In the usual case, where the solicitor is acting for both the lender and the borrower, the best practice is to have the affidavit, renunciation or consent granted at the same time as the standard security. Where different solicitors were acting, the solicitor who was acting for the lender had to ensure that the documentation was dated prior to the date of delivery of the standard security.

With effect from 1 January 1991 the 1981 Act has been amended by the Law Reform (Miscellaneous Provisions) (Scotland) Act 1990, Schedule 8, paragraph 31. The 1990 Act deletes the words 'at or before the time of the dealing' in section 6 and the words 'before the granting of the loan' in section 8. The effect of these changes are that the seller need no longer produce the affidavit at or before the time of dealing and may produce one after the dealing to the effect that the subjects were not at the time of the dealing a matrimonial home. Similarly where the interest of heritable creditors is concerned the affidavit need not be produced at or before the time of the granting of the security but may be produced afterwards and may be to the effect that a spouse of the granter has not, or had not, at the time of the granting of the security occupancy rights in the subjects. These changes apply also to renunciations.

There are two other changes worth noting. One relates to a residence provided or made available by one spouse to reside in separately from the other spouse. Such a residence is not now a matrimonial home[3] and so, if a security is to be granted over it, no renunciation or consent is required and an affidavit is appropriate. Under the previous law such a residence was a matrimonial home and so in theory a renunciation or consent was required. Because in many cases, it was difficult to obtain either, affidavits were granted but many will not be in the form required by the Act. The other reform is that occupancy rights now prescibe in five years[4], but as the 1981 Act is not retrospective, it would seem that occupancy rights acquired prior to 30 December 1985 prescribe after 20 years. Fortunately, although perhaps not correctly, the Keeper seems to treat all occupancy rights as having prescribed after five years.

It is outwith the scope of this book to consider the details of the 1981 Act but inquiring readers will find Colin Miller's and, George Gretton's PQLE Lectures on the conveyancing aspects most helpful[5].

1 There is no prescribed form for affidavits or renunciations, but there is for consents. The form is found in the Matrimonial Homes (Form of Consent) (Scotland) Regulations 1982, SI 1982/971.
2 Matrimonial Homes (Family Protection) (Scotland) Act 1981, s 8(2A).
3 Ibid, s 22.
4 Ibid, s 6(3)(f).
5 C B Miller 'The Matrimonial Homes (Family Protection) (Scotland) Act 1981' PQLE General Conveyancing Course (November 1988) p 51; G L Gretton 'The Matrimonial Homes Act: The Conveyancing Aspects' PQLE General Conveyancing Course (November 1989) p 156.

FORMS

4.17 General

Section 9(1) of the 1970 Act requires the standard security to be 'in conformity' with one of the forms described in Schedule 2 of the Act. At first sight, that might appear to preclude any departure from the forms except possibly those of a trivial nature. However, section 53(1) provides that it shall be sufficient if any 'deed, notice, certificate or procedure' conforms 'as closely as may be' to what the Act lays down. The parliamentary draftsman opted to call the first form 'Form A', and probably after a great deal of cerebral agitation opted to call the other one 'Form B'. Form A is used where the personal obligation which is being secured is created in the same deed as the security, whereas Form B is used where there is a separate (unrecorded) deed creating the personal obligation. The forms are set out in Schedule 2 to the Act and both Forms are relatively short. Brevity has been acheived in part by defining the import and effect of the documents in the Act itself rather than in the standard security and partly by setting out, again in the Act, standard conditions which apply to all securities subject, when permissible, to any variation by the parties. Form A is generally used by building societies and for standard securities which are governed by the Consumer Credit Act 1974. It may also be used by banks. Form B is generally used by other lending institutions both for domestic and other properties. (Both forms are shown below at Appendix [87], [88]). Some other examples of standard securities are given at the end of this chapter.

The forms are identical in that they design the granter and grantee, they contain an undertaking to perform the obligation, almost certainly an obligation to pay, they then grant a security over a specified interest in land, the standard conditions (with any variation) are applied, and warrandice is granted.

The forms differ in that in Form A, the details of the personal obligation are spelt out and because the personal obligation is set out in full, there is a consent to registration for execution.

Form B specifies the documentation which contains the personal obligation and that documentation, usually a personal bond or minute of agreement, will contain a consent to registration for execution. It states only the nature of the debt and identifies the deeds by which it is constituted and it then goes on to create the security. Form B does not contain a clause of consent to registration for execution but, as has been said, that will almost certainly be in the separate documentation.

In order to give the creditor a real right, the standard security must be recorded in the Register of Sasines, or registered in the Land Register where it will appear in the Charges Section of the title sheet. Where the granter is a company, registration of the charge constituted by the standard security is also required in the Register of Charges, about which more will be said in chapter 11 below.

If a creditor attempted to enforce an *unrecorded* standard security and was *per incuriam* granted a warrant to sell the property, there is no doubt that the personal obligations entered into would be valid. However, there would be no security and so only the personal obligations could be enforced, either by court action or by registration in the Books of Council and Session, or the books of the sheriff court. The creditor could then obtain a decree, or its equivalent, which would allow him to enforce the obligations, but the property could not be sold automatically and if this remedy was sought, further diligence would be required and none of the other remedies under standard condition 10 would be available.

4.18 Clauses common to both Forms

The following clauses are common to both forms. In sequence these are (1) a description of the security subjects; (2) a reference to the standard conditions; and (3) a clause of warrandice.

4.19 Description of the security subjects

Sasine transactions

Both forms require the security subjects to be described by means of a particular description, or a statutory description by reference, or a description by general name[1]. In strict conveyancing parlance, a particular description is one where the subjects are fully described by reference to boundaries[2]. That being so, the statute does not permit the security subjects to be described in other ways which are acceptable in a conveyance, for example a general description, such as a postal address, or a common law description by reference. I have developed this issue elsewhere[3], but it is worth noting that while a statutory description by reference is bungled in a disposition, the subjects may nevertheless be adequately described if there is a common law description, (usually the postal address) but that safety net is not available where the subjects are being described in a standard security. Some secondary lenders have forms of standard security which contain no more than the postal address. These are, however, accepted by the Keeper in both Sasine and Land Register transactions.

Operational areas

If the security subjects are situated in an area which is operational for the purposes of registration of title, the subjects may or may not yet be registered and the security transaction may or may not induce registration.

The general rules are set out below, and further details are given by Professor Halliday[4].

(1) If the security transaction consists of the granting of a new security, or a dealing with an existing security, for example a deed of variation and that transaction does not induce registration, the security transaction is recorded in the Register of Sasines. However, while the creditor may in theory apply for voluntary registration of his interest, the Keeper does not have the resources to deal with such a matter

(2) However, certain dealings in heritable securities will induce registration on the basis that they are transfers for value and extinguish the security. The most common example is a disposition by the heritable creditor in the exercise of his power of sale. An extract decree of foreclosure and a disposition by a heritable creditor in his own favour after he has unsuccessfully attempted to sell the security subjects also induces registration.

(3) Where the security transaction relates to subjects in an operational area which have been registered, then all new standard securities, assignations, variations, etc must be registered. Descriptions need refer only to the title sheet[5] and a description by reference is not competent[6].

1 1970 Act, Sch 2, Note 1; App [89].
2 *Halliday* vol II, para 18-09.
3 D J Cusine 'Descriptions' PQLE Course General Conveyancing (November 1989), pp 72–73; 'Descriptions in Standard Securities' (1990) 35 JLSS 98.
4 *Halliday* vol III, paras 42-05–42-20.
5 *Halliday* vol II, paras 18-74; A McDonald *Registration of Title Manual* paras 15-66 *et seq. Registration of Title Practice Book* para C94.
6 *Registration of Title Practice Book* para C94; Richard S H Girdwood 'Conveyancers Cornered: Invalid Descriptions by Reference' (1987) 32 JLSS 307.

4.20   Standard conditions

After the description the standard security then states, '[t]he standard conditions specified in Schedule 3 to the Conveyancing and Feudal Reform (Scotland) Act 1970, and any lawful variation thereof operative for the time being, shall apply'. There is a discussion of these conditions in chapter 5 below.

4.21   Warrandice

The clause of warrandice in the forms has the same statutory meaning as in the bond and disposition in security[1]. In other words, the debtor grants absolute warrandice as regards the subjects and the titles thereto and fact and deed warrandice so far as the rents are concerned. The warrandice can, and indeed should, be qualified according to the circumstances. If, for example, there is a prior security, the 1970 Act provides that it should be referred to immediately before the clause of warrandice which should be qualified accordingly. Appropriate ranking clauses would be inserted before the warrandice clause[2].

1 1970 Act, s 10(2); App [10].
2 For ranking, see chapter 7 below.

4.22   Reference to burdens

Like the bond and disposition in security, the standard security does not contain a reference to burdens.

4.23 Assignation of writs

Although the standard security does not contain an express clause of
assignation of writs, such an assignation is implied under the 1970
Act[1]. Accordingly, unless the standard security is qualified there is an
assignation to the creditor of the title deeds including searches and all
the conveyances which affect the security subjects or any part thereof.

1 1970 Act, s 10(4); App [12].

4.24 Assignation of rents

There is no assignation of rents clause imported into the standard
security but by virtue of the standard conditions, the creditor has the
right on default to enter into possession and uplift rents[1] (the
equivalent of an action of maills and duties).

1 1970 Act, Sch 3, standard condition 10(3); App [105].

4.25 Consent to registration

This clause in Form A means that the debtor consents to registration
for execution in either the Books of Council and Session or those of
the appropriate sheriff court[1]. A clause of consent will invariably
appear in the separate documentation for a Form B standard security.
Such a clause permits summary diligence to be done[2]. However, if the
obligation is *ad factum praestandum*, that cannot automatically be
enforced by imprisonment if there is default[3]. The creditor would
need to raise an action based on the obligation and in the event of the
debtor's failure to obtemper the decree, apply to the court for an order
to imprison the debtor. the court has a discretion whether or not to
grant this[4].

1 1970 Act, s 10(3); App [11].
2 See G Maher and D J Cusine *The Law and Practice of Diligence* paras 2.16–2.26.
3 Debtors (Scotland) Act 1987, s 100.
4 Law Reform (Miscellaneous Provisions) (Scotland) Act 1940, s 1.

4.26 The personal obligation

The import of the clause or document containing the personal obligation in Form A is defined in section 10 of the 1970 Act.
    Where the security is for a fixed amount, the clause containing the

personal obligation imports three things: (1) an acknowledgement of the receipt by the debtor of the principal sum advanced; (2) a personal obligation to repay that sum with interest at the rate stated, on a written demand by the creditor; and (3) an obligation to pay all expenses for which the debtor is liable under the standard security or by virtue of the Act.

Where the security is for a fluctuating amount, there is a similar provision in section 11, but with the necessary modifications. The debtor undertakes to repay to the creditor the amount which has been advanced and where it is subject to maximum amount, then he is liable only for that maximum amount. Interest is due on each advance from the date of the advance.

The fact that the debtor's liability is to pay on demand means, of course, that, as in a bond in disposition in security, a personal action is always competent against him. Furthermore, the clause of registration for execution, which is the last clause in Form A and will almost certainly also appear in the separate personal bond or minute of agreement relating to Form B, will permit summary diligence against the debtor.

4.27 Variations of the personal obligation

While such variations are something different from variations to the standard conditions, most lenders incorporate the variations to the standard conditions and the personal obligation in the one document. Furthermore, it is usually provided that the debtor will be in default if there is any breach of the terms of this composite document. In building society loans, the debtor may be bound by the terms of the society's rules. The variations in the personal obligation which are commonly encounted are dealt with here. Variations of the standard conditions are dealt with in chapter 5 below.

4.28 (1) Further advances

In a building society standard security, it will usually be expressly stated that the security is not only for the initial advance but also for any further advances, and for all money which may be due by the debtor 'on any account'. The society will not release any property held as security until all money due by the debtor has been repaid. If, as is sometimes the case, the building society suggests to the debtor that, rather than redeem the full amount, a token figure, for example £5 should be left outstanding, the security over the property will still remain. It may also be provided that a failure to pay two instalments of the loan will amount to default.

Securities in favour of banks may provide that the security covers not only all sums lent to the debtor, including future advances, but also sums due under any bank account operated by the debtor as an individual or jointly with any person, whether as a principal or as a guarantor. Some building societies have a similar provision.

4.29 (2) Interest

Section 10 of the 1970 Act requires the debtor to repay the principal sum with interest and in the case of a fluctuating advance, interest on each advance. The security documentation will usually provide details of the rates of interest, how interest is calculated, for example on a daily basis, and how it is applied, for example to reduce interest, then capital. The following are the provisions most commonly encountered:

(a) Interest will be charged on the full amount advanced or becoming due during the year and it will be due from the date of the advance or the date on which it becomes due.

(b) Interest shall accrue from day to day, but it shall be payable in equal instalments as part of the monthly repayments.

(c) If the amount due by way of interest in any year exceeds the monthly payments due in that year, the surplus will be an additional sum payable by the debtor in that year.

(d) The interest shall be payable at the rate stated from time to time.

(e) The rate of interest may be varied upon giving not less than one month's notice in writing.

(f) The debtor may be required to pay an increased monthly payment if the interest rate is increased, the object being to ensure that the loan is repaid by the original date. He may, however, be given the option of continuing to pay at the current rate and thus extend the period of the loan.

(g) No part of any monthly payment, or other payment made by the debtor shall be regarded as repayment of the initial advance or subsequent advance unless all interest due has been paid.

(h) Interest outstanding may be added to the capital and interest will run on the principal and interest, ie compound interest.

4.30 (3) Repayments

Section 10 of the 1970 Act requires the debtor to repay the sum or sums advanced, but the security documentation will, again, be more

specific. Repayment will usually be on a monthly basis, the first
payment usually being due one month after encashment of the loan
cheque but some lenders seek monthly payments in advance after the
loan cheque has been encashed. The debtor will be advised from time
to time of any variations in the monthly repayments and he may be
permitted either to continue paying the existing monthly account, or
to increase it or decrease it as appropriate. While a letter advising of
the decrease in the monthly payment is a thing of beauty, it is unlikely
that it will be a joy for ever. The documentation may also deal with the
situation in which monthly payments are suspended by the creditor.

It is commonly stated in the standard security rather than in the
supporting documentation that the amount due by the debtor at any
time shall be the amount certified as being due by a named official of
the lender. If that is not done, the lender would either have to state in
any calling-up notice the exact sum due, or provide that it is subject to
adjustment. If the latter course is chosen, the debtor may call upon the
creditor to state the correct amount 'within . . . one month from the
date of service of the calling-up notice'. A shrewd debtor who wishes
to 'buy time' might request this information the day before the month
expired and if the creditor did not comply, he would have to re-
commence the calling up procedure[1].

The debtor may agree that any compulsory purchase monies or
similar payments will be applied to reduce the amount of capital due.

1 1970 Act, s 19(9); App [45].

4.31 (4) Indemnification

The debtor may be required to indemnify the lender against all
actions, proceedings, claims etc, caused by any breach of any undertaking, obligation, stipulation or the non-payment of any outgoing.
This clause may further provide that the debtor will advise the creditor
of all notices of such claims.

4.32 (5) Cautioners (guarantors)

If there is a cautioner/guarantor, it will usually be provided that the
cautioner is to be regarded as a principal debtor with joint and several
liability and that his liability will not be affected by anything which
would not have resulted in his being discharged had he been the
principal debtor. In particular, his liability will remain despite (a)
release of the security subjects; (b) anything having been done which
would prevent recovery from the debtor; (c) the principal debt

becoming unenforceable; (d) the legal incapacity of the debtor. These provisions are designed to avoid the cautioner being discharged at common law[1].

1 W M Gloag and R C Henderson *Introduction to the Law of Scotland* (9th edn) para
  21-20; D J Cusine and A D M Forte *Scottish Cases and Materials in Commercial Law*
  pp 196–204.

4.33 (6) Endowment policies

Where there is an endowment policy, the lender will take full powers to deal with any insurance policy if the debtor is in default, which would involve assignation and sale, or surrender. The lender will apply any proceeds to reduce or discharge the amount due. These powers would be available only if the policy was assigned and in many instances, building societies do not require this. The debtor may also agree that there will be no obligation on the lender to account to the debtor for any commission earned by the lender on the policy. Some lenders appoint themselves as executors under the policy (for example, the Halifax Building Society).

4.34 (7) Assignation of rights

The debtor will assign all rights which he has under any statute or upon the compulsory acquisition, etc, of the property.

4.35 (8) Discharge

The debtor will agree that any discharge documentation may be drawn up by the lender and any signature required for recording or registering discharge documentation may be adhibited by a solicitor in the employment of, or instructed by the lender. That covers, for example, a signature on the warrant of registration of a discharge and permits the lender to frame and record/register the same.

4.36 Additions to the Forms, etc

The 1970 Act provides that nothing shall preclude the addition of material to a deed, or a notice, or a certificate, or a procedure[1]. It is not uncommon to find additional material in calling-up notices and notices of default, the object of which is to advise the debtor of the consequences of a failure to comply. It is, however, an open question whether such additions would be given effect to where the additions were greater in size than the deed, etc. In that situation, the deed, notice, etc would be the additional material and not the other way round. It might therefore be argued, where a lengthy loan document has a security attached to in such a way that the debtor would have to read the documentation with great care in order to find out that he was granting a standard security, that the document is not a standard security within the meaning of the Act.

1 1970 Act, s 53(1).

STYLES

4.37 General

The following styles are ones which are in common use, the first two, the building society and the bank being more commonly encountered than the third, the insurance company. The fourth is a 'discount' standard security which is granted in respect of a loan given to a tenant to finance a purchase by the tenant.

4.38 Building society

The style is that of the Halifax Building Society and the standard security is in Form A, which incorporates the personal obligation. As with most building societies securities, the debtor is taken bound by the Society's Rules and the Schedule of Variations and the Standard Conditions, which in the case of the Halifax and many others are registered in the Books of Council and Session. The Schedule of Variations contains variations not only to the standard conditions in the 1970 Act, but also to the personal obligation. This again is common among building societies and it has the advantage of setting everything out in the one document.

4.39 Bank

The style is that of the Royal Bank of Scotland, which is also in Form A. In this standard security (like that of the Clydesdale Bank) the variations to the personal obligation are set out first and then the variations to the standard conditions. The Bank of Scotland style is also Form A, but it uses a separate booklet as the building societies do.

SS10

HALIFAX BUILDING SOCIETY - STANDARD SECURITY

In this deed the expressions set out below shall have the meanings and effect respectively set opposite to them:—

The Debtor	
	Where the Debtor is more than one person the singular includes the plural and all obligations of the Debtor are undertaken jointly and severally
The Society	Halifax Building Society of Halifax, West Yorkshire
The Property	The heritable subjects known as being the subjects more fully described below.

The Debtor hereby undertakes to pay to the Society the Advance made by the Society to the Debtor with interest computed in accordance with the practice of the Society at the Interest Rate by Monthly Payments the first of which is to be made on the date specified by the Society and notified to the Debtor and subsequent payments at successive intervals of one Month thereafter until the whole sums hereby secured are paid and satisfied: And the Debtor also undertakes to pay to the Society any further advance or payment that may be made by or be due to the Society secured over the Property and all relative interest and consequents: For which the Debtor grants a Standard Security in favour of the Society over the Property, being ALL AND WHOLE

The standard conditions specified in Schedule 3 to the Conveyancing and Feudal Reform (Scotland) Act 1970, as varied by the Schedule of Variations made by the Society dated the Twentieth day of July nineteen hundred and ninety and registered in the Books of Council and Session on the Twenty-third day of July nineteen hundred and ninety receipt of a copy whereof is hereby acknowledged by the Debtor and any lawful variation thereof operative for the time being shall apply: And the Debtor grants warrandice: And the Debtor consents to registration for execution.

IN WITNESS WHEREOF these presents are executed by the Debtor at

on the   day of   Nineteen

hundred and   before these witnesses:—

Signature..

Name in block capitals...................................

Address...

....

Occupation...

....

Signature of Debtor

Signature..

Name in block capitals...................................

Address...

....

Occupation...

Register on behalf of the within named Halifax Building Society in the Register of the County of

Solicitors,   Agents.

I,.., spouse of the within-named Debtor, consent to the within-written Standard Security for the purposes of the Matrimonial Homes (Family Protection) (Scotland) Act 1981.

I confirm that:—

a.   this consent shall relate to the making of the Advance and any further advances or payment secured by the Standard Security

b.   the effect of this form of consent has been explained

c.   I have been advised of the right to have independent legal advice on its effect

d.   this consent was given before any part of the Advance was made to the within-named Debtor.

IN WITNESS WHEREOF these presents are executed by the said..

....at

on the   day of   Nineteen

hundred and   before these witnesses:—

Signature....................................

Name in block capitals....................................

Address....................................

....

Occupation....................................

....

      Signature of consenting spouse

Signature....................................

Name in block capitals....................................

Address....................................

....

Occupation....................................

1

SCHEDULE OF VARIATIONS

REGISTERS OF SCOTLAND

AT EDINBURGH the Twenty-third day of July Nineteen hundred and ninety the Deed hereinafter reproduced was presented for registration in the Books of the Lords of Council and Session for preservation and is registered in the said Books as follows:-

WE, HALIFAX BUILDING SOCIETY of Halifax, West Yorkshire (hereinafter referred to as 'the Society') considering that we are about to make advances in accordance with our Rules to be secured by standard securities to be granted in our favour over heritable property in Scotland have resolved and hereby declare that the said standard securities shall be regulated by the standard conditions specified in Schedule 3 to the Conveyancing and Feudal Reform (Scotland) Act 1970 as amended by the Redemption of Standard Securities (Scotland) Act 1971 and by the following variations, videlicet:-

One

In construing these presents the following expressions shall have the meanings hereby assigned to them respectively, videlicet:-

'Added Rate'	The additional rate of interest (if any) specified in the Offer of Mortgage as the Added Rate or prescribed in accordance with Condition Ten (h) of these Conditions or any variation of the same made in accordance therewith
'The Advance'	The sum specified in the Offer of Mortgage as the Amount of the Advance receipt of which (or where the advance is to be made in instalments the first instalment of which) is acknowledged by the Debtor
'Base Rate'	The rate of interest specified in the Offer of Mortgage as the Base Rate or any variation of the same made in accordance with these Conditions but excluding any Added Rate
'The Consumer Credit Act'	The Consumer Credit Act 1974 or any statutory re-enactment thereof
'The Debtor'	The person to whom the Advance has been made including his legal representatives and successors in title and any person (other than a guarantor) who undertakes the obligations of the Debtor
'The Initial Repayment Period'	The period specified in the Offer of Mortgage as the Initial Repayment Period
'Interest Rate'	The Base Rate and (where appropriate) the Added Rate
'Month'	A calendar month
'Monthly Payment'	The monthly sum specified in the Offer of Mortgage as the Gross Monthly Payment or any variation of the same made in accordance with these Conditions
'Offer of Mortgage'	The written notice described as the Offer of Mortgage and received by the Debtor before the date of the Standard Security stating that the Society is prepared to make the Advance (including any variation of that notice)
'The Policy Owner'	The person who is entitled to the benefit of the policy of life assurance referred to in Condition Thirteen

2

'The Property'	The heritable subjects over which the Standard Security is secured or any part or parts thereof
'The Redemption Money'	The aggregate of the moneys outstanding for the time being on the security of the Standard Security
'Relevant Loan Interest'	Relevant Loan Interest to which Section 369 (1) applies
'The Rules'	The Rules of the Society in force from time to time including rules adopted and amendments made after the date of the Standard Security
'Section 369 (1)'	Section 369 (1) of the Income and Corporation Taxes Act 1988 or any statutory modification or re-enactment thereof
'The Society'	The Society and its successors and assigns
'The Standard Security'	The Standard Security granted by the Debtor over the Property
'Year'	The financial year of the Society

Words importing the masculine gender shall include the feminine gender. Words importing the singular number shall include the plural number and vice versa, and where there are two or more persons included in the expression 'the Debtor' and 'the Policy Owner' obligations and conditions expressed to be made by the Debtor and the Policy Owner shall be held to bind such persons jointly and severally.

Two   (a) Subject to paragraph (b) of this Condition the Standard Security shall be security not only for the moneys primarily provided for by it but also for all moneys which may be or become owing by the Debtor to the Society on any account including any further advances and at the discretion of the Society no property held by the Society as security for the indebtedness of the Debtor shall be released until all moneys owing by the Debtor to the Society have been paid.

(b) Paragraph (a) of this Condition shall not apply to moneys owing under an agreement which is either (i) a regulated agreement under the Consumer Credit Act unless the requirements of Section 58 of that Act have been satisfied in respect of the agreement or (ii) secured by a separate standard security.

Three   The Debtor shall be bound by and comply with the Rules of the Society in respect of the Advance and the security created by the Standard Security.

Four   (a) Subject to paragraphs (b) and (c) of this Condition the Debtor will pay to the Society a Monthly Payment in every Month (after making such deductions as he may be entitled to make under Section 369 (1)) until the Advance and all further advances on the security of the Standard Security with interest and all other moneys to be paid to the Society by the Debtor have been fully paid and satisfied

(b) If and so long as the Debtor is entitled to make deductions under Section 369 (1) then instead of paying the amount referred to in paragraph (a) of this Condition the Debtor will (subject to paragraph (c) of this Condition) pay the gross equivalent of the net monthly amount specified for this purpose by the Society (from which gross monthly amount he will be entitled to make the said deductions) and for this purpose the gross equivalent of a net amount is such amount as after deducting income tax at the basic rate from that part of it which consists of Relevant Loan Interest is equal to the said net amount PROVIDED that if no net monthly amount has been specified by the Society for

3

the purpose of this paragraph the Debtor shall make payments in accordance with paragraph (a) or (c) as the case may be

(c) If and so long as the Debtor is entitled to make deductions under Section 369 (1) and the Debtor and the Society agree or the Society gives notice in writing to the Debtor that this paragraph shall apply then instead of paying either of the amounts specified in paragraphs (a) and (b) of this Condition the Debtor will pay the gross equivalent of the net monthly amount and for this purpose

(i) the net monthly amount throughout any Year means the Monthly Payment payable in the first month of that Year reduced by income tax at the basic rate then in force on that part of it which consists of Relevant Loan Interest (having regard to Condition Ten)

(ii) the gross equivalent of the net amount is such amount as after deducting income tax at the basic rate for the time being in force from that part of it which consists of Relevant Loan Interest is equal to that net amount

(d) The first payment under this Condition shall be made on the date specified by the Society and notified to the Debtor and subsequent payments at successive intervals of one Month thereafter

(e) If the Debtor shall allow two of the Monthly Payments to remain unpaid the Debtor shall be held to be in default.

(f) In addition to the payments made under the other paragraphs of this Condition and unless otherwise agreed by the Society the Debtor will before the end of the Year in which the Advance is made and before the end of any Year in which a further advance is made to him pay to the Society (subject to any deduction which he may be entitled to make under Section 369 (1) a sum equal to the amount by which the interest due to accrue in any such Year exceeds the interest to be paid as part of the Monthly Payments in that Year

Five If a further advance shall be made to the Debtor in accordance with the Rules he will pay to the Society such payments and at such times as may be prescribed by the Society in respect of the Advance and such further advance, and if he shall allow two of such payments to remain unpaid the Debtor shall be held to be in default.

Six (a) Notwithstanding the provisions of Condition Four the Society will not require repayment of principal to be made under that Condition in respect of any amount covered by a subsisting policy of endowment assurance included in the Society's security and by means of which at maturity such amount is intended to be repaid

(b) If the making of Monthly Payments shall be suspended either in whole or in part either by the operation of paragraph (a) of this Condition or otherwise by permission of the Society the Debtor will duly pay such interest and reduced monthly instalments (if any) as the Society may require as a condition of the suspension and on cesser of the suspension the Debtor will resume or begin and complete the making of Monthly Payments or pay such other amounts as shall be necessary to discharge the Redemption Money within the Initial Repayment Period.

Seven The Debtor shall keep the Society indemnified from and against all actions, proceedings, claims, expenses and damages occasioned by any breach of any undertaking, obligation or stipulation or the non-payment of any outgoing.

Eight The Debtor shall not at any time during the continuance of the security without the consent in writing of the Society (1) make any alteration to or in the use of the Property or (2) part with the possession of the Property or any part thereof.

4

Nine

Should the Debtor after receiving a part of the Advance or any further advance leave any building forming part of the Property unfinished the Society may either sell the Property in its then condition or complete the building at the cost of the Debtor and the money so expended with all relative expenses and outlays shall be recoverable from the Debtor on demand and until paid by him shall be a charge on the Property.

Ten

(a) The Society shall be entitled for any Year to charge interest on the full amount of any money advanced to or becoming owing by the Debtor during the Year as from the date on which it was advanced or became owing and on the amount of the Redemption Money at the beginning of the Year and the Debtor will pay interest accordingly

(b) Subject to paragraph (f) of this Condition interest for any Year shall accrue from day to day but shall be payable (subject to paragraph (f) of Condition Four) in equal instalments as part of the Monthly Payments payable in that Year

(c) If such interest for any Year shall exceed the Monthly Payments payable in that Year the excess shall be an additional sum payable by the Debtor in that Year

(d) Interest shall be charged by the Society at the Interest Rate as well after as before any decree for payment

(e) Where only part of an intended advance has been made interest shall not be charged on more principal money than has actually been advanced

(f) Where at any time a premium or part thereof in respect of any insurance of the Property is unpaid by the Debtor his next available Monthly Payment or Payments shall be credited first against the unpaid premium. Subject thereto at the end of any Year payments made in that Year shall be credited first against Relevant Loan Interest payable, secondly against other interest payable and thirdly so as to reduce the Redemption Money

(g) The Society may from time to time vary the Base Rate

(h) The Society may also from time to time prescribe an Added Rate to be chargeable in addition to the Base Rate in respect of all or any part of the Redemption Money and the Society may from time to time vary the Added Rate

(i) To vary the Base Rate or to prescribe or vary the Added Rate the Society must give notice either by advertising the same in accordance with the Rules in newspapers circulating in Edinburgh London Belfast and Halifax or by writing to the Debtor and in either case the rate so prescribed or varied shall take effect from the date specified in the notice

Eleven

(a) Notwithstanding any other provisions in these Conditions the Monthly Payment may be varied from time to time by written notice to the Debtor from the Society so as to provide for the payment of the Redemption Money by such time (not being earlier than the end of the Initial Repayment Period) as shall be specified in the notice

(b) The Debtor may on receipt of a notice under this Condition or on any variation in the Interest Rate elect to increase the Monthly Payment to any amount which is sufficient to discharge the Standard Security within the Initial Repayment Period

(c) Notwithstanding anything contained in this Condition the Monthly Payment may be varied at any time by agreement between the Society and the Debtor.

5

Twelve   (a) The Debtor may with the Society's written consent but not otherwise insure and keep insured the Property in the joint names of the Debtor and the Society against fire and such risks as the Society may from time to time require with insurers and in a sum approved by the Society from time to time

(b) Where the Debtor insures the Property he will produce to the Society on demand particulars of the terms of the insurance and evidence that the required insurance cover is in force

(c) The Debtor will promptly notify the Society of any damage to the Property which may give rise to a claim under the insurance of the Property

(d) The Debtor will not do or permit or suffer to be done anything whereby any insurance on the Property may become void or voidable or may lapse or be vitiated or is altered without the consent of the Society

(e) If any insurance is effected by the Debtor (whether after application to and with the consent of the Society or not) he will hold all moneys receivable by him or under his control in respect of such insurance in trust for the Society to be paid to it or at the option of the Society it may as his agent on his behalf and in his name receive and give a good discharge for such moneys

(f) If the Debtor does not insure or keep insured the Property, or if there is a breach or failure to comply with any of the foregoing paragraphs, then unless some other person has covenanted to do so the Society may insure the Property against fire and other contingencies for such sums as it may from time to time think fit and money expended for that purpose will be recoverable from the Debtor and until repaid will (subject to any agreement to the contrary) carry interest and be a charge on the Property

(g) Any insurance effected by the Society shall be in such insurance office and through such agency as the Society may from time to time think fit

(h) The Society shall have full power to settle and adjust with the insurers

(i) Any moneys receivable by the Society or the Debtor on any insurance of the Property whether effected by the Society or any other person shall be applied at the option of the society either in or towards making good the loss or damage in respect of which the moneys are received or in or towards the payment of the Redemption Money

Thirteen   (a) This Condition applies to any and every policy of life assurance from time to time deposited with the Society by the Policy Owner

(b) Where the Debtor is in default the Society shall have full power to deal with the policy as absolute owner thereof including the power to sell, assign, transfer, surrender or otherwise deal with the policy and to collect the policy moneys and any sums received from such sale, assignation, transfer, surrender or other dealing may be applied by the Society in the reduction or discharge of the Redemption Money

(c) In case of default in payment of any moneys payable in respect of the policy the Society may

(i) pay the same and all moneys expended by the Society and all costs and expenses of keeping the policy in force or restoring any voidable policy or effecting a new policy shall be a charge both on the policy and on the Property and all moneys expended by the Society shall carry interest

(ii) convert the policy into a paid up policy and retain it as collateral security

(iii) surrender the policy

(d) When the policy moneys are received by the Society they shall be applied in reducing or discharging the Redemption Money

6

(e) Upon repayment to the Society of the Redemption Money the Society (subject to paragraph (f) of this Condition) will at the request and cost of the person entitled to the policy retrocess it

(f) Upon repayment to the Society of the Redemption Money the Society may (with the concurrence of the Policy Owner) retain the policy as security for the repayment to the Society of other moneys advanced or to be advanced by the Society

(g) The Policy Owner waives all right to compete with the Society in claiming any security or money unless and until all the indebtedness of the Debtor to the Society has been discharged in full

(h) Unless and until the policy has been legally assigned to the Society and so long as the Redemption Money remains owing to the Society

   (i) the Policy Owner appoints the Society irrevocably to be the Agent of and Attorney for the Policy Owner and in his name to assign (including an assignation in security of the Society itself), transfer, surrender or otherwise deal with the policy and to collect the policy moneys, and

   (ii) the Policy Owner nominates and appoints the Society to be his testamentary executor quoad the policy and assigns to the Society as executor foresaid any life policy belonging to the Policy Owner which is deposited with the Society but that in trust always for the purpose of keeping in force and uplifting the proceeds of the said policy and applying the same towards the Redemption Money and thereafter accounting to the Policy Owner's representatives for any surplus proceeds in the hands of the Society and the Policy Owner provides and declares that this appointment of executor is irrevocable by the Policy Owner either by inter vivos or testamentary deed.

Fourteen The Society may at any time assign the Standard Security to any person and in case of any such assignation the assignee shall have the benefit of all obligations by the Debtor and provisions contained in the Standard Security and these Conditions and may at any time thereafter exercise all rights and remedies of the Society for securing the Redemption Money and interest and every statement of fact contained in such assignation shall as against the Debtor be deemed conclusive.

Fifteen The Debtor will not without the written consent of the Society grant any transfer of the Property but the Society will not unreasonably withhold its consent to the vesting of the Property in a beneficiary on the death of a debtor.

Sixteen Every deed vesting the Property in a purchaser, transferee or beneficiary subject to the Standard Security shall be approved by a Solicitor of the Society at the expense of the Debtor and shall when executed be deposited with the other title deeds held by the Society.

Seventeen Every sale or transfer or purported sale or transfer of the Property under burden of the Standard Security (otherwise than by operation of law) except in accordance with the Rules and the provisions of these presents shall render the Redemption Money immediately due and payable.

7

Eighteen

(a) As soon as practicable after repayment to the Society of all moneys due under the Standard Security the Society shall grant a formal discharge to the Debtor and shall deliver to him the whole deeds and documents relating to the Property, and

(b) A Solicitor to the Society shall prepare or revise such formal discharge and his fees and outlays shall be payable by the Debtor

(c) The Debtor authorises a Solicitor to the Society as agent for the Debtor to procure the registration in the Register of Sasines or the Land Register of Scotland of such formal discharge and to sign a warrant of registration for that purpose.

Nineteen

The Society upon entering into possession of the Property shall (but only in respect of the matters hereinafter mentioned) become and be the agent of the Debtor with authority at his expense to remove store preserve sell or otherwise dispose of any furniture or effects of the Debtor which the Debtor shall refuse or omit to remove from the Property in such manner as the Society may think fit.

Twenty

The Debtor hereby irrevocably appoints the Society his attorney with full power in his name and on his behalf to receive any money payable to the Debtor under the provisions of any agreement insurance or guarantee relating to the repair or condition of the Property or the rectification of defects in the title to the Property. Any money receivable by the Society under this condition shall be applied as in paragraph (i) of Condition Twelve.

Twenty-one

The Society shall be entitled to all expenses properly incurred (including costs of legal proceedings whether brought by or against the Debtor or any other person) on a basis of full indemnity and expenses shall carry interest from the date of expenditure.

Twenty-two

Where a retention is made by the Society from the Advance or where the Advance is paid in instalments as the building of the Property proceeds the Society will pay the balance of the Advance to the Debtor by such instalments and at such times as the Society shall determine having regard to any conditions upon which the Advance was made PROVIDED ALWAYS that the Society shall not be bound to pay the balance of the Advance or any part of it unless the Debtor shall have duly performed and observed the obligations contained or referred to in the Standard Security.

Twenty-three

The Society shall permit the Debtor to hold and enjoy the Property and to receive the rents and profits thereof so long as he shall not be in default under the Standard Security or until the Redemption Money shall become due in terms of Condition Twenty-four.

Twenty-four

The Debtor agrees to vacate the Property in so far as occupied by him, his family and servants and to give the Society immediate possession thereof on the expiry of a period of seven days after the posting of a notice by recorded delivery given by or on behalf of the Society and addressed to the Debtor at his last known address given at any time after the Society shall have become entitled to enter into possession of the security subjects; and the Debtor agrees that a warrant of summary ejection may competently proceed against him in the Sheriff Court of the District in which the Property is situated at the instance of the Society. The Society shall, notwithstanding the terms of the Standard Security, be entitled at any time to require the Debtor to pay the Redemption Money by calling up the Standard Security in accordance with the Conveyancing and Feudal Reform (Scotland) Act 1970 as amended by the Redemption of Standard Securities (Scotland) Act 1971.

8

Twenty-five   The Debtor shall be held to be in default under the Standard Security if there is a breach of any other obligation contained or implied in the Standard Security, these Conditions or the Rules or otherwise undertaken by the Debtor in connection with the Standard Security. In addition the Debtor, if a company, will be held to be in default in the event of an administration order being made in respect of its affairs, business and property.

Twenty-six   (a)   This Condition applies to any insurance effected by the Debtor in respect of which the Society is the policyholder.

                             (b)   In default of payment of any moneys payable in respect of the insurance the Society may pay the same and all moneys expended by the Society and all costs and expenses of keeping the insurance in force or restoring any voidable insurance or effecting any new insurance shall be a charge on the Property and until paid by the Debtor shall carry interest.

Twenty-seven   The powers available to the Society under the Standard Security are in addition to and without prejudice to and not in substitution for all other powers and remedies competent to the Society under the Rules or by statute or at common law.

                    IN WITNESS WHEREOF these presents are sealed with the seal of the Society on Twentieth day of July Nineteen hundred and ninety and countersigned by RICHARD GEORGE BELL Assistant General Manager by order of the Board of Directors in the presence of these witnesses:

STEPHEN ARNOLD MILLINGTON
Trinity Road, Halifax
Solicitor

JACK WILD
Trinity Road, Halifax
Legal Executive

R. G. BELL

Note. Pages 9–11 of the Halifax Schedule of Variations comprise the Conveyancing and Feudal Reform (Scotland) Act 1970, Sch 3, standard conditions, and are not reproduced here. For the standard conditions, see App [96]–[107A].

I/WE

(hereinafter referred to as "the Obligant") hereby undertake to pay to THE ROYAL BANK OF SCOTLAND plc (hereinafter referred to as "the Bank", which expression includes its successors and assignees whomsoever) on demand all sums of principal, interest and charges which are now and which may at any time hereafter become due to the Bank by the Obligant whether solely or jointly with any other person, corporation, firm or other body and whether as principal or surety;

DECLARING THAT;

(1) the interest hereinbefore referred to shall be at the rate(s) agreed between the Bank and the Obligant or (failing such agreement) determined by the Bank and shall be payable at such dates as may be so agreed or determined by the Bank;

(2) in the event of the foregoing personal obligation being granted by more than one person the expression "the Obligant" means all such persons together and/or any one or more of them; and in all cases the obligations hereby undertaken by the Obligant shall bind all person(s) included in the expression "the Obligant" and his, her or their executors and representatives whomsoever all jointly and severally without the necessity of discussing them in their order;

(3) if there shall be any breach of the obligations contained or referred to in this document the Bank shall (without prejudice to all other rights and powers available to it) be entitled, without notice to the Obligant, to withhold further banking facilities from the Obligant and to return without making payment thereof Cheques, Bills of Exchange, Direct Debits and other like documents drawn on the Bank by the Obligant or otherwise bearing to be payable by the Bank to the Obligant's order;

(4) if the Bank receives notice of any subsequent charge or other interest affecting all or any part of the security subjects as hereinafter defined the Bank may open a new account or accounts with the Obligant and, if or insofar as the Bank does not open a new account or accounts, it shall nevertheless be treated as if it had done so at the time when it received such notice and as and from that time all payments made by the Obligant to the Bank shall, notwithstanding any instructions by the Obligant to the contrary, be credited or treated as having been credited to the new account or accounts and shall not operate to reduce the amount due from the Obligant to the Bank at the time when it received the notice;

(5) the sums due by the Obligant shall be conclusively ascertained by a statement under the hand of a Director, General Manager, Assistant General Manager, Secretary or Chief Accountant of the Bank;

(6) the Bank may (without releasing, modifying, rendering unenforceable or otherwise prejudicing the security and liabilities hereby constituted, except insofar as the Bank expressly so agrees) allow any person(s) any time or indulgence or enter into, renew, vary or end any arrangement security or guarantee with any person(s);

(7) any person who under this document is liable for the debts of another shall not in competition with or in priority to the Bank make any claim against that other nor take or share in or enforce any security in respect of such debts, until such debts have been paid to the Bank in full, nor shall such liability be affected by the existence of any other security or guarantee nor by any other security or guarantee being or becoming void or unenforceable; and the Bank may place to the credit of a suspense account for so long as it considers desirable any moneys received in respect of such debts without any obligation to apply them towards payment of such debts; and in applying moneys towards payment of such debts the Bank may appropriate them towards such part(s) of the debts as it thinks fit.

For which sums (except any sums due or to become due under any agreement to which Section 61 of the Consumer Credit Act 1974 applies unless such agreement provides that it is secured over the security subjects aftermentioned)

Insert full name(s) and designation(s) of the proprietors of the security subjects, or where the proprietor(s) is/are named above "the said............"

*delete if not applicable

*(with the consent, as testified by, his/her subscription hereof, of

presently residing at,

the spouse of the said,   for the purposes of the Matrimonial Homes (Family Protection) (Scotland) Act 1981 (as amended)) hereby grant(s) a Standard Security in favour of the Bank over ALL and WHOLE

which subjects hereinbefore described are herein referred to as "the security subjects";
The Standard Conditions specified in Schedule 3 to the Conveyancing and Feudal Reform (Scotland) Act 1970, and any lawful variation thereof operative for the time being, shall apply; And the Standard Conditions shall be varied to the effect that

(FIRST)   The Definitions in the said Schedule 3 shall have effect also for the purposes of the following variations;

(SECOND) The insurance to be effected in terms of Standard Condition 5(a) shall provide cover to the extent of the reinstatement value of the security subjects and not the market value thereof;

(THIRD)   All policies of insurance affording cover in respect of the security subjects shall be disclosed to the Bank by the debtor in order that they may be written or endorsed for the interests of the Bank and the debtor as the Bank may require and shall in other respects be deemed for the purpose of this Standard Security to have been effected under Standard Condition 5(a). All rights and claims under policies effected or deemed to have been effected under Standard Condition 5(a) are hereby assigned by the debtor to the Bank and all monies becoming payable under any such policies shall be applied in making good the loss or damage in respect of which such monies become payable or, if the Bank so requires, in or towards the discharge of the sums secured by this Standard Security;

(FOURTH) It shall be an obligation on the debtor not to create or agree to create a subsequent security over the security subjects or any part thereof or convey or assign the same or any part thereof (otherwise than by *mortis causa* deed) or make directly or indirectly any application for planning permission in relation to the security subjects or any part thereof or make application for an improvement grant or other grant in respect of the security subjects or any part thereof, without the prior consent in writing of the Bank in each case which consent if granted may be so granted subject to such conditions as the Bank may see fit to impose;

(FIFTH)   If the Bank shall enter into possession of the security subjects the Bank shall be entitled (if it thinks fit) at the expense and risk of the debtor to remove, store, sell or otherwise deal with any furniture goods, equipment or other moveable property left in or upon the security subjects and not removed within fourteen days of the Bank entering into possession, without the Bank being liable for any loss or damage occasioned by the exercise of this power. The Bank shall however be subject to an obligation to account for the proceeds of any such sale after deducting all expenses incurred by the Bank in relation to such furniture, goods, equipment or other moveable property.

If the warrandice is subject to
a prior security or there is
any other qualification of
absolute warrandice insert
before the warrandice
"subject to............" and give
details

The person(s) granting the foregoing security (jointly and severally if more than
one) grant warrandice: And the parties hereto consent to registration of these
presents and of the said statement for execution: IN WITNESS WHEREOF

NB Any Consentor named
must sign the document

REGISTER on behalf of the within named THE ROYAL BANK OF SCOTLAND plc
in the REGISTER of the COUNTY of

Agents

We, THE ROYAL BANK OF SCOTLAND plc, CONSIDERING that we have agreed to disburden of the within written Standard Security the subjects over which the same was constituted, hereby DISCHARGE the foregoing Standard Security by

in our favour recorded in

the Register for the County of

on the   day of   in the year Nineteen Hundred

: IN WITNESS WHEREOF

REGISTER on behalf of the within named

in the REGISTER of the COUNTY of

Agents

4.40   Insurance company

The style is that used by Guardian Assurance plc and is in Form B.
Once again, reference is made to separate documentation which contains the alterations to the personal obligation as well as the variations
to the standard conditions.

Insurance company style

⟨4⟩ Hereby in security of all sums principal interest premiums and others now payable or which may become payable by ⟨5⟩ under a Minute of Agreement signed by ⟨6⟩ of even date with ⟨7⟩ execution of these presents and entered into between ⟨8⟩ and Guardian Assurance plc aftermentioned and any future Minute or Minutes of Agreement entered into between ⟨9⟩ and the said Guardian Assurance plc and of the whole obligations and conditions therein expressed GRANT a Standard Security in favour of the said Guardian Assurance plc incorporated under the Companies Acts 1862 and 1900 and re-registered under the Companies Acts 1948 to 1980 and having their Registered Office at Royal Exchange in the City of London over ALL and WHOLE ⟨10⟩

The Standard Conditions specified in Schedule 3 to the Conveyancing and Feudal Reform (Scotland) Act 1970 (as amended by the Redemption of Standard Securities (Scotland) Act 1971) as varied by the said Minute of Agreement and any lawful variation thereof operative for the time being shall apply; And ⟨11⟩ grant warrandice:

SIGNED by the said ⟨12⟩

at ⟨13⟩ on the ⟨14⟩
day of ⟨15⟩ Nineteen hundred
and ninety ⟨16⟩ in the presence of:—

Witness:

Address:

Occupation:

Witness:

Address:

Occupation:

⟨17⟩ REGISTER on behalf of the within named Guardian Assurance plc in the Register of the County of ⟨18⟩.

W.S., Solicitors,
Glasgow & Edinburgh, Agents.

4.41   'Discount' standard security

The style is that of the City of Aberdeen District Council and is in a form not dissimilar to other councils. It sets out the circumstances in which the discount is repayable and narrates the standard security (if any) which already exists to finance the purchase and to which the 'discount' standard security is postponed.

I/WE, (1) (hereinafter referred to as 'the debtor(s)'), WHEREAS, THE CITY OF ABERDEEN DISTRICT COUNCIL constituted under the Local Government (Scotland) Act 1973 (hereinafter referred to as 'the Council') have sold to the debtor(s) ALL and WHOLE (2) being the subjects more particularly described in and disponed by the Feu Disposition by the Council in my/our favour recorded in the Division of the General Register of Sasines applicable to the County of (3) of even date with the recording of these presents (hereinafter referred to as 'the property') the date of entry being the (4) day of (5) Nineteen Hundred and (6) and that at the price of (7) POUNDS STERLING (£(8)); AND CONSIDERING THAT the said price has been calculated by deducting from the market value of the property a discount of (9) POUNDS STERLING (£) (hereinafter referred to as 'the discount') in accordance with the provisions of Section 62 of the Housing (Scotland) Act, 1987: THEREFORE the debtor(s) hereby agree(s) and (jointly and severally) underetake(s) in the event of the property being conveyed, disponed, sold or otherwise disposed of except in the following circumstances:—

(a) where a successor in title to the debtor(s) disposes of the property in the capacity of executor of the debtor(s);

(b) when the property is sold as the result of an order for compulsory purchase;

(c) where the disposal is of part of the property and is by one debtor to another debtor where both are parties hereto;

(d) where the disposal is of part of the property and the remainder continues to be the only or principal home of the debtor(s) disposing of the part;

(e) where the disposal is to a member of the debtor's (debtors') family (as defined in the said lastmentioned Act) who has lived with the debtor(s) for a period of twelve months prior to the said disposal and the disposal is for no consideration on the understanding that in such circumstances in the event of the said member disposing of the house before the expiry of the three year period hereinafter mentioned the provisions of Section 72 of the said Act shall apply to him as if his disposal was the first disposal and he was the original purchaser;

to pay to the Council the proportion hereinafter specified of the discount at the date of entry in respect of the sale or disposal of the property or part thereof; and the debtor(s) agree(s) that the specified proportion is as follows, videlicet:—

Within One year from (10) the proportion is 100% of the discount;

More than One but not more than Two years after (11) the proportion is 66% of the discount;

More than Two but not more than Three years after (12) the proportion is 33% of the discount;

More than Three years after (15) the proportion is Nil;

for which the debtor(s) grant(s) a Standard Security in favour of the Council over the property being ALL and WHOLE (16) being the subjects more particularly described in and disponed by the said Feu Disposition recorded as aforesaid: The standard conditions specified in Schedule 3 to the Conveyancing and Feudal Reform (Scotland) Act 1970 and any lawful variation thereof operative for the time being shall apply: Provided that the whole discount hereby secured shall be ranked and preferred on the property and on the rents thereof and on the proceeds thereof in the event of a sale of the property after and postponed to the whole amount secured or to be secured by a Standard Security for (17) granted by the debtor(s) in favour of (18) recorded in the said Division of the General Register of Sasines of even date with the recording of these presents: And the debtor(s) grant(s) warrandice excepting therefrom the said Standard Security in favour of (19): And the debtor(s) consent(s) to registration hereof for execution: IN WITNESS WHEREOF

REGISTER on behalf of the within-named THE CITY OF ABERDEEN DISTRICT COUNCIL in the Register of the County of (20).

Solicitor, Aberdeen Agent.

4.42 Other styles and *verb sap*[1]

The styles which have been used are no more than illustrations. Other building societies, banks, insurance companies and local authorities will use different styles although the result may not be vastly different.

Clearly, however, other transactions, for example loans over businesses, especially where trade agreements are involved, will require different and possibly more detailed documentation and many solicitors have devised their own form of security to meet the needs of particular clients.

If one is acting for a borrower, there may be no opportunity to revise the style of standard security which is offered, but particularly where one is acting for lenders, it is essential to consider whether the style needs to be altered or adapted in any way. The office style should never become the client's standard security without passing through someone's mind first.

1 *Verbum sapienti sat est*—a word to the wise is enough.

CHAPTER 5

The standard conditions

INTRODUCTION

5.01 General

Both forms of standard security adopt the standard conditions which appear in Schedule 3 of the 1970 Act. These standard conditions impose a variety of obligations on the debtor and one object, as has been said previously, is to standardise and minimise the documentation involved. Another is to reproduce those conditions which one would normally expect in an agreement qualifying an *ex facie* absolute disposition, but stopping short of including conditions which are unduly slanted in favour of either the creditor or the debtor. Apart from the standard conditions regarding enforcement of the security, they are aimed, in general, at preserving the security subjects intact and ensuring there is no unnecessary diminution in their value. The standard conditions which are set out below in their unamended form relate to (1) maintenance and repair; (2) completion of buildings and the prohibition of alterations, etc; (3) observation of title conditions; (4) compliance with planning notices; (5) insurance; (6) restriction on letting; (7) powers of the creditor to perform the debtor's obligations; (8) calling-up; (9) default; (10) the remedies available to the creditor on default; (11) the exercise of the right of redemption; and (12) expenses. Some comment is offered on these shortly.

5.02 Variable and non-variable conditions

The 1970 Act provides that the standard conditions may be varied by agreement between the parties, except those relating to the powers of sale and foreclosure and the exercise of these powers[1]. Not only can these conditions not be altered directly, but the Act also provides that if another standard condition is varied in a way which is inconsistent with the non-variable nature of the conditions about sale and foreclosure, then the purported variation is ineffective[2]. The object of making these conditions non-variable is obviously to protect the debtor. He may not be in a position where he can negotiate the terms of any other variations, but at least he knows that the conditions about sale and foreclosure cannot be altered to his prejudice. Variations of the standard conditions are dealt with later in this chapter. As the object of section 11 is to protect the debtor, Professor Halliday suggests that the standard conditions governing sale, etc, may be altered in a way which is more favourable to the debtor[3]. So far as is known, no lender has taken this step.

1 1970 Act, s 11(3); App [15].
2 1970 Act, s 11(4); Appl [16].
3 Halliday *Commentary* para 8-07; *Halliday* vol III, para 38-96.

THE STANDARD CONDITIONS

5.03   Maintenance and repair

[1] It shall be an obligation on the debtor—
   (a) to maintain the security subjects in good and sufficient repair to the reasonable satisfaction of the creditor;
   (b) to permit, after seven clear days' notice in writing, the creditor or his agent to enter upon the security subjects at all reasonable times to examine the condition thereof;
   (c) to make all necessary repairs and make good all defects in pursuance of his obligation under head (a) of this condition within such reasonable period as the creditor may require by notice in writing.

This standard condition does not merit any comment, except to say that any repairs or maintenance which are required as a condition of the loan may result in a retention, but it is unlikely that this standard condition will be altered to deal with this, because such repairs and maintenance are intended to be done immediately after the loan has been granted.

1 1970 Act, Sch 3, standard condition 1; App [96].

5.04   Completion of buildings, etc and prohibitions of alterations, etc

[2] It shall be an obligation on the debtor—

(a) to complete, as soon as may be practicable, any unfinished buildings and works forming part of the security subjects to the reasonable satisfaction of the creditor;

(b) not to demolish, alter or add to any buildings or works forming part of the security subjects, except in accordance with the terms of a prior written consent of the creditor and in compliance with any consent, licence or approval required by law;

(c) to exhibit to the creditor at his request evidence of that consent, licence or approval.

The debtor is required to complete any unfinished buildings, an obligation which would arise if the debtor was obtaining a loan in order to extend his property or where he was being financed for the purchase of a house which he was having built for him. The loan would probably be made in stage payments, hence the obligation on the debtor to complete any unfinished building. It is unlikely that the condition will be altered to deal with the situation in which the debtor is having only one house built, where the payments will be made in stages and only after a certificate from a surveyor or architect. That being so, the matter may be regulated entirely by correspondence between the parties, or in the offer of loan.

The condition also imposes on the debtor an obligation not to demolish, alter or add to any of the buildings except with the written consent of the creditor. It is quite clear that any of these activities could adversely affect the value of the subjects and that would not be in the creditor's interests. The debtor, for example, may have in mind what he regards as being a tasteful extension of his property to provide a sun-lounge, but the debtor's tastes may prove to be unique and the existence of any horrendous addition could reduce the value of the subjects quite considerably. It is important to draw this to the client's attention. In many instances, the client will need extra finance for this and so the original lender may become involved, but the client may obtain a loan from another lender, or may not require an additional loan at all. Whatever the circumstances, the consent of the original creditor should be sought.

1 1970 Act, Sch 3, standard condition 2; App [97].

5.05 Observance of conditions in title, payment of duties, charges, etc, and general compliance with requirements of law relating to security subjects

[1]3 It shall be an obligation on the debtor—

(a) to observe any condition or perform any obligation in respect of the security subjects lawfully binding on him in relation to the security subjects;

(b) to make due and punctual payment of any ground burden, teind, stipend, or standard charge, and any rates, taxes and other public burdens, and any other payments exigible in respect of the security subjects;

(c) to comply with any requirement imposed upon him in . relation to the security subjects by virtue of any enactment.

The debtor is under an obligation (as he would be as the proprietor) to adhere to the conditions in the title including such things as paying the feu-duty. It is obvious that any failure by the debtor to do so could result in an irritancy of the feu which would bring to an end the creditor's rights in the security subjects[2]. It is unusual for this standard condition to be altered.

1 1970 Act, Sch 3, standard condition 3; App [98].
2 *Sandeman v Scottish Property Investment Co* (1885) 12 R(HL) 67.

5.06 Planning notices, etc

[1]4 It shall be an obligation on the debtor—

(a) where he has received any notice or order, issued or made by virtue of the Town and Country Planning (Scotland) Acts 1947 to 1969 or any amendment thereof, or any proposal so made for the making or issuing of any such notice or order, or any other notice or document affecting or likely to affect the security subjects, to give to the creditor, within fourteen days of the receipt of that notice, order or proposal, full particulars thereof;

(b) to take, as soon as practicable, all reasonable or necessary steps to comply with such a notice or order or, as the case may be, duly to object thereto;

(c) in the event of the creditor so requiring, to object or to join with the creditor in objecting to any such notice or order or in making representations against any proposal therefor.

The debtor is required to notify the creditor of any notice which he receives from the local planning authority whether this relates to the security subjects or to adjacent subjects. If he is required to do so by the creditor, he must lodge objections to any notices which are issued. An example would be a proposal by a neighbouring proprietor to do something to his property which might adversely affect the value of the security subjects. In these circumstances, it would be reasonable to expect the debtor to object to these proposals and the creditor may require him to do so. It may be that the notice from the local authority directly affects the debtor's own property. He must obviously comply with the local authority's requirements, because if he fails to do so, the local authority could require him to carry out repairs, or carry out the repairs themselves and, in the case of a dangerous building could demolish it.

In commercial transactions, this standard condition may be expanded to include specifically notices under the environmental health legislation, the Fire Precautions Act 1971, the Health and Safety at Work, etc Act 1974, the Offices, Shops and Railway Premises Act 1963, etc.

1 1970 Act, Sch 3, standard condition 4; App [99].

5.07 Insurance

[1]5 It shall be an obligation on the debtor—
  (a) to insure the security subjects or, at the option of the creditor, to permit the creditor to insure the security subjects in the names of the creditor and the debtor to the extent of the market value thereof against the risk of fire and such other risks as the creditor may reasonably require;
  (b) to deposit any policy of insurance effected by the debtor for the aforesaid purpose with the creditor;
  (c) to pay any premium due in respect of any such policy and, where the creditor so requests, to exhibit a receipt therefor not later than the fourteenth day after the renewal date of the policy;
  (d) to intimate to the creditor, within fourteen days of the occurrence, any occurrence which may give rise to a claim under the policy and to authorise the creditor to negotiate the settlement of the claim;
  (e) without prejudice to any obligation to the contrary enforceable against him, to comply with any reasonable requirement of the creditor as to the application of any sum received in respect of such a claim;
  (f) to refrain from any act or omission which would invalidate the policy.

Little need be said about the import of this clause but, at this stage, it is worth noting that the standard condition is almost always altered to insert 'reinstatement value' in place of 'market value' and that most building societies insist on dealing with the insurance themselves.

1 1970 Act, Sch 3, standard condition 5; App [100].

5.08 Restriction on letting

> [1]6 It shall be an obligation on the debtor not to let, or agree to let, the security subjects, or any part thereof, without the prior consent in writing of the creditor, and 'to let' in this condition includes to sub-let.

The debtor is not permitted to let or agree to let the security subjects without the agreement in writing of the creditor[1]. If the creditor does agree to a let, that may result in an increase in the insurance cover. One reason for the prohibition is to avoid any person who leases the security subjects having security of tenure under the Housing (Scotland) Act 1988 as an assured tenant or short assured tenant[2]. If there is security of tenure and the debtor defaults, the creditor may not be able to obtain vacant possession of the subjects. Under the 1988 Act, the sheriff will not make an order for possession of an assured tenancy or a short assured tenancy except on one of the grounds set out in Part I of Schedule 5. Ground 2 is that the house is subject to a heritable security which was granted before the creation of the tenancy and the creditor, following on default by the debtor, wishes to dispose of the house with vacant possession. The sheriff can decide whether in such circumstances it is reasonable to dispense with the requirements that the tenant should be given prior notice that possession might be recovered under this head. It is thought that sheriffs will dispense with notice especially where the heritable creditor has not been asked for permission to lease the subjects. Heritable creditors should, however, insist on a clause being inserted in any lease to cover this, rather than leave it to the discretion of the sheriff. If possession is given to the heritable creditor, the local authority may be required to house the tenant under the Housing (Homeless Persons) Act 1977. Very often, however, the accommodation which is offered to such persons is in less desirable areas and the amenities available may be fewer than the tenant currently enjoys. In such a case, some sheriffs may not be prepared to dispense with the requirement of prior notice. Similar considerations arise in relation to agricultural property where a lease could become an agricultural tenancy with the protection which that affords. Whether or not there is security of tenure, court proceedings may be required to remove the person occupying the subjects.

1 1970 Act, Sch 3, standard condition 6; App [101].
2 See also paras 5.30 *et seq* below.
3 Housing (Scotland) Act 1988, ss 18, 33.

5.09   General power of creditor to perform obligations, etc, on failure of debtor and power to charge debtor

[1]**7** (1) The creditor shall be entitled to perform any obligation imposed by the standard conditions on the debtor, which the debtor has failed to perform.

(2) Where it is necessary for the performance of any obligation as aforesaid, the creditor may, after giving seven clear days' notice in writing to the debtor, enter upon the security subjects at all reasonable times.

(3) All expenses and charges (including any interest thereon), reasonably incurred by the creditor in the exercise of a right conferred by this condition, shall be recoverable from the debtor and shall be deemed to be secured by the security subjects under the standard security, and the rate of any such interest shall be the rate in force at the relevant time in respect of advances secured by the security, or, where no such rate is prescribed, shall be the bank rate in force at the relevant time.

The creditor is given a general power to perform any of the obligations imposed by the standard conditions if the debtor fails to perform these. If the creditor is forced to perform the obligations, the debtor will be liable for all the expenses which are reasonably incurred in connection with that performance. While it is not possible for the heritable creditor to alter the feuing conditions to permit him to perform obligations imposed by the titles, the heritable creditor will be made aware of any action of irritancy which is raised[2]. While there are restrictions on the exercise of the right to irritate leases[3], there is no statutory requirement to notify heritable creditors and so it is desirable to ensure that a lease permits heritable creditors to perform the tenant's obligations.

1 1970 Act, Sch 3, standard condition 7; App [102].
2 Conveyancing Amendment (Scotland) Act 1938, s 6.
3 Law Reform (Miscellaneous Provisions) (Scotland) Act 1985, ss 4–6.

5.10 Calling-up

[1]8 The creditor shall be entitled, subject to the terms of the security and to any requirement of law, to call-up a standard security in the manner prescribed by section 19 of this Act.

1 1970 Act, Sch 3, standard condition 8; App [103].

5.11 Default

[1]9 (1) The debtor shall be held to be in default in any of the following circumstances, that is to say—
  (a) where a calling-up notice in respect of the security has been served and has not been complied with;
  (b) where there has been a failure to comply with any other requirement arising out of the security;
  (c) where the proprietor of the security subjects has become insolvent.

(2) For the purposes of this condition, the proprietor shall be taken to be insolvent if—
  (a) he has become notour bankrupt, or he has executed a trust deed for behoof of, or has made a composition contract or arrangement with, his creditors;
  (b) he has died and a judicial factor has been appointed under section 11A of the Judicial Factors (Scotland) Act 1889 to divide his insolvent estate among his creditors, or his estate falls to be administered in accordance with an order under section 421 of the Insolvency Act 1986;
  (c) where the proprietor is a company, a winding-up order has been made with respect to it, or a resolution for voluntary winding-up (other than a members' voluntary winding-up) has been passed with respect to it, or a receiver or manager of its undertaking has been duly appointed, or possession has been taken, by or on behalf of the holders of any debentures secured by a floating charge, of any property of the company comprised in or subject to the charge.

1 1970 Act, Sch 3, standard condition 9; App [104].

5.12 Rights of creditor on default

[1]10 (1) Where the debtor is in default, the creditor may, without prejudice to his exercising any other remedy arising from the

contract to which the standard security relates, exercise, in accordance with the provisions of Part II of this Act and of any other enactment applying to standard securities, such of the remedies specified in the following sub-paragraphs of this standard condition as he may consider appropriate.

(2) He may proceed to sell the security subjects or any part thereof.

(3) He may enter into possession of the security subjects and may receive or recover feu-duties, ground annuals or, as the case may be, the rents of those subjects or any part thereof.

(4) Where he has entered into possession as aforesaid, he may let the security subjects or any part thereof.

(5) Where he has entered into possession as aforesaid there shall be transferred to him all the rights of the debtor in relation to the granting of leases or rights of occupancy over the security subjects and to the management and maintenance of those subjects.

(6) He may effect all such repairs and may make good such defects a are necessary to maintain the security subjects in good and sufficient repair, and may effect such reconstruction, alteration and improvement on the subjects as would be expected of a prudent proprietor to maintain the market value of the subjects, and for the aforesaid purposes may enter on the subjects at all reasonable times.

(7) He may apply to the court for a decree of foreclosure.

1 1970 Act, Sch 3, standard condition 10; App [105].

5.13   Exercise of right of redemption

[1]**11** (1) The debtor shall be entitled to exercise his right (if any) to redeem the security on giving notice of his intention so to do, being a notice in writing (hereinafter referred to as a 'notice of redemption').

(2) Nothing in the provisions of this Act shall preclude a creditor from waiving the necessity for a notice of redemption, or from agreeing to a period of notice of less than that to which he is entitled.

(3)(a) A notice of redemption may be delivered to the creditor or sent by registered post or recorded delivery to him at his last known address, and an acknowledgement signed by the creditor or his agent or a certificate of postage by the person giving the notice accompanied by the postal receipt shall be sufficient evidence of such notice having been given.

(b) If the address of the creditor is not known, or if the packet containing the notice of redemption is returned to the sender with intimation that it could not be delivered, a notice of redemption may be sent to the Extractor of the Court of Session and an acknowledgment of receipt by him shall be sufficient evidence of such notice having been given.

(c) A notice of redemption sent by post shall be held to have been given on the day next after the day of posting.

(4) When a notice of redemption states that a specified amount will be repaid, and it is subsequently ascertained that the whole amount due to be repaid is more or less than the amount specified in the notice, the notice shall nevertheless be effective as a notice of repayment of the amount due as subsequently ascertained.

(5) Where the debtor has exercised a right to redeem, and has made payment of the whole amount due, or has performed the whole obligations of the debtor under the contract to which the security relates, the creditor shall grant a discharge in the terms prescribed in section 17 of this Act.

1 1970 Act, Sch 3, standard condition 11; App [106].

5.14 Comment

Standard conditions 8–11 are dealt with at chapter 8 below.

5.15 Expenses

[1]**12** The debtor shall be personally liable to the creditor for the whole expenses of the preparation and execution of the standard security and any variation, restriction and discharge thereof and, where any of those deeds are recorded, the recording thereof, and all expenses reasonably incurred by the creditor in calling-up the security and realising or attempting to realise the security subjects, or any part thereof, and exercising any other powers conferred upon him by security.

It is common to alter the standard conditions to provide that any expenses due by the debtor shall be part of the sums owed to the creditor.

1 1970 Act, Sch 3, standard condition 12; App [107].

VARIATION OF THE STANDARD CONDITIONS

5.16 General

Although the standard conditions are intended to simplify the documentation, they may nevertheless be varied, subject to the exceptions which have already been noted. Any variation which is agreed at the time of the creation of the security should be set out, or referred to, in the standard security. If there is a separate deed, the deed need not be recorded so long as it is identified in the standard security.

A separate deed of variation is favoured by building societies and because they employ a large number of variations which will apply to each loan, deeds of variation have been prepared and many are registered in the Books of Council and Session[1]. These variations are then referred to in each standard security which avoids the need to repeat them at length. In practice, building societies have booklets which set out the standard conditions as varied and the debtor will have a copy of such a booklet at or before the execution of the standard security.

1 Eg Bradford and Bingley; Britannia; Century; Dunfermline; Halifax; National and Provincial; Newcastle; Northern Rock, Skipton; Woolwich; Yorkshire.

5.17 Variations commonly encountered

As has been said, it would be rare to find a standard security in favour of an institutional lender where the standard conditions have not been altered in any way. The variations which are commonly encountered can be classified under the following headings: (1) insurance; (2) parting with possession; (3) transfer of the security subjects; (4) alterations in use; (5) improvement grants; (6) compulsory purchase; (7) assignation by the creditor; (8) dealing with moveables belonging to the debtor; (9) other things which may prejudice the security; (10) other securities; (11) the definition of 'default'; and (12) notice.

5.18 (1) Insurance

In their altered form, the standard conditions may require the property to be insured for re-instatement value, rather than market value[1]. In many cases, the cost of re-instating a building will be far in excess of its market value, particularly where the building is constructed of materials which would be difficult or costly to acquire, for example Aberdeen granite, or Ballachulish slates. An alternative is to require that the property is insured by the lender against fire or such other risks as the lender may specify[2]. If the property is not insured by the lender, but by the debtor, he may be required to exhibit details to the lender and evidence that the insurance is still in force[3]. In addition, the lender may require the debtor to disclose the figure for which the insurance is required[4]. In some cases, the lender has the option to insure or require the debtor to do so[5]. The debtor may also be required to notify the lender of any damage to the property[6] and will be required to refrain from doing anything which may render the insurance void[7]. If the debtor defaults, the lender may be given the power to effect the necessary insurance and charge the debtor for that[8].

The lender may have taken power to adjust and settle any insurance claims on behalf of the debtor[9] and it may be provided that any money received by the lender or the debtor from any insurance claim shall, at the option of the lender, be applied to make good the loss, or towards repairing the amount due[10]. That would be important where the property was so severely damaged that it was a total loss or a constructive total loss. One final provision is that any money received by the debtor, where he effects the insurance, shall be held in trust for the lender[11].

1 Eg Clydesdale; Royal Bank; Bank of Scotland.
2 Eg Abbey, Bradford and Bingley; Britannia; Century; Dunfermline; Newcastle; National and Provincial; Skipton; Yorkshire.
3 Eg Abbey; Clydesdale; Halifax; National and Provincial; Royal Bank; Yorkshire.
4 Eg Abbey; Halifax; National and Provincial; Royal Bank.
5 Eg Alliance and Leicester.
6 Eg Abbey; Halifax.
7 Eg Abbey; Alliance and Leicester; Bradford and Bingley; Century; Halifax; Newcastle; Skipton; Yorkshire; Royal Bank.
8 Eg Halifax; Clydesdale.
9 Eg Alliance and Leicester; Bradford and Bingley; Britannia; Century; Halifax; Newcastle; Skipton; Yorkshire; Royal Bank.
10 Eg Abbey; Alliance and Leicester; Bradford and Bingley; Britannia; Century; Dunfermline; Halifax; Newcastle; Skipton; Yorkshire, Royal Bank.
11 Eg Alliance and Leicester; Bradford and Bingley; Britannia; Century; Dunfermline; Halifax; National and Provincial; Newcastle; Skipton.

5.19 (2) Parting with possession

The debtor will frequently be prohibited from parting with possession of the security subjects in whole or in part[1]. Framed in that way, the prohibition is wider than the prohibition against letting[2], because a person who does not have a lease may nevertheless be in possession of the security subjects. Although that possession may not give the occupant any security of tenure, he may have to be removed by court proceedings, whether as a matter of law or merely one of practicality. The creditor will obviously not wish to have to resort to such measures.

1 Eg Abbey; Alliance and Leicester; Bradford and Bingley; Britannia; Century; Dunfermline; Halifax; National and Provincial; Newcastle; Skipton; Yorkshire; Bank of Scotland; Clydesdale.
2 1970 Act, Sch 3, standard condition 6; App [101].

5.20   (3) Transfer of the property

The debtor may be prohibited from selling or otherwise transferring the property subject to the security without the creditor's consent[1]. Although such a transfer replaces the original debtor with a new debtor, the original debtor would remain liable under the personal obligation[2]. Having transferred the property, however, the original debtor might disappear and, while the lender's rights against the property would normally be regarded as more valuable than the personal obligation, the lender would not wish to be deprived of any means of enforcing the security and the personal obligation. In one case, the conditions provide that the lender 'will not unreasonably withhold its consent to the vesting of the property in a beneficiary on the death of the debtor[3].'

1 Eg Alliance and Leicester; Bradford and Bingley; Britannia; Century; Dunfermline; Halifax; Skipton; Woolwich; Bank of Scotland; Clydesdale; Royal Bank; Yorkshire.
2 Conveyancing (Scotland) Act 1874, s 47 (amended by the Conveyancing (Scotland) Act 1924, s 15).
3 Eg Halifax.

5.21   (4) Alterations in use

The standard conditions already prohibit the debtor from making alterations to the security subjects[1], but they may add a prohibition against altering the use[2]. Any alteration in use may be an infringement of the conditions of the title which could, in theory, result in irritancy. However, even where there is no infringement of the title conditions, an alteration in use may require consents or some other form of approval under the Town and Country Planning (Scotland) Act 1972, the Building (Scotland) Act 1959 and the Fire Precautions Act 1971. However, even if none of these consequences would follow from a change of use, the fact that the security subjects are put to a different use may make them less marketable, for example the conversion of office premises into a private dwelling-house.

1 1970 Act, Sch 3, standard condition 2(b)(1); App [97].
2 Eg Abbey; Bradford and Bingley; Britannia; Century; Dunfermline; Halifax; National and Provincial; Skipton; Woolwich; Yorkshire; Bank of Scotland; Clydesdale.

5.22 (5) Improvement grants

Some variations of the standard conditions prohibit the debtor from applying for an improvement grant[1]. Although at first sight this may seem odd since the clear object is to improve the property, there are conditions attached to these grants, viz: that the house must be used only as a dwelling-house, that it must be occupied as a main residence and it must be maintained in good repair[2], which, while they are not onerous, may have implications where the subjects are sold by the creditor.

Other conditions go slightly further by prohibiting the debtor from applying for any grants[3] and two such grants which are specifically mentioned are grants for agricultural subjects under the Agriculture (Scotland) Act 1948[4] and for crofts under the Crofters (Scotland) Act 1955[5].

1 Eg Abbey; Alliance and Leicester; Bradford and Bingley; Dunfermline; National and Provincial; Newcastle; Woolwich.
2 Housing (Scotland) Act 1987, s 246.
3 Eg Bradford and Bingley; Century; Dunfermline; Bank of Scotland; Clydesdale; Royal Bank.
4 Agriculture (Scotland) Act 1948, s 77.
5 Crofters (Scotland) Act 1955, s 22(2).

5.23 (6) Compulsory purchase

The standard conditions, as varied, may provide that any rights which the debtor may have on compulsory acquisition of the security subjects shall be held to be assigned to the creditor who will have full power in relation thereto[1]. While there can be no doubt about the intention behind this provision, it would be necessary for the debtor to assign his claim and intimate that to the acquirer and there must therefore be doubt as to whether the mere statement is sufficient. As an alternative, the debtor may be obliged to pay any compensation to the creditor[2].

1 Eg Bradford and Bingley; Skipton.
2 Eg Newcastle; Woolwich; Clydesdale.

5.24 (7) **Assignation by the creditor**

While the debtor may not assign the standard security without the consent of the creditor, the creditor may be able to do so[1]. In recent years, a 'secondary mortgage market' has developed in which 'securitisation' takes place. A typical transaction would involve the sale of mortgages by lenders in exchange for further money, for example by an issue of Euronotes. The 'new' lender will demand that all rights under the existing mortgages are transferred. That is the reason why some Reports on Title (for example TSB) are framed in terms that the solicitor guarantees the Report to anyone acquiring rights from the lender[2].

1 Eg Abbey; Alliance and Leicester; Bradford and Bingley; Britannia; Century; Halifax; National and Provincial; Skipton; Woolwich; Bank of Scotland; Clydesdale.
2 See para 2.08 above.

5.25 (8) **Dealing with moveables belonging to the debtor**

The variation of the standard conditions may permit the creditor to deal with the debtor's belongings in the event of their being left in the subjects after the creditor has taken steps to enforce the security[1]. The provision might be in the following terms:

> 'On or after taking possession of the property the company may, as agent of the debtor and at his expense, remove, store, sell or otherwise deal with any furniture or goods which the borrower shall fail or refuse to remove, and the company shall not be liable for any loss or damage thus occasioned to the debtor[2].'

If the creditor does not take this power, he will be under an obligation to store the debtor's goods and take reasonable care of them. The creditor will have to pay any charges for storage with little or no hope of ever recoving the cost from the debtor.

It is not uncommon for a heritable creditor to sell the security subjects with some moveable items included in the sale. The obvious example is carpets. In such a case, the heritable creditor may refuse to warrant ownership of the moveables[3].

1 Eg Abbey; Alliance and Leicester; Bradford and Bingley; Britannia; Century; Dunfermline; Halifax; National and Provincial; Newcastle; Skipton; Woolwich; Bank of Scotland; Clydesdale; Royal Bank.
2 For a discussion of 'entering into possession', see para 8.36 below.
3 See para 8.31 below.

5.26 (9) Other things which may prejudice the security

In addition to prohibiting the debtor from parting with possession or transferring the security subjects, the variations may also prohibit him from doing various other things which may prejudice the security[1]. For example, he may not be able to 'grant any servitude, wayleave, real burden, water or drainage rights or other continuing rights upon or affecting the security subjects or any part thereof'[2]. Some of these rights could be quite onerous and could adversely affect the value of the property.

1 Eg Century; Dunfermline; Yorkshire; Clydesdale.
2 Eg Clydesdale; Bank of Scotland.

5.27 (10) Other securities

There may be a prohibition against the granting of other securities, or a prohibition against granting such securities without the lender's consent[1]. If the debtor grants a second security without the original creditor's knowledge, intimation of the existence of the second security could limit the scope of the first security in a way that was not intended[2]. Many debtors may be unaware that the documentation which they sign, for example in connection with double glazing or kitchen units, is a standard security. They may therefore be in contravention of a provision in their existing security prohibiting other securities.

1 Eg Bradford and Bingley; Britannia; Century; Dunfermline; National and Provincial; Newcastle; Skipton; Woolwich; Yorkshire; Bank of Scotland; Clydesdale; Royal Bank.
2 1970 Act, s 13, App [20].

5.28 (11) Definition of default

Although the issue of default is dealt with later, it is useful to note the definition of default in standard condition 9 (see para 5.11 above).

That standard condition is frequently altered to add other circumstances in which the debtor will be in default. For example, a failure to pay a specified number of monthly instalments[1] and a failure to comply with any obligations imposed under the standard conditions[2] (as varied) or any breach of the building society's rules[3]. There may also be default if the security subjects are compulsorily acquired, or requisitioned or a notice to treat is served[4].

1 Eg Alliance and Leicester; Bradford and Bingley; Century; Halifax; National and Provincial; Newcastle; Skipton; Woolwich; Bank of Scotland.
2 Eg Alliance and Leicester; Century; Halifax; National and Provincial.
3 Eg Alliance and Leicester; Century; Halifax; National and Provincial.
4 Eg Alliance and Leicester; Bradford and Bingley; National and Provincial; Skipton; Bank of Scotland.

5.29 (12) Notices

The 1970 Act contains provisions for serving calling-up notices[1] and notices of default[2]. In addition, the creditor may serve notice of intention to inspect the security subjects[3], and notice of intention to enter the subjects to perform any obligations which have not been performed by the debtor[4].

While the Act sets out in detail the methods by which calling-up notices and notices of default can be served, it says nothing about the service of other notices. It is common to find a general provision about notice which covers any situation in which a notice has to be served on the debtor[5]. It is also almost universal to find that the heritable creditor is empowered at any time after 'he shall have been entitled to enter into possession' to give the debtor seven days' notice to quit. While this is a useful provision, a heritable creditor who applies to the court under section 24 will also seek warrant to evict the debtor[6]. If the heritable creditor serves a calling-up notice and it is not complied with, that would entitle him to enter into possession. It is unlikely that officers of court would seek to evict the debtor except on the basis of a court warrant, and so the sending of a 'seven-day' letter may not be of much use if the debtor fails to comply.

1 1970 Act, s 19(6); App [42].
2 1970 Act, s 21(2); App [54].
3 1970 Act, Sch 3, standard condition 1; App [96].
4 1970 Act, Sch 3, standard condition 7; App [102].
5 Eg Abbey; Alliance and Leicester; Britannia; Century; Dunfermline; National and Provincial; Newcastle; Woolwich; Yorkshire; Bank of Scotland.
6 See paras 8.20, 8.21 below.

5.30 Breach of the standard conditions

Although the 1970 Act, and probably also standard conditions as varied, deal with default, there was always an obligation on the debtor at common law not to do anything which would prejudice the creditor's security. In *Reid v McGill*[1], the debtor granted a lease of mineral rights which was on very favourable terms and the lease was also of a long duration. The court held that the lease was not valid against the creditor because the debtor's actions were not reasonable, having regard to the creditor's interests. The point was that because the security subjects would have burdened with a long lease at an uneconomic rent, the value of the security subjects was considerably reduced.

This principle is probably applicable to standard securities[2], but the standard conditions will usually deal with this.

1 1912 2 SLT 246.
2 See, however, Lord Kissen in *Trade Development Bank v Warriner and Mason* 1980 SC 74 at 107.

5.31   Third party rights

While the common law has been altered in that the standard conditions now provide that the debtor cannot grant leases without the written consent of the creditor, an important issue which still arises is what is the position of a third party who enters into a lease, or indeed any other arrangement with the debtor, which contravenes the terms of the standard security? Does it make any difference whether the contravention is obvious *ex facie* of the standard security, or whether the fact that there is a contravention appears only after an examination of other documentation which may not appear on the Register of Sasines, or the Land Register? These issues have been discussed in three cases, all involving the Trade Development Bank.

These decisions have been commented upon and the decision in the *Warriner and Mason*[1] case has been criticised as being incorrectly decided[2]. For that reason, it would be helpful to set out the facts of these cases and indicate the basis of the criticism. That said, however, it must be remembered that no matter how well-founded the criticism may seem, these cases still represent the law until such time as they are overturned by a larger bench of the Court of Session, or by the House of Lords.

1 *Trade Development Bank v Warriner and Mason* 1980 SC 74.
2 K G C Reid 'Real Conditions in Standard Securities' 1983 SLT (News) 169, 189.

5.32   The Trade Development Bank cases

The three cases are *Trade Development Bank v Warriner and Mason (Scotland) Ltd*[1], *Trade Development Bank v David W Haig (Bellshill) Ltd*[2] and *Trade Development Bank v Crittall Windows Ltd*[3]. The effect of these cases can be summarised in the following way. If a debtor, in contravention of standard condition 6 which prohibits the granting of leases of the security subjects without the consent of the heritable creditor, grants a lease, that lease, or a sub-lease, may be reduced by the heritable creditor, unless the creditor knew at the time when the security was granted that the lessee had a real right or one which was capable of being made real. If the heritable creditor has this knowledge, then he would not be acting in good faith, if he attempted to reduce the lease.

1 1980 SC 74.
2 1983 SLT 107, 510.
3 1983 SLT 107, 510.

5.33   Trade Development Bank v Warriner and Mason (Scotland) Ltd[1]

Lyon Group Ltd were the tenants of part of an industrial estate. The lease was for 120 years and it was recorded in the General Register of Sasines on 9 April 1973. At the same time, Lyon granted a Form B standard security over the lease in favour of the Trade Development Bank and the reference to the standard conditions was in its usual form, ie 'the standard conditions specified in Schedule 3 to the Conveyancing and Feudal Reform (Scotland) Act 1970 and any lawful variation thereof operative for the time being shall apply and we agree that the standard conditions shall be varied in accordance with the said minute of agreement.' The personal obligation was in the separate, unrecorded minute of agreement just referred to.

In 1975, The Lyon Group purported to sub-lease part of the security subjects to Warriner and Mason and later went into liquidation. TDB served a calling-up notice and raised an action for reduction of the sub-lease. Warriner and Mason, referred to standard condition 6, ie 'It shall be an obligation on the debtor not to let, or agree to let, the security subjects, or any part thereof, without the prior consent in writing of the creditor, and "to let" in this condition includes to sub-let'. They contended that, notwithstanding the terms of standard condition 6, Lyon had power to grant the sub-lease by virtue of its radical right in the subjects, provided that did not adversely affect the security. The decision at first instance was upheld on appeal.

The First Division held (Lord Kissen dissenting) that because the minute of agreement was unrecorded, Warriner and Mason could not tell from the standard security whether standard condition 6 applied, or did not apply, or applied in some varied form. Nevertheless the terms of the standard security should have put them on their inquiry and because they failed to make the necessary inquiries, they were in bad faith and accordingly, the lease fell to be reduced.

The opinion of Lord President Emslie, who gave the leading judgment, was that standard condition 6 had not been made a real condition, but that it was nevertheless enforceable against the sub-lessees, because they did not make the appropriate enquiries and hence were not in good faith. In both the *Haig*[2] case and in *Crittall Windows*[3], the issue of good faith was stressed and it was stated, correctly it is submitted, that if the heritable creditor knew about the existence of a right which might become real, he would not be entitled to enforce the security in a way prejudicial to that right.

1 1980 SC 74.
2 *Trade Development Bank v David W Haig (Bellshill) Ltd* 1983 SLT 107.
3 *Trade Development Bank v Crittall Windows Ltd* 1983 SLT 107.

5.34   The counter-argument

Kenneth Reid's argument is that it is incorrect to say that the standard conditions are not real unless they appear on the face of the standard security. At one point in his judgment, the Lord President had this to say,

> 'Variations at the time of the granting of a standard security . . . may, but need not, enter the register at all. If they do enter the register either in gremio of the standard security, or by endorsement thereon . . . or in a duly recorded deed then there can be no doubt that the standard conditions so varied are published to the world and affect the granter's title. The provisions governing the making of variations by an unrecorded variation are to be regarded as having entered the granter's title, or that third parties are to be affected by those variations which do not appear on the face of the register'[1].

That comment introduces a distinction between standard conditions which appear on the register and those which do not, and this appears to be in conflict with the terms of section 11(2) of the Act which says that the standard conditions whether in their original form or in their varied form 'shall regulate every standard security'. In so far as the Lord President was suggesting that no condition can be real unless it appears on the register, then it is submitted with respect, that is incorrect. Servitude rights for example, can be acquired by prescription, and they are nevertheless real even although they do not appear on the register. Leases under the Leases Act 1449 are also real rights.

Kenneth Reid's further point, however, is that although the standard conditions are real, the prohibition against granting leases was a personal obligation and so that prohibition could not have any effect on the real right granted by Lyon to Warriner and Mason. There is a great deal of force in Kenneth Reid's argument, but, as he points out, it does not follow that the heritable creditor is without other remedies. He refers to the cases which are authority for the proposition that a debtor must not do anything which would prejudice the security. *Reid v McGill*[2] is only one such case where a lease was reduced on that ground[3] and there does not appear to be any reason why this principle cannot apply equally to standard securities. In *Warriner and Mason*, however, Lord Kissen made an obiter remark to the effect that the principle had no such application[4].

So far as good faith is concerned, a distinction has to be drawn between real rights or rights which are capable of being made real and personal rights which are incapable of being made real. A person dealing with a debtor under a standard security will be deemed to know about real rights which appear on the registers and will be affected by other real rights or rights capable of being made real if he knows about them[5]. However, so far as personal rights are concerned, he is not affected by these even if he does know about them[6]. In order to get round that well-recognised distinction, it would have to have been argued in *Warriner and Mason* that the prohibition against letting in standard condition 6, which in practice is never altered, rendered null any real right which would otherwise have been created.

1 *Trade Development Bank v Warriner and Mason (Scotland) Ltd* 1980 SC 74 at 93.
2 1912 2 SLT 246.
3 Other cases are *Mitchell v Little* (1820) Hume's Dec 661 and *Edinburgh Entertainments Ltd v Stevenson* 1926 SC 363.
4 1980 SC 74 at 107.
5 *Rodger (Builders) Ltd v Fawdry* 1950 SC 483.
6 *Mann v Houston* 1957 SLT 89; *Wallace v Simmers* 1960 SC 255. See also G L F Henry 'Personal Rights' 1961 Con Rev 193.

5.35   Trade Development Bank Ltd v David W Haig (Bellshill) Ltd[1]

Lyon leased subjects from the local county council in 1971, and part of the subjects were sub-leased to Haig. Neither of the leases was at the time registrable. In the offer to sub-let, it was provided that Haig should have the option to lease another part of the subjects, but the option had to be exercised within three years. In January 1973 Lyon had surrendered the original lease and had taken in its place three leases of the original subjects. These leases were registered and Lyon granted a standard security over them in favour of the Trade Development Bank. In August 1973, Haig intimated that they wished to exercise the option and that was accepted in 1974. In 1975, Lyon went into liquidation.

The Trade Development Bank wished to exercise their rights under the standard security and raised an action against Haig for reduction of the missives in exercise of the option and declarator that Haig had no right, title, or interest in the subjects. Haig argued *inter alia* that they were 'excusably ignorant' of the existence of the standard security. The First Division held that Haig could not be regarded as 'excusably ignorant' because the registers gave public notice of the existence of the standard security.

1 1983 SLT 510.

5.36 Trade Development Bank Ltd v Crittal Windows Ltd[1]

This case concerned the same 1971 lease as the *Haig* case above. In 1972, Crittal offered to purchase Lyon's whole right, title and leasehold interest in part of the subjects and that was accepted. In January 1973, the new leases were substituted and the standard security granted. In June 1973, Lyon granted in a recordable assignation of one of the leases and that was recorded in May 1974. After Lyon went into liqudation, the Trade Development Bank raised a similar action against Crittal. Crittal's argument was that the standard security had been entered into in bad faith. The Trade Development Bank argued that a security holder could not be in bad faith if it knew the third party had acquired enforceable rights and that the leases had ceased to apply to the subjects and so the 1972 missives ceased to be enforceable against Lyon. The First Division held that if it was established that the Trade Development Bank had knowledge that there was a right which was capable of being made real, Crittal could prevent the Trade Development Bank from exercising their rights and also that the missives of 1972 remained enforceable against Lyon.

1 1983 SLT 510.

5.37 Comment

The result of these decisions is that a tenant must take steps to protect himself against being ousted by a heritable creditor of the landlord who has not consented to the lease. The reasoning which was applied in the *Trade Development Bank* cases (and indeed the counter argument) can be applied to any other arrangement which the debtor may enter into in contravention of the standard conditions. Thus, as we have noted[1], the standard conditions may prohibit the debtor inter alia from (1) parting with possession of the security subjects, (2) transferring them, (3) granting other securities, and (4) granting other rights, eg servitude rights. On the basis of the cases, any right which was purportedly conferred on a third party would be void, unless the heritable creditor knew that the third party either had a real right or a right which was capable of being made real. That is the current legal position. Using the counter argument, the arrangement with the third party would be valid, but *qua* the heritable creditor, the debtor might be in breach of his obligation not to do anything which would prejudice the heritable security.

That said, it would be prudent for anyone who is contemplating taking a lease, an assignation of a lease, or a sub-lease to ascertain whether there is a standard security over the landlord's, or tenant's interest, or both, and if there is, to ensure that the security holder (or holders) has given written consent to the proposed transaction. There is an argument in relation to assignations, that if the heritable creditor consented to the lease, his consent to the assignation is not required, but there is nothing to be lost by a 'belt and braces' approach.

1 See paras 5.16–5.27 above.

CHAPTER 6

Variation, restriction, assignation and transmission of standard securities

VARIATION

6.01 General

We have already considered the possibility of the variation of standard conditions, but it is possible also to vary the terms of a standard security which has already been recorded. This facility appears in section 16(1) of the 1970 Act, but it should be noted, however, that it is not available if the contemplated alteration can competently be achieved by other means, for example, assignation, or discharge, or restriction of the standard security. In other words, it is not possible to use the simple process of variation where other specific methods are laid down by the Act. The Act does provide for assignation, discharge and restriction of a standard security and accordingly, it is not possible to use section 16 instead of these other provisions. It is also provided that section 16 cannot be used if the variation involves a variation to, or an extension of, the interest in land over which the security extends. Thus, if a standard security exists over Plot A and the creditor wishes a standard security over Plot B which the debtor also owns, a fresh standard security would have to be granted over Plot A or over Plots A and B and the original standard security over Plot A would then be discharged. It is not, however, competent to *vary* the standard security over Plot A and provide that it now extends to Plot B as well.

Section 16 is available if the amount of the loan is to be altered or where there is a change in the name of the creditor or the debtor, or where the debtor, for example, amalgamates with somebody else to form a new entity.

It is important to distinguish two situations. If the provisions to be altered have already been recorded, then the variation must also be recorded and that may be done by endorsing the variation on the standard security in accordance with Schedule 4 of the Act or alternatively a separate deed may be drawn up and recorded.

If, on the other hand, the provisions which are to be altered are contained in a deed which has not been recorded, then the variation may be made in any form of deed appropriate for the purpose and that deed need not itself be recorded[1]. Nevertheless some such deeds are recorded/registered, but it is not clear why.

Any variation which is made in accordance with section 16 will not prejudice any other security over the same interest in land which has been effectively constituted before the variation is recorded or where the variation is effected by a deed which has not been recorded then before that deed has been executed. The term 'constituted' must refer to recording or execution whichever is appropriate. That is specifically provided for in section 16(4) and contemplates a problem which arose at common law[2].

1 1970 Act, s 16(2); App [28].
2 *National Bank of Scotland v Union Bank of Scotland* (1885) 13 R 380 especially Lord Rutherfurd Clark at 394.

6.02   Uninfeft granter, or creditor

If a deed of variation which has to be recorded is to be granted by a person who does not have a recorded title to the standard security, a clause of deduction of title would have to be inserted in the deed of variation. Such a clause would also be required where the creditor whose consent to a variation is required, does not have a recorded title. Where the security appears in the Land Register, a clause of deduction of title is not required, but the links in title should be submitted to the Keeper with the application for registration of the deed of variation.

6.03   When deeds of variations are used

Deeds of variation are used in a variety of circumstances, for example for an additional loan, or an increase in the rate of interest. Power to make additional advances and vary interest rates are commonly provided for in the initial documentation and, in that event, no deed of variation will be needed. A common situation in which a deed of variation will be required is where the granter dies and a beneficiary, or some other person, takes on the loan. A deed of variation will also be required in a divorce or separation which the responsibility for the loan is being transferred, for example, from the husband, or husband and wife, to the wife[1]. If in such a case, the property is also being transferred, as is most likely, it is desirable to check that any special destination has been evacuated[2].

1 For possible problems, see D J Cusine 'Property Transfer Orders: Some Conveyancing Imponderables' (1990) 35 JLSS 52; E M Clive (1990) 35 JLSS 188. For ranking implications, see para 7.11 below.
2 For the consequences of failing to do so, see the letter from D A Johnstone in 1985 SLT (News) 18.

6.04 Styles of variation

Various styles of variation are to be found in Professor Halliday's book[1]. The style below can be used in a situation where there is a *divorce, or separation, and there is a disposition transferring the title from the husband to the wife, and where only the husband was infeft.*

> I, Mrs. Mary Donoghue or Stevenson hereby agree that the foregoing standard security granted by William Stevenson in favour of the Rest Assured Building Society recorded in the Division of the General Register of Sasines applicable to the County of Erewhon on Nineteenth February, Nineteen hundred and eighty-two [registered on Nineteenth February, Nineteen hundred and Eighty-two over the Subjects in Title Number REN 123456789] shall with effect from Seventh May, Nineteen hundred and Ninety be varied so that I, the said Mrs. Mary Donoghue or Stevenson undertake the whole obligations undertaken by the said William Stevenson in the said standard security in so far as they remain outstanding, the balance thereunder as at the said Seventh May, Nineteen hundred and Ninety being £45,067.83; and shall be entitled to the whole rights competent to the said William Stevenson thereunder and that on the terms and conditions contained in the said standard security: Which subjects were last vested in the said William Stevenson whose title thereto is recorded in the said Division of the General Register of Sasines of even date with the said standard security and from whom I acquired right by Disposition granted by the said William Stevenson in my favour dated Fourth May, Nineteen hundred and Ninety and to be recorded of even date with these presents: And We, the said Rest Assured Building Society consent to the variation hereby effected; And we discharge the said William Stevenson absolutely of all liability under the said standard security IN WITNESS WHEREOF[2].

The variation is not frequently done by a separate deed. Separate deeds are used and are desirable where the ranking clauses are complex, for example, where one heritable creditor ranks first, but only to the extent of £X of principal and interest, then the second heritable creditor ranks to the extent of £Y of principal and interest, and after that the first heritable creditor is secured over the balance. This kind of arrangement is common in brewers' loans.

1 Halliday *Commentary* paras 9.43–9.45; *Halliday* vol III paras 40-06–40-12.
2 The clause of deduction of title would be omitted in a registered transaction.

RESTRICTION

6.05 General

Section 15 deals with the release of part of the security subjects and it provides a form of deed of restriction to be used where there is no payment, and a form of partial discharge and deed of restriction which will be used when the loan is partly repaid in consideration for release of part of the property. The appropriate forms are C and D of Schedule 4. Thus if a standard security has been granted over three plots and one of these is sold, the proceeds may be used to pay off part of the loan. A deed of restriction combined with a partial discharge would be appropriate. A practical problem may arise in connection with large developments. The developer may have granted a security over the subjects at the time of his purchase. If he then builds houses and sells them, each house will be affected the standard security granted by the developer unless there is a deed of restriction. In practice, the builder and his lender may agree at the outset that the necessary deeds of restriction will be granted (possibly in exchange for specified payments). The disadvantage of that is that the solicitors acting for the builder may not be able to deliver an executed deed at settlement and that factor would have to be taken account of in any letter of obligation. The preferable approach is to incorporate the consent to the restriction by the creditor in the conveyance by the builder in favour of the purchaser.

ASSIGNATION

6.06 General

A standard security may be transferred in whole or in part[1]. This is done by assignation and two forms are to be found in Schedule 4. The first form is used where the assignation is to be in a separate document and the second is used where the assignation is to be endorsed on the standard security. The recording of the assignation vests the security in the assignee to the same effect as if it had been granted originally in his favour[2].

1 1970 Act, s 14(1); App [23].
2 1970 Act, s 14(2); App [24].

6.07 Assignation or discharge?

An assignation may be at the instance of either the creditor or the debtor. Where a loan is being rearranged, it may be difficult for the incoming creditor to decide whether to take an assignation of the existing security, or to take a fresh standard security. The advantages of taking an assignation are that an assignation retains the ranking of the original creditor and it is also a simpler process. On the other hand, there are disadvantages. There is a risk that part of the loan has been repaid and that the part repayment has not been disclosed. Partial repayment would not be obvious from either the Register of Sasines or the Land Register. In *Jackson v Nicoll*[1], the assignee found out that the whole debt had been repaid and accordingly, his security was valueless. One other disadvantage is that the assigner will be liable for warrandice given in respect of the validity of the security and the existence of the debt[2]. One last problem is that the personal obligation of the debtor will not automatically transmit to the assignee[3].

1 (1870) 8 M 408.
2 *Reid v Barclay* (1879) 6R 1007; J Burns *Conveyancing Practice* (4th edn) pp 556–557.
3 See para 6.10 below.

6.08 Effect of an assignation by the creditor

The effect of an assignation by the creditor is dealt with in section 14(2).

> (2) An assignation of a standard security shall, except so far as otherwise therein stated, be deemed to convey to the grantee all rights competent to the grantor to the writs, and shall have the effect *inter alia* of vesting in the assignee—
>
> (a) the full benefit of all corroborative or substitutional obligations for the debt, or any part thereof, whether those obligations are contained in any deed or arise by operation of law or otherwise,
>
> (b) the right to recover payment from the debtor of all expenses properly incurred by the creditor in connection with the security, and

(c) the entitlement to the benefit of any notices served and of all
    procedure instituted by the creditor in respect of the
    security to the effect that the grantee may proceed as if he
    had originally served or instituted such notices or
    procedure.

Thus apart from the benefits of ranking, the creditor also has the
benefit of any additional security which may exist, the right to recover
any expenses incurred by the original creditor, for example, in carry-
ing out repairs on the property and, in particular, the advantage of any
steps which the original creditor may have taken to enforce the
security. If, therefore, the original creditor had served a calling-up
notice and after the expiry of the two-month period, he assigned the
standard security, the assignee could proceed to exercise any of the
powers in standard condition 10.

What was said about deduction of title in Sasine transactions and the
position in relation to a registration of title applies here also[1].

1 See para 6.02 above.

6.09 Assignation by the creditor of the personal obligation in a Form B standard security

As Professor Halliday observes[1] the phrase 'all corroborative or
substitutional obligations for the debt' which appears in section 14(2)
may not cover the personal obligation contained in the separate documentation for a Form B standard security. It would therefore be
prudent to follow his advice that the assignation of the standard
security should incorporate an assignation of the debt.

1 Halliday *Commentary* para 9-02; *Halliday* vol III, para 40-04.

6.10 Assignation by the debtor

In most instances, the standard conditions will have been varied to
prevent the debtor from assigning the standard security without the
consent of the creditor[1], but that prohibition may be implied by law[2].

Assuming the creditor gives consent to the assignation, it should be
borne in mind by the original debtor, the creditor and the new debtor
that the assignation per se does not discharge the original debtor. This
was the position with an assignation of a bond and disposition in
security[3], and the position is the same under a standard security. In
order to ensure that discharge under the bond and disposition in

security, the assignee had to sign the 'conveyance' indicating his willingness to assume responsibility for the loan[4]. The term 'conveyance', as defined in the Conveyancing (Scotland) Acts of 1874 and 1924[5], excludes heritable securities and so it may not be possible to achieve the aim in a standard security by having the new debtor sign the assignation. The alternative is to have the new obligation enshrined in a bond of corroboration[6].

While, at common law, the debtor has a right to demand that the creditor grants an assignation, instead of a discharge, the creditor cannot be compelled to do so if that would be prejudicial to him. In *Fleming v Black*[7], the creditor made two advances and he received two bonds over the same property, one being postponed to the other. In due course, he demanded repayment of the first advance. The debtor agreed to pay, but insisted on an assignation to the third party who was willing to renew the loan. It was held that the first creditor was not bound to grant an assignation and that the onus is always on the party demanding the assignation to show that the other will not be prejudiced. It is submitted that that also applies to a standard security.

1 See para 5.20 above.
2 Ie if the relationship between the heritable creditor and the debtor involves *delectus personae*.
3 Conveyancing (Scotland) Act 1874, s 47 (amended by the Conveyancing (Scotland) Act 1924, s 15); see *Carrick v Rodger* (1882) 9 R 242.
4 Conveyancing (Scotland) Act 1924, s 5.
5 Conveyancing (Scotland) Act 1874, s 3; Conveyancing (Scotland) Act 1924, s 2.
6 Halliday *Commentary* para 9.29; *Halliday* vol III, para 40-42.
7 1913 1 SLT 386.

6.11 Assignation of standard securities for fluctuating amounts

While there is no theoretical objection to assigning a standard security for a fluctuating amount, there are practical problems which make it undesirable. If the creditor is assigning, he will be warranting the amount due by the debtor and exposes himself to liability if the amount due is incorrectly stated[1]. If it is the debtor who is assigning, the creditor's consent will be required and the creditor may again have to warrant the amount due. However, if the original debtor wishes to assign, the creditor will almost certainly not have any further dealings with him. Any further advance to be made to the assignee will require a variation of the standard security, or a new standard security. Where the original standard security is a Form B, there will have to be an assignation of the debt constituted by the separate agreement[2].

1 See para 6.07 above.
2 Halliday *Commentary* para 9.07; *Halliday* vol III, para 40-19.

6.12 Uninfeft granter

If the granter of the assignation is uninfeft, the advice set out in para 6.02 above applies.

6.13 Transmission

The person to whom a standard security has been transmitted on succession or by operation of law, for example, an executor or trustee in bankruptcy, may complete title in exactly the same manner as with any disposition or other heritable security. That is done by a notice of title in accordance with the Conveyancing (Scotland) Act 1924 using the previous recorded title and the confirmation or docket as a link. As an alternative, without completing title, he may deduce title in accordance with Schedule 4, when he is called upon to grant a subsequent assignation, discharge or deed of restriction. That stems from section 32 of the Act which extends the existing statutory provisions dealing with completion of title to standard securities.

6.14 Death of the debtor

The debtor's liability is heritable in his succession, but the debt must be satisfied from his general estate if the security subjects, when realised, are insufficient to cover the amount due. The standard security should be inserted in the inventory as a debt.

In the usual case, the standard security will be paid on death either from the proceeds of an insurance policy which has been assigned to the creditor, or from the general estate. The liability lies with the executor[1].

If the security subjects are bequeathed, the beneficiary will be liable for the amount due under the standard security[2], but he would have to give his consent before summary diligence would be available against him[3].

1 Succession (Scotland) Act 1964, s 14(3).
2 *Douglas's Trs v Douglas* (1866) 2M 223.
3 Conveyancing (Scotland) Act 1924, s 15(2).

6.15 Death of the creditor

On the death of the creditor, a standard security is moveable except *quoad fiscum* and for the calculation of legal rights[1]. A standard security should therefore be included as an item of moveable property in the inventory.

1 Titles to Land Consolidation (Scotland) Act 1868, s 117; *Halliday* vol IV, para 43-06.

6.16 Sequestration

By virtue of the permanent trustee's act and warrant, the whole estate of the bankrupt vests in the trustee, *tantum et tale* as it was held by the bankrupt[1]. However, where the heritable property is burdened by a standard security, the trustee may sell only if the heritable creditor agrees or if he obtained a high enough price to discharge every heritable security[2]. If, however, the heritable creditor intimates to the trustee that he intends to sell, the trustee cannot prevent the sale[3]. The other party may sell if the party who has intimated an intention to sell delays in selling, but that sale requires the authority of the court[4].

If the property is the debtor's family home, then the trustee in bankruptcy must inform any non-entitled spouse of his appointment and of the right of that spouse to apply to the Court of Session for an order protecting any occupancy rights[5]. The trustee must also obtain the consent of the debtor's spouse or former spouse who occupies the home, or the consent of the debtor where he occupies the house along with a child of the family[6]. If that consent is not obtained, the sale can take place only with permission of the court[7].

1 Bankruptcy (Scotland) Act 1985, s 31(1).
2 Ibid, s 39(4). For the problems in this area, see W W McBryde *Bankruptcy* pp 131–133.
3 Bankruptcy (Scotland) Act 1985, s 39(4).
4 Ibid, s 39(4).
5 Ibid, s 41.
6 Ibid, s 40.
7 Ibid, s 40(2); *Salmon's Trs v Salmon* 1989 SLT (Sh Ct) 49. See also *Halliday* vol IV, paras 51-46–51-48.

6.17 Liquidator

A liquidation does not vest any property in the liquidator unless the court so directs[1]. On the winding up of the company, the liquidator has the same powers of realisation as the permanent trustee[2].

1 Involvency Act 1986, s 145.
2 Ibid, s 185.

6.18   Receiver

A floating charge attaches to the company's property on the appointment of a receiver. However, although in relation to heritable
property, the receiver is deemed to have a fixed security, that does not
affect the position of any prior ranking (or *pari passu* ranking) heritable
creditor who may exercise the powers under the security without
reference to the receiver[1]. The receiver may sell with the consent of
such a heritable creditor or, if the consent is not forthcoming, he may
apply to the court for power to sell[2].

1 Insolvency Act 1986, s 55(3)(b).
2 Ibid, s 61; *Armour and Mycroft Petitioners* 1983 SLT 453.

6.19   Administrator

While an administrator is required to give notice to a floating charge
holder and the holder of a fixed charge of his appointment[1], he seems
to be able to sell the company's property without requiring to notify
the charge holders[2]. The reasoning must be that the holder of a fixed
security is secured while the floating charge holder cannot take any
further steps in relation to his charge once the administrator is
appointed.

1 Insolvency Act 1986, s 10.
2 Ibid, s 15.

6.20   Completion of title

The person to whom a standard security has been transmitted on
succession or by operation of law, for example an executor or trustee
in bankruptcy, may complete title in exactly the same manner as with
any disposition or other heritable security. That is done in a Sasine
transaction by a notice of title in accordance with the Conveyancing
(Scotland) Act 1924 using the previously recorded title and the confirmation or docket as a link. As an alternative, without completing
title, he may deduce title in accordance with Schedule 4 of the 1970
Act, when he is called upon to grant a subsequent assignation,
discharge or deed of restriction. That stems from section 32 of the
1970 Act which extends the existing statutory provisions dealing with
completion of title in bonds and dispositions in security to standard
securities.

In the case of a title to a property in a registration area which is not yet registered, the title of the executor, or transferee from the executor or trustee in bankruptcy is recordable in the Register of Sasines[1].

Where the title is registered, the confirmation to the estate is registerable[2] and where the property vests in a trustee in bankruptcy, he may have his title registered by production of his act and warrant[3].

1 *Halliday* vol IV, para 48-47.
2 *Halliday* vol IV, para 48-46.
3 *Halliday* vol IV, para 51-28.

CHAPTER 7

Ranking of standard securities and competition

7.01 Introduction

The object of this chapter is to consider the ranking of standard securities inter se and competition between standard securities and other charges and diligences.

RANKING OF STANDARD SECURITIES FOR SPECIFIC SUMS

7.02 General

Ranking will take place where there is more than one heritable security over the same security subjects. It is not uncommon nowadays for someone who wishes to raise capital, particularly for business purposes, to borrow from two or more sources. Each creditor will want a security, but there is only one property over which a security can be granted. If there is more than one security over the same subjects, the question which arises is in which order do the securities rank inter se. There are two possibilities (1) *pari passu* ranking ie equal ranking or (2) postponed ranking. Ranking is usually dealt with expressly in the security deeds or in a separate ranking agreement, but, in the absence of express provision, it is implied by law.

7.03 Express ranking

Express ranking can be achieved in two ways. If the loans are being made at the same time, the standard securities will contain reciprocal ranking clauses. If one takes the example of two standard securities, one for £20,000 in favour of A and another for £24,000 in favour of B, which are both executed on the same date, it may be agreed between the parties that the standard security for £20,000 in favour of A will rank before B's standard security. In that event, the ranking clauses will be as follows. In the standard security in favour of A, there will be a clause in something like the following terms: 'Declaring that the standard security hereby created is to be preferred to the extent of £20,000 to a standard security by the grantor in favour of B recorded of even date herewith'. The other deed will have an almost identical clause but it will narrate 'it is postoned to the extent of £20,000'. If the security subjects are later sold for £40,000, in these circumstances, A will get his whole loan out of the proceeds of sale, but B will get only £20,000 and accordingly there will be a shortfall of £4,000. B will therefore have to rank along with the unsecured creditors on the remainder of the estate for that £4,000. Reciprocal arrangements like this can be made only if the transactions are being entered into at the same time.

If one security is already on the record and, as we shall see, this implies preferential ranking, then it is important to note that any alteration in that ranking can only be made if the holder of the first security consents in writing to it. In other words, if it is agreed to alter that implied preferential ranking in order to give a subsequent security *pari passu*, or perhaps less likely, preferential ranking, then a ranking clause will be required in the second deed or a separate ranking agreement. However, the creditor in the first security will require to be a party to that deed or give his consent in some other way to the alteration in his pre-existing ranking position. In the absence of such consent, any ranking clause in a subsequent standard security will be of no effect.

7.04   Delay in recording the 'first' security

A problem may arise where a second security is described as being postponed to an earlier security, but, for some reason, the earlier security is recorded after the second security.

An example should make matters clearer. The debtor, A, is buying his house with a loan from the Rest Assured Building Society. He grants a standard security in their favour on 5 January 1990 and it is sent for recording or registration immediately. However, following a customary polite telephone call from the Keeper's office, the standard security is withdrawn, for correction. On 30 March 1990, A grants another standard security in favour of the Smashing Loan Company Ltd, this time for double glazing. That standard security contains the following clause: 'But the standard security hereby granted is subject to the standard security in favour of the Rest Assured Building Society dated 5 January 1990', and the warrandice clause is suitable qualified also. The 'second' security is recorded on 5 April 1990. The standard security in favour of the building society, in its amended form, is sent to the Keeper on 15 April and recorded on 22 April. *Quid iuris*, as they say in the best examination papers?

There are two possible views. The first is that the second security is postponed because its terms make clear that it is a security right only over the reversionary interest and so infeftment in the second security is infeftment in the right as qualified by its own terms. Section 11(1) of the 1970 Act provides that where a standard security is recorded, it vests the interest over which it is granted in the grantee as a security for performance of the contract to which it relates. The contract to which the second security relates is a contract which accepts that there is a pre-existing standard security and related contract. The right under the first security is personal, but is capable of being made real and hence, because the second security holder knows of it, his right cannot prevail over it.

The other argument is simpler and it is to the effect that at the time of the recording of the second security, there was no other validly-recorded standard security and no real right vested in any other creditor. On that basis, the second security holder would be preferred because his real right was created earlier. If the position was otherwise, the holder of the second security, upon default of the debtor, would have to redeem the earlier security, albeit it did not appear on the record. Likewise, the rights of a trustee in bankruptcy would be subject to both securities, albeit one of them did not appear on the record. If one takes the first argument to its logical conclusion, the position of the second security holder would be postponed to that of the first, even if the first security was never subsequently recorded and the second security holder would become a first-ranking security holder only once the first security has prescribed. This matter has never been the subject of any court decision and so any conclusion can, at best, be tentative, but the writer's own preference would be for the second argument. This problem could be avoided by the parties entering into a separate ranking agreement.

7.05   Implied ranking

Implied ranking will apply where there are no express provisions. *Pari passu* ranking can be implied by law as can postponed ranking.

7.06   *Pari passu* ranking: deeds received by the Keeper simultaneously

The first situation is dealt with by the Land Registers (Scotland) Act 1868, which provides that where two or more writs which are transmitted by post and are received by the Keeper of the Registers of Scotland at the same time, they shall be deemed to be recorded or registered contemporaneously and there is no presumption in favour of the one or the other[1]. Accordingly, if two standard securities are received at the same time, they will be deemed to rank equally. It is unlikely that two creditors who wish their standard securities to be ranked equally would rely upon what the law implies. There are two reasons for this. One is the uncertainty of the postal or other delivery services and the other is the possibility that the Keeper might notice an error in one security which would require that it be returned for amendment. In that situation, the other security, which did not require amendment, would go on the record first.

1 Land Registers (Scotland) Act 1868, s 6.

7.07 *Pari passu* ranking: partial assignations

The other example of *pari passu* ranking is somewhat more specialised and relates to partial assignations of a creditor's interest in a standard security. The law deems such partial assignations to rank equally regardless of the respective dates of their recording[1]. Partial assignations of a creditor's interest are somewhat unusual. An example would be where A has granted a standard security to B for £10,000. Let us assume that this is a long term-loan, but, for some reason, at a later stage and before the expiry of the term loan, B wants his money. He cannot demand repayment from A, unless A is in default. It may be, however, that he can find two other people, C and D, who are willing to step into his shoes. C and D will pay B (probably less a discount) and B will then assign his interest to C and D. Let us assume that he assigns his interest to the extent of £4,000 to C and £6,000 to D. It may be that C records his assignation first, but that does not matter. The law implies that the two new creditors step simultaneously into the same position as the original creditor (B) and accordingly they rank *pari passu*.

1 *Halliday* vol III, para 42-29.

7.08 Postponed ranking

The rule here is clear, viz: standard securities rank in accordance with their dates of recording. If, therefore, a standard security is recorded today and there is already one in favour of someone else which was recorded five years ago, then the law will imply, in the absence of any other agreement, that the standard security recorded today will rank after the one recorded five years ago.

RANKING OF SECURITIES FOR UNCERTAIN SUMS

7.09 General

In the discussion of ranking so far, it has been assumed that each of the competing securities is for a specific sum.

If, as is not uncommon, the first ranking security is for 'all sums due and to become due' then, if there is no limit on the amount which can be lent under the first security, the second security could be rendered valueless by subsequent advances made under the first security. The 1970 Act, however, introduces a 'freezing' provision, but in order to appreciate the significance of the provisions, it is necessary to look at the pre-1970 case law.

7.10 Position pre-1970

The question of ranking of securities for uncertain sums did not come before the courts until almost the end of the nineteenth century, the reason being that, under the bond and disposition in security until latterly, it was not possible to create a security for fluctuating and future advances. The matter, therefore, arose in the context of *ex facie* absolute dispositions. The leading case was *Union Bank of Scotland v National Bank of Scotland*[1] (the decision which forms the basis of the provisions of the 1970 Act). In that case, property was conveyed by the debtor to the National Bank by way of an *ex facie* absolute disposition. There was a back letter stating that the subjects were held in security of the present advance and all future advances to be made to the debtor by the National Bank. Subsequently, the debtor assigned his reversionary interest in the property to the Union Bank as security for advances which the Union Bank had made to him. The assignation in favour of the Union Bank was intimated to the National Bank. When the debtor subsequently went bankrupt, it was held that the National Bank, as the original lender, could not claim any preference over the security subjects for advances which had been made after the assignation had been intimated. The decision was, therefore, that, when there was a security for a future sum or a fluctuating sum, then immediately the existence of a second security was intimated to the holder of the first security, that first security was limited to the amount which had then been advanced. The reason for the decision was that the court would recognise an *ex facie* absolute disposition as effectively securing future advances without further documentation, provided that, at the time of each further advance or fluctuation in the amount due, the borrower was in a position to renew his security. If, however, he had conveyed away his reversionary interest either outrightly, or as in the *Union Bank* case, by way of a second security, then he was no longer in a position to renew the pledge of his property and accordingly the first security was good only for advances prior to the date of the intimation.

A number of practical results flowed from the decision. In the first place, it opened the door to postponed securities. Secondly, however, someone who was receiving a conveyance of the reversionary interest by way of security, or outrightly, would immediately intimate the conveyance to the prior lender in order to secure his position and to 'freeze' the position of the prior lender. The third consequence was that the prior lender would not make any further advances on the strength of his security. If the loan came from a bank, it would be usual for the bank to open another account usually called a 'Number 2 account' for all sums later paid in, so that if the relationship was to continue on roughly the same basis their original security would not gradually dwindle away to nothing on the basis of the rule in *Clayton's* case[2].

The next development in the law in this area was *Campbell's Judicial Factor v National Bank of Scotland*[3]. In that case, it was held that the appointment of a judicial factor on the bankrupt estate of a borrower was equivalent to an intimated assignation of the reversionary interest. The judicial factor acquires title by the operation of law and accordingly the debtor ceases to have a right to the reversion. That was not the main point of the case, but the court went on to hold that the effect of the decision in *Union Bank v National Bank* was to limit the security not only to the advances then outstanding, but also to the interest then due.

While there was a certain logic in this, the extention of the principles set out in the *Union Bank* case in *Campbell's Judicial Factor* was thought to be an unfortunate one. The original creditor might have been bound by contract not to demand immediate repayment of his loan. Alternatively, he might not have wished to do so if, for example, the customer, in the continuing overdraft agreement, was a good customer. However, if he allowed matters to stand after the creation of the second security, then, while he would still have a security for the principal sum then due, he would have no security for the daily interest accruing after that time. That was the position as it stood prior to 1970.

1 (1886) 14R (HL) 1.
2 (1816) 1 Merr 529.
3 1944 SC 495.

7.11 The Conveyancing and Feudal Reform (Scotland) Act 1970

The principles which were laid down in the *Union Bank*[1] case albeit arising out of an *ex facie* absolute disposition were generally regarded as being fair and reasonable, and were adopted in the 1970 Act for standard securities[2].

Section 13 of the 1970 Act[2] broadly restates the position in the *Union Bank* case, but reverses the decision in *Campbell's Judicial Factor*. The effect of section 13 is that where the creditor in a recorded standard security receives intimation of the *creation*, ie the execution of a subsequent standard security, or indeed notice of the outright conveyance of the debtor's interest, then the first security is 'frozen'. On intimation, the first security is restricted to (a) existing advances; (b) further advances which the first creditor is contractually obliged to make; (c) interest present and future on these advances; (d) expenses which have been or may be incurred by the creditor in the exercise of any of the powers in the standard security.

There are a number of points to note here.

(1) the first security is limited to existing advances: that is a restatement of the decision in *Union Bank*;
(2) future interest on these advances is secured, and the effect of that is to reverse the decision in *Campbell*;
(3) expenses are secured: this is a new provision;
(4) future advances which the creditor is contractually bound to make will also be secured: this is also new, but it is a useful addition;
(5) It is now clear that actual notice by the postponed creditor must be given and so the mere recording/registration of the subsequent standard security in the Register of Sasines/Land Register is not enough to constitute notice to the prior creditor. The only exception is a judicial transmission, ie a conveyance by operation of law, which in itself is sufficient notice. Notice is usually given by the solicitor acting for the second lender. However, where the second security is a 'discount' security[3], intimation is frequently made by the creditor.

There is a further and more important point to note which arises out of the phrase 'or of the subsequent assignation or conveyance of that interest in whole or in part'. The result is that if the debtor assigns or conveys his interest in the security subjects, and the creditor receives notice of it, that, like the grant of another security has the 'freezing' effect mentioned above. It is common for the title to properties to be taken in joint names, frequently of spouses, and hence for the security to be granted in joint names. If the joint owners subsequently go their separate ways, for example on divorce, the title to the subjects may be transferred to one of the original owners who will agree to take on the obligations under the standard security. The new arrangement under the standard security may be achieved by a deed of variation in terms of which the lender agrees that one of the original borrowers is discharged and the other takes on the whole obligations.

However, it the title is to be transferred, that conveyance or assignation comes within the terms of section 13 and thus restricts the security as described above. If, therefore, the original lender makes any other advances, these could be postponed to the borrowings under any other security, even if a new standard security has been entered into when the title was transferred. If that construction of section 13 is sound, the solicitor acting for the original lender would be under an obligation to advise that lender of the consequences of discharging the original security and having a new one granted. The matter could, however, be resolved by the parties entering into a ranking agreement.

1 *Union Bank of Scotland v National Bank of Scotland* (1886) 14 R (HL) 1.
2 1970 Act, s 13; App [20]–[22].
3 See para 11.22 below.

7.12 Further advances by first creditor after intimation

The only issue which is not entirely clear is what happens if the first creditor does actually make further advances after the intimation of the second security. There is no doubt that the holder of the second security will have a preference as against any such further advance. It may be, however, that the value of the security subjects is sufficient not only to cover the original advance and the second advance, but also leave a balance. The question which remains unanswered is whether the effect of section 13 is that the first creditor has no security at all for these further advances or whether he ranks after the postponed creditor. The answer to that is clearly crucial in either a bankruptcy or a liquidation because it could mean the difference between recovering the whole of any such further advance as against merely ranking for it along with the other unsecured creditors. Professor Halliday's opinion is that such sums are still covered by the security albeit postponed to the second security in the ranking, because section 13 deals with the first creditor's secured preference or ranking[1]. In practice, however, it appears that holders of first-ranking securites in these circumstances rarely, if ever, make further advances after intimation of the granting of a second security.

1 Halliday *Commentary* para 5.39; *Halliday* vol III, para 36-20; G L Gretton 'Ranking of Heritable Creditors' (1980) 25 JLSS 275; J M Halliday (1981) 26 JLSS 26; G L Gretton (1981) 26 JLSS 280.

RANKING AND WARRANDICE

7.13 General

Where there were two bonds and dispositions in security, it was held at common law that an exception from warrandice in one bond did not, of itself, confer a preferential ranking on the other bond holder, but did no more than regulate the liabilities of the parties in respect of warrandice[1]. Thus, in order to regulate ranking, there had to be ranking clauses in the respective bonds. Although the common law authority has been overruled[2], the rule itself, it is submitted still stands, given the terms of the 1970 Act. Schedule 2 which sets out the forms of standard security, requires that, where there is another standard security, there should be inserted before the warrandice clause in the later standard security, a clause indicating that the second security is 'subject to' the other one[3].

It may be argued that the phrase 'subject to' regulates ranking, but it is submitted that Professor Halliday and the Keeper to whom he refers are correct in their view that an express ranking clause is required[4]. The warrandice clause indicates that there is another security in existence, but says nothing about how it ranks with the later one. The intention of the parties may be that the later security should rank after, or *pari passu* with, the earlier one and it submitted that in order to achieve what would otherwise be a preferential ranking for the deed which went on the record first, there must be a ranking clause in the second security and the consent of the pre-existing security holder, or a ranking agreement.

1 *Leslie v McIndoe's Trs* (1824) 2 S 48.
2 *Trade Development Bank Ltd v Crittal Windows Ltd* 1983 SLT 510 at 517, per Lord President Emslie.
3 App [93], note 5.
4 Halliday *Commentary* para 42-30.

CATHOLIC AND SECONDARY SECURITIES

7.14 General

The rules on catholic and secondary securities arise where one creditor (the catholic creditor) has securities over two subjects and the other creditor (the secondary creditor) has a postponed security over one of the subjects. While the securities may be either moveable or heritable, the rules are most frequently applied in the case of heritable securities.

In such a situation, the prior (catholic) creditor must exercise his rights in such a way as to leave the largest amount possible for the secondary creditor[1]. That does not prevent the catholic creditor from releasing one of the subjects from the security, even if that results in the whole debt being exigible from the other subjects, ie the subjects over which there is a postponed security[2]. Nor does it prevent him from realising both subjects, or either of them[3]. Where the catholic creditor realises the subjects over which there is a postponed security, he must assign his interests in the other subjects to the secondary creditor. Where both subjects have been realised, the secondary creditor has a preference over any balance remaining after the catholic creditor has been paid[4].

1 Bell *Comm* II, 417.
2 *Morton (Liddell's Curator)* (1871) 10M 292.
3 *Preston v Erskine* (1715) M 3376.
4 Bell *Comm* II, 417.

COMPETITION BETWEEN HERITABLE SECURITIES AND INHIBITIONS

7.15 Inhibition against the debtor

Where a debtor has granted a heritable security and is thereafter inhibited, the inhibition has no effect on the heritable security[1]. If the inhibiting creditor wishes to secure a preference over the free proceeds of sale, on one view he must either arrest these proceeds, or adjudge[2]. It has been held, however, that he already has a preference by virtue of the inhibition[3].

Where the debtor's heritable security post-dates the inhibition, the heritable security may be reduced by the inhibiting creditor. In any ranking, the inhibitor is entitled to rank as if the postponed creditors did not exist, and the inhibitor draws back from the posterior creditors, the amount which he would have received had they not existed.

The principles of ranking governing this situation were laid down by Bell[4] and subsequently approved by the courts[5]. Further details are available in the various works on diligence[6].

1 *Campbell's Tr v De Lisle's Exrs* (1870) 9 M 252.
2 Bell *Comm* II, 139.
3 *Bank of Scotland v Lord Advocate* 1977 SLT 24; *Halifax Building Society v Smith* 1985 SLT (Sh Ct) 25.
4 Bell *Comm* II, 413.
5 *Baird and Brown v Stirrat's Tr* (1872) 10 M 414.
6 J Graham Stewart *The Law of Diligence* pp 551 et seq; G L Gretton *The Law of Inhibition and Adjudication* ch 6; G Maher and D J Cusine *The Law and Practice of Diligence* paras 9.13–9.17. See also para 8.34 below.

7.16   Inhibition against the creditor

An inhibition which post-dates the security has no effect on it and the creditor cannot be prevented from granting a discharge[1]. So far as advances made after the inhibition are concerned, it is thought that they are struck at only if the creditor is not contractually obliged to make them[2]. However, they would be unsecured only *quoad* the inhibiting creditor and not against other creditors.

1 *Mackintosh's Trs v Davidson and Garden* (1898) 25 R 554.
2 *Campbell's Trs v De Lisle's Exrs* (1870) 9 M 252; *Halliday* vol II, para 21-80; *Gretton* p 113.

THE EFFECT OF SEQUESTRATION

7.17   General

The debtor's estate vests *tantum et tale* and so sequestration does not affect a standard security. However, while the permanent trustee may sell estate over which there is a standard security, he may do so only with the consent of the heritable creditor unless he secures a price which is great enough to discharge every heritable security[1]. The heritable creditor may intimate his intention to sell to the permanent trustee and vice versa and that situation prevents the other party from proceeding to sell, but if the party selling delays, the other party may be authorised by the court to sell or enforce the security as the case may be[2]. A purchaser's title is not challengeable on the ground that there has been a failure to comply with these procedures[3].

1 Bankruptcy (Scotland) Act 1985, s 39(3), (4).
2 Ibid, s 39(7). See also W W McBryde *Bankruptcy* pp 131–133.
3 Ibid, s 39(8).

THE EFFECT OF LIQUIDATION

7.18   General

A liquidator may sell property which is affected by a standard security. What has been said about sales by the permanent trustee applies to a liquidator[1].

1 Companies Act 1985, s 623(4).

THE EFFECT OF FLOATING CHARGES

7.19   General

In the unlikely event that there is no ranking agreement, a fixed (standard) security which has been constituted as a real right (recorded/registered) before a floating charge has crystallised is preferred to the floating charge, irrespective of their dates[1].

1 Companies Act 1985, s 464.

THE EFFECT OF RECEIVERSHIP

7.20   General

The rights which a heritable creditor has as the result of the constitution of his real right are not affected by the subsequent appointment of a receiver[1]. The receiver may, however, sell the property but must obtain the consent of the heritable creditor. Failing such consent, the receiver may apply to the court for power to sell[2].

1 Companies Act 1985, s 471(2).
2 Insolvency Act 1986, s 61.

THE EFFECT OF THE APPOINTMENT OF AN ADMINISTRATOR

7.21   General

The position is the same as with the receiver[1].

1 Insolvency Act 1986, s 16.

THE EFFECT OF STATUTORY CHARGES

7.22 General

Various statutes impose charges on heritable property[1], and it is
essential to look at the relevant statutory provisions in order to
determine what effect such a charge has and, in particular, how it
ranks in relation to heritable securities[2].

Apart from stipend which is exigible from the teinds of any land, the
statutory charges now commonly encountered are those which are
created by local authorities in respect of works done or services
provided. These include charges in respect of repairs to houses, or
demolition of houses[3], or the supply of water to houses[4]. These
charging orders are recorded in the Register of Sasines or registered in
the Land Register.

1 Building (Scotland) Act 1959, Sch 6; Sewerage (Scotland) Act 1968, s 47; Housing
   (Scotland) Act 1987, Sch 9; Water (Scotland) Act 1980, s 65; Civic Government
   (Scotland) Act 1982, s 102; Agricultural Holdings (Scotland) Act 1949, ss 70, 82;
   Civil Legal Aid (Scotland) Regulations 1987, SI 1987/381, reg 40.
2 *Sowman v City of Glasgow District Council* 1985 SLT 65.
3 Building (Scotland) Act 1959, ss 10, 11, 13 and Sch 6 (all as amended).
4 Water (Scotland) Act 1980, s 65.

CHAPTER 8

Remedies: the 1970 Act or the standard security

8.01 Introduction

The main remedies available to the heritable creditor in respect of the property may be conferred by the 1970 Act or by the standard security, and it is these which are considered in this chapter. There are, however, other remedies available at common law, such as enforcing the personal obligation, which are dealt with in chapter 9 below.

8.02 Where the debtor is in default

Where the debtor is in default, the remedies which arise by virtue of the Act, or the terms of the standard security are (1) power to sell the security subjects[1]; (2) power to enter into possession of the security subjects[2]; (3) power to carry out necessary repairs[3]; and (4) power to apply for a decree of foreclosure[4]. Before he can exercise any of these remedies, the creditor has to take some preliminary steps. These steps are the serving of a calling-up notice, the service of a notice of default or an application to the sheriff court under section 24.

1 1970 Act, Sch 3, standard condition 10(2); App [105].
2 1970 Act, Sch 3, standard condition 10(3); App [105].
3 1970 Act, Sch 3, standard conditions 1, 7, 10(6); App [96], [102], [105].
4 1970 Act, Sch 3, standard condition 7; App [102].

8.03 Calling-up notice

A creditor who wishes the debt to be discharged may serve a calling-up notice, and failing that discharge, he may wish to sell the security subjects or exercise one of the other powers available. It would also be appropriate to serve a calling-up notice in respect of a default which cannot be remedied.

It is always competent to serve a calling-up notice, unless the

110

creditor is debarred from doing so by the terms of the standard security, or the related documentation, or by law[1]. For example, there may be a provision in the standard security to the effect that repayment is to be made by instalments over a period of years. This is always the case in domestic mortgages. In these cases, it is not competent to demand earlier repayment by serving a calling-up notice unless, of course, the debtor defaults in making his monthly payments, or there is some other default under the security. Likewise, the trustee in sequestration may have intimated an intention to sell the security subjects[2]. Additional material may appear in the notice, for example advising the debtor of the consequences of failing to comply[3].

1 1970 Act, Sch 3, standard condition 8; App [103].
2 Bankruptcy (Scotland) Act 1985, s 39(4)(b).
3 1970 Act, s 53(1).

8.04   The form of the calling-up notice

The form of the notice is set out in Schedule 6 of the 1970 Act and it must be served in accordance with section 19. Although that section does contain details of how the notice has to be served, it is commonly the case that the standard conditions will have been altered and the procedure for giving notice will be simpler than that specified in the Act. This has been dealt with earlier[1].

1 See para 5.29 above.

8.05   The sum in the notice

Section 19(1) of the 1970 Act specifies that the calling-up notice should be served only in respect of the debt secured by the standard security. It is therefore essential to examine the precise terms of the standard security, the standard conditions and any variation because the various sums secured by the security will be detailed there. The sum secured will probably include future advances, expenses incurred by the creditor and it may include any sums due by the debtor to the creditor no matter how they arise and whether the sums have been advanced to the debtor as an individual, or, for example, as a partner[1]. Some securities also cover guarantees. The sum due may be in respect of a fluctuating debt, for example an overdraft, or of an uncertain amount and it is necessary to have a certificate from the creditor which certifies exactly what is due. It is almost universal practice for the security documentation to provide that a certificate under the hand of a stated authorised person will be final as regards any amount which has to be stated in a calling-up notice[2]. That does not mean that that is necessarily what is due by the debtor, but it does mean that the debtor cannot challenge the calling-up notice merely on the ground that the sum stated in it is not correct. If there is no such provision, the terms of section 19(9) apply, and the creditor must give the debtor a note of the full amount due within one month of the date of service of the calling-up notice.

It is probably essential that the amount stated in the calling-up notice should be the amount which is due when the notice is served. If the security documentation provides that the amount due will be certified by an authorised individual, that person may be in the head office of the creditor and he or she may make up the calling-up notice. If, however, it is then sent to the local solicitor, or the local branch to be served, there is a possibility that the amount due at that stage may differ from the amount stated in the calling-up notice. Theoretically, the person on whom the notice is served could object if there was a discrepancy.

1 See para 4.28 above.
2 See para 4.30 above.

8.06 Obligation *ad factum praestandum*

In the unlikely event that the standard security is granted solely in respect of an obligation other than an obligation to pay money, the calling-up notice would have to set out clearly the obligation which the creditor wished to be performed. Any obligation which, in court parlance, is 'lacking in specification' will not be enforceable[1].

1 *Hendry v Marshall* (1878) 5 R 687.

8.07 Persons on whom and by whom notice is served

This matter is dealt with in Professor Halliday's books and little more needs to be said here[1], except about two matters. The first is the need to serve notice on all other persons who may be affected by the initiation of the calling-up procedure. These include postponed-ranking and *pari passu* ranking security holders, the proprietor (if that is not the debtor), co-obligants, guarantors and anyone who may be liable under the personal obligations. So far as guarantors are concerned, the standard conditions will usually provide that their potential liability will not be affected by any steps taken in relation to, or arrangements entered into with, the debtor[2]. It would be prudent to serve the notice on any non-entitled spouse because the entitled spouse requires the consent of the non-entitled spouse to any waiver or shortening of the period specified in the notice[3]. The second is that section 19 does not deal with service where the debtor is a non-natural person, for example a partnership, or a company. In practice, a calling-up should be served on the firm and the individual trustees who hold the property for the firm as well as those who were the grantors of the standard security. Any partners who were assumed as partners thereafter should receive notice also. In the case of a company, it should be served at the registered office and also on any liquidator, or receiver, at this place of business.

1 Halliday *Commentary* paras 10.07–10.09; *Halliday* vol III, paras 39.08–39.10.
2 See para 4.32 above.
3 1970 Act, s 19(10); App [46]. See also para 8.08 below.

8.08 Period of notice

The person on whom the notice is served is given two months within which to pay, or otherwise perform the obligations[1]. It is not entirely clear whether the standard conditions relating to calling-up notices may be altered[2], but in practice they are not. It is open to the person on whom the notice should be served to agree to a shorter period of notice, or to waive the requirement for any notice at all[3]. However, it will be necessary to obtain the consent of postponed-ranking and *pari passu* ranking security holders to such a move in order to give them time to come to an arrangement with the creditor who has served the calling-up notice[4].

Where the standard security is over a matrimonial home as defined in the Matrimonial Homes (Family Protection) (Scotland) Act 1981, the spouse on whom the notice is served may not dispense with or shorten the period of notice without the consent in writing of the non-entitled spouse[5].

1 1970 Act, Sch 6, Form A; App [120].
2 1970 Act, s 11(3) (App [15]) deals with the powers of sale and foreclosure and 'the exercise of these powers', which may include calling-up notices and notices of default.
3 1970 Act, s 19(10); App [46].
4 Halliday *Commentary* para 10.09; *Halliday* vol III, para 39-10.
5 1970 Act, s 19(10) proviso; App [46].

8.09 Duration of notice

The notice endures for five years, which is calculated from the date of the notice where there has been no exposure for sale, or, in the situation where the subjects have been put up for sale, the date on which that took place[1].

1 1970 Act, s 19(11); App [47].

8.10 Mistake in the notice

Section 19(1) of the 1970 Act provides that the calling-up notice shall be 'in conformity with' Form A of Schedule 6 of the Act. It follows therefore that if the notice does not conform, it is a nullity, but it may be that trivial errors would not render the notice null. Under the legislation dealing with bonds, the calling-up notice must be 'in or as nearly as may be' in the terms of Form No 1 of Schedule M to the Conveyancing (Scotland) Act 1924[1]. There is authority for the view that, in that context, trivial errors may be overlooked[2], but two points are worth noting. The first is that the case concerned a failure to specify either the date of the bond, or the register, or the date of recording and the sheriff held that these omissions could not be overlooked. The second point is that the wording of the 1970 Act is different and it could therefore be argued that any departure from the terms of Form A of Schedule 6 to the 1970 Act would be fatal. What has been said above applies equally to a notice of default[3].

1 Conveyancing (Scotland) Act 1924, s 33.
2 *Strathclyde Securities Co Ltd v Park* 1955 SLT (Sh Ct) 79.
3 1970 Act, s 21(2); App [54].

8.11 Failure to comply with notice

Failure to comply with a calling-up notice amounts to default within the meaning of standard condition 9(1)(a) and in that event, the creditor may exercise any of the powers contained in standard condition 10[1].

1 1970 Act, s 20(1); App [48].

8.12 Problems with calling-up notices

If the Keeper's experience is anything to go by, there seem to have been very few problems with calling-up notices. Three problems which the Keeper kindly drew to my attention are, however, worth mentioning. It should be pointed out that they were raised with the Keeper to find out whether he would exclude indemnity under section 12 of the Land Registration (Scotland) Act 1979, but they are, of course, pertinent also to a Sasine transaction.

Case 1

There were two borrowers. Calling-up notices were served on 1 April 1987. One of the borrowers signed an acknowledgement on 1 April, but the second did not do so until 18 June. During the intervening period, the property was advertised for sale and an offer received, but the offer was not accepted before 18 June. The Keeper's view was that there would be no exclusion of indemnity, possibly on the ground that what is important is the service and not the acceptance of service.

Case 2

A calling-up notice was not served on the party last infeft. That party, however, said that he would dispense with notice under section 19(10) of the 1970 Act, but, that subsection allows notice to be dispensed with, or shortened by the person *on whom it is served* and so, strictly, it has no application where the notice has not been served at all. The debtor, of course, might be personally barred from saying that the notice had not been served, but the Keeper's view was that any such action on the part of the debtor would not be binding upon a trustee or liquidator who might be under an obligation to challenge the sale. Accordingly his view was that the calling-up process had to start again.

Case 3

The standard security apparently provided that unless the parties otherwise agreed, the debtor was obliged to repay the loan only from the proceeds of the sale of the property. The debtor abandoned the property and a calling-up notice was served. The sellers argued that the calling-up notice was *ex facie* valid and therefore the purchasers were protected. On the other hand, the purchasers said that they were entitled to be assured that the serving of the calling-up notice was justified and the Keeper agreed with that view. Accordingly, the calling-up process had to begin again.

8.13   Notice of default

This procedure is available only where the debtor is in default within the meaning of standard condition 9(1)(b)[1] and the default can be remedied[2]. What is being considered here, for example, is a failure to keep the property in good order and repair, a failure to observe some title condition or a failure to pay some instalment of the loan, all of which are breaches of the debtor's obligations and all can, of course, be remedied. In these circumstances, the creditor may serve a notice calling on the debtor to purge the default within one month. The form of notice is contained in Form B of Schedule 6[3] and the requirements as to service and dispensing with, or shortening the period of notice are the same as in the case of a calling-up notice[4]. A notice of default similarly ceases to be effective after five years[5]. As with the calling-up notice, it is permissible to have additional matters in the notice[6].

1 See para 8.14 below.
2 1970 Act, s 21(1); App [53].
3 1970 Act, s 21(2); App [54].
4 1970 Act, s 21(3); App [55]. See also para 8.07 above.
5 1970 Act, s 21(4); App [56].
6 1970 Act, s 53(1).

8.14   'Default' in standard condition 9(1)(b)

Standard condition 9(1)(b) provides that the debtor will be in default 'where there has been a failure to comply with any other requirement arising out of the security'. There is some doubt about what that means.

In the Commentary, Professor Halliday says:

'Any failure by the debtor to implement an obligation enforceable under a standard security will entitle the creditor to serve a notice of default. Default in payment of interest or of a periodic instalment of capital and interest or breach of an obligation under standard conditions 1, 2, 3 or 5, or failure to implement an obligation undertaken in the personal obligation or in the variation of the standard conditions are obvious examples. The only qualification is that the failure should be remediable[1].'

Standard condition 1 deals with maintenance and repair, condition 2 deals with completion of buildings etc, condition 3 deals with observation of conditions in title and condition 5 deals with insurance). At a later point in the same paragraph, however, he says

'The debtor may not be in default under standard condition 9(1)(b) simply because he has failed to implement any of his obligations under the security: failure to comply with a "requirement" may infer something more formal than a breach of an obligation of the security contract, although arguably that may be too strict an interpretation.'

In volume III of *Conveyancing Law and Practice in Scotland*[2], these two comments are omitted.

In a later passage in the Commentary[3] which also appears in volume III[4] he says 'Standard Condition 9(1)(b) refers to non-compliance with a "requirement arising out of the security". It is thought that this phrase is intended to refer primarily to a requirement made in a notice of default which has not been complied with.' The Act, however, is not particularly well drafted, because in terms of section 21 where the debtor is in default within the meaning of standard conditions 9(1)(b), the creditor may serve a notice of default and it is submitted that a 'failure to comply with any other requirement arising out of the security' must be wider than a failure to comply with something mentioned in a notice of default, because there has to be default before a notice of default can be served. In the writer's opinion, 'failure to comply with any other requirement arising out of the security' means a failure to comply with any condition of the standard security, or the standard conditions, ie anything except failure to comply with a calling-up notice. Having said that, there is still some doubt about whether the phrase is wide enough to cover obligations imposed in any separate agreement, for example, under a Form B standard security. In a domestic transaction where there is a life policy as additional security, is a failure to pay the premiums a default and in a commercial transaction, is a failure to keep the liquor licence in force, a default? The solution would appear to be to provide in any such documentation that any breach of the debtor's obligations will amount to 'default' within the meaning of standard condition 9(1)(b).

1 *Halliday*, vol III, para 10-19.
2 *Halliday*, vol III, para 39-19.
3 *Halliday*, vol III, para 10-55.
4 *Halliday*, vol III, para 39-56.

8.15 Objection by the debtor

The debtor may object to a notice of default by applying to the court and the court may order the notice to be set aside, varied, or it may uphold it[1]. Notice of the objections must be served on the creditor and any others on whom the original notice was served.

1 1970 Act, s 22; App [57]–[60].

8.16   Calling-up notice or notice of default?

When advising a creditor whether to proceed by way of a notice of default or a calling-up notice or both[1], the right which the debtor has to object to a notice of default is a major factor. Proceeding by way of a notice of default is quicker in that the period of notice is shorter, but the fact that the debtor has the right to object may mean that he can delay matters for much longer than he could do under a calling-up notice. The debtor will probably not be able to sustain the objection, but all he has to do is to make an application to the court in order to hold up proceedings. Should he do so, the creditor can counter this by making an application to the court for immediate warrant to exercise any of the remedies available to him under standard condition 10 and the court can, if it thinks proper, grant such a warrant[2].

The right of the creditor to make this counter claim is clearly designed to prevent debtors from making completely spurious objections simply with a view to delaying matters. The creditor's position is strengthened further by section 22(4) which provides that a certificate by the creditor as to the nature of the default will be treated as *prima facie* evidence of the default itself.

1 A failure to pay the instalments would justify both a calling-up notice and a notice of default.
2 1970 Act, s 22(3); App [59].

8.17   Failure to comply

Should the debtor fail to comply with the notice of default which is not objected to, or which is upheld, or varied, that entitles the creditor to exercise the rights conferred upon him by standard condition 10(2), 10(6) and 10(7), ie power of sale, power to carry out repairs and the power to apply for a decree of foreclosure. It should be noted that this does not include the right to enter into possession, but the creditor may apply for this under section 24. However, the debtor or proprietor may redeem the security by giving notice at any time before an enforceable contract has been concluded for the sale of the security subjects[1]. In normal circumstances, the debtor would require to give two months' notice of redemption and it therefore seems a little surprising that the debtor is allowed to redeem without giving notice at all in circumstances where he is in default. By doing so, he could render null the time and effort expended by a creditor in advertising and attempting to sell the subjects. In practice, slightly more use seems to be made of the calling-up procedure rather than the default procedure, perhaps because of the debtor's right to object and his power to redeem under a notice of default.

1 1970 Act, s 23(3); App [63].

8.18   Problems with notices of default

Although the writer's impression is that notices of default are used less often than calling-up notices, nevertheless more problems seem to have been drawn to the Keeper's attention of which the following are examples:

Case 1

A notice of default was served on the debtor requiring payment of arrears. The debtor was given the usual one month period to purge the default. However, there was a second paragraph in the notice of default and one question which arose (and indeed arose in another case) was whether it was competent to have additional material in the notice of default. That point is expressly provided for in section 53(1) of the 1970 Act, which says 'and nothing in this Act shall preclude the inclusion of any additional matter in such notices'. The second paragraph of the notice of default required the debtor to vacate the premises on the expiry of seven days from the date of service of the notice. The Keeper's view was that there would be no exclusion of indemnity. In my opinion, however, the second paragraph of the notice was incompetent. The standard conditions provided that the building society could serve such a notice at any time after 'it shall have become entitled to enter into possession of the security subjects'. The fact that a debtor is in default does not of itself entitle the heritable creditor to enter into possession.

Even if the default has not been purged after service of the notice, the only rights available to the creditor are those under standard condition 10(2), (6) and (7), which are to sell the subjects, to make good defects and to obtain a decree of foreclosure. The agents acting for the building society may have assumed that the creditors were entitled to enter into possession immediately the debtor was in default. It is of course, competent to vary the standard condition to that effect, but that had not been done.

Case 2

The notice of default was served, but was returned. The Keeper's view, rightly in my opinion, was that the notice was a sufficient link in title.

Service of a notice of default is no different from the service of a court action and the important thing is service in the proper form.

Case 3

There was a duplicate of the notice of default, but no evidence that it had been sent by recorded delivery, as the Act requires[1]. However, the debtor wrote to the heritable creditor relinquishing his rights in the subjects and the letter made reference to the service of the notice. The Keeper was prepared to accept the notice, presumably because the debtor would have been personally barred from denying that the notice had been served. Such a bar may not affect a trustee in bankruptcy, etc[2].

Case 4

The original borrowers were Mr A and Miss B. However, two years later, Mr A and Miss B disponed the whole subjects to Miss B. Presumably, she undertook the responsibility of the obligations under the original standard security. A notice of default was subsequently served but only on Miss B. The Keeper's view, again correctly in my opinion, was that service need only be made on Miss B.

1 1970 Act, s 19(6); App [42].
2 See para 8.12, case 2, above.

8.19 Default on the proprietor's insolvency

The final situation in which the debtor is in default is where the proprietor of the subjects is insolvent[1]. Usually the debtor will also be the properietor but if he is not, for example where the proprietors are the husband and the wife and only the husband grants the personal obligation in the standard security, it is the proprietor's insolvency which matters. If the debtor is insolvent, he will presumably have failed to make his payments or failed to comply with a calling-up notice or will be in default for other reasons. When the default arises because the proprietor is insolvent, the creditor must apply to the court before he can exercise any of the powers in standard condition 10. The proprietor will be insolvent if, as an individual, he is in apparent insolvency, or has executed a trust deed or entered into another arrangement with his creditors. If the proprietor has died and a judicial factor has been appointed under section 11A of the Judicial Factors (Scotland) Act 1889[2], he will be insolvent and hence in default.

Where the proprietor is a company, it will be insolvent and hence in default if a winding-up order has been made, or a resolution for voluntary winding-up has been passed (other than member's voluntary) or a receiver or administrator manager has been appointed, or possession has been taken by debenture holders or their agents under a floating charge over any property secured by the charge[3].

In the case of an individual's insolvency, the heritable creditor wishing to exercise his power of sale may find that the permanent trustee wishes to sell also. This matter has been dealt with[4].

1 1970 Act, Sch 3, standard condition 9(1)(c); App [104].
2 Judicial Factors (Scotland) Act 1889, s 11A (added by the Bankruptcy (Scotland) Act 1985, s 75(1), Sch 7, para 4).
3 1970 Act, Sch 3, standard condition 9(2); App [104].
4 See para 6.16 above; W W McBryde *Bankruptcy* pp 131–133.

8.20   Application under section 24 of the 1970 Act

If the debtor is in default within the meaning of standard condition 9(1)(b) or 9(1)(c), the creditor may apply to the court for warrant to exercise any of the powers in standard condition 10. The court is the sheriff court and the Act states that applications (and counter applications) should be summary applications[1]. If the creditor lodges in court a certificate specifying the nature of default, that is *prima facie* evidence of the facts in it[2]. It is common for creditors to apply to the court for these powers, rather than, or in addition to, serving a notice of default in terms of standard condition 9(1)(b). In any such application, the creditor should specify the remedies he wishes and these should appear in the extract decree. Many of the reported cases under section 24 relate to the issue of the 'ejection' of the debtor of which more will be said later, but other issues were raised in three cases, all involving United Dominions Trust Ltd[3]. If the creditor uses the 'belt and braces' approach of serving a calling-up notice, or a notice of default on both and also obtains a decree under section 24, the decree would give the creditor whatever powers he wished under standard condition 10. That being so, any defects in the calling-up or default procedure could be ignored[4].

1 1970 Act, s 24(1) (App [64]); 1970 Act, s 29(2); App [81].
2 1970 Act, s 24(2); App [65].
3 *United Dominions Trust Ltd Noters* 1977 SLT (Notes) 56; *United Dominions Trust Ltd v Site Preparations Ltd (No 1)* 1978 SLT (Sh Ct) 14; *United Dominions Trust Ltd v Site Preparations Ltd (No 2)* 1978 SLT (Sh Ct) 21.
4 See para 8.10 above.

8.21   The United Dominions Trust Ltd cases

In the first of these cases, *United Dominions Trust Ltd, Noters*[1] the issue was how to reconcile section 24 of the 1970 Act with what is now section 127 of the Insolvency Act 1986. Section 24(1) permits the heritable creditor to apply to the sheriff for a warrant to exercise any of the remedies in standard condition 10 if the debtor is in default within the meaning of standard condition 9(1)(b). Standard condition 9(1)(a) provides that the debtor is in default if he has failed to comply with a calling-up notice, and standard condition 9(1)(b) provides that he is in default if there has been a failure to comply with any other requirement arising out of the security. Section 127 of the Insolvency Act 1986 provides that in a winding up by the court, any disposition of the company's property made after the commencement of the winding up is void unless the court otherwise directs. The court for this purpose is the Court of Session. United Dominions Trust Ltd therefore presented a note in a winding up process in which they asked the Court of Session to authorise the sale of heritable property where a sheriff had previously granted a warrant to sell under section 24. Lord Kincraig dismissed the application as unnecessary. The point which he made was that since the 1970 Act envisaged the sheriff granting the power of sale, it was a necessary consequence of that that the heritable creditor, when selling, would grant a valid disposition of the subjects to the purchaser and accordingly the sheriff's warrant entitled the seller to grant a valid disposition. It was unnecessary to apply to the Court of Session for further permission where the debtor was in liquidation.

In *United Dominions Trust Ltd v Site Preparations Ltd (No 1)*[2] two issues were raised. The first was whether the court had a discretion under section 24 to grant warrant to sell or not, and the second was whether a failure to pay interest or capital amounted to default under standard condition 9(1)(b). The court held that if it was satisfied that there had been default under standard condition 9(1)(b), then it had no discretion but to grant the creditor the warrant to exercise any of the powers under standard condition 10. The real issue was whether the debtors were in default by virtue of their admitted failure to pay capital and interest. It was argued that the obligation did not arise out of the standard security, but out of the existence of the debt which was secured by the standard security. Against that it was argued that the term 'security' was not restricted to the physical subjects and that in terms of the 1970 Act 'security' means the contract and all the rights secured thereby. The court held that the liability to pay interest or capital arose out of the standard security and accordingly, failure to pay either was a default under standard condition 9(1)(b).

In the third case, *United Dominions Trust Ltd v Site Preparations Ltd*

(No 2)[3], the issues raised were (1) whether a failure to pay interest or capital amounts to default within the meaning of standard condition 9(1)(b); and (2) whether a company can be notour bankrupt (now apparently insolvent) within the meaning of standard condition 9(2)(a). So far as the second matter was concerned, while there was clear authority for the proposition that a company could be notour bankrupt, the sheriff's opinion was that standard condition 9(1)(a) applied only to individuals who are notour bankrupt and not companies. On this matter, the sheriff differed from Sheriff Smith, in the No 1 case.

On the first issue, counsel for the defenders contended that liability to pay capital and interest arose from the debt and not from the security (standard condition 9(1)(b) talks of 'failure to comply with any other requirement arising out of the security') and he suggested that there was a distinction between the word 'security' in standard condition 9(1)(b) and 'standard security', the term used elsewhere in the Act. The pursuers had proceeded by way of an application under section 24, whereas the defenders' contention was that they should have served a calling-up notice.

The sheriff rejected the defenders' contention. He was not 'persuaded that a failure [to pay either capital or interest] . . . cannot be regarded as falling under para 9(1)(b)'. Furthermore, the security documentation set out the dates on which payments had to be made and the rates of interest and in his opinion these were 'every bit as much requirements arising out of the security as the other standard conditions'. In his opinion, standard condition 9(1)(b) covered 'any default apart from failure to comply with a calling-up notice'[4]. From these cases, the following propositions arise:

(a) 'Default' within the meaning of standard condition 9(1)(b) has a wide meaning and includes anything except a failure to comply with a calling-up notice. In particular, it covers a failure to pay capital or interest. It follows therefore that if there is such a failure, the creditor may serve a calling-up notice (unless he is contractually barred from doing so) or a notice of default, or apply to the court under section 24.

(b) The court has no discretion but to grant the warrant if any application is made under section 24. Some doubt has been cast on that proposition by the decision in *Armstrong Petitioner*[5].

There is a difference of opinion about whether standard condition 9(2)(a) covers a company which is notour bankrupt or only individuals, but it is submitted that the better view is that taken in the third *United Dominions Trust Ltd* case, viz that it does cover the notour bankruptcy/apparent insolvency of a company[6].

1 1977 SLT (Notes) 56.
2 1978 SLT (Sh Ct) 14.
3 1978 SLT (Sh Ct) 21.
4 1978 SLT (Sh Ct) at 23.
5 1988 SLT 255. See para 8.25 below.
6 See W M Gordon on *Scottish Land Law* para 20-192.

8.22 Summary of procedure and remedies

Procedure	Calling-Up Notice	Notice of Default	Application to Court
Authority	Sections 19–20	Sections 21–23	Sections 24, 29(2)
Pre-Condition	Creditor wishes payment or performance	Remediable Default standard condition 9(1)(b)	Default under standard condition 9(1)(b); standard condition 9(1)(c)
Notice	Two months	One month	None
Remedies	All in standard condition 10 viz sale, entering into possession (and leasing), repairs, foreclosure	Sale Repairs Foreclosure	All in standard condition 10 viz sale, entering into possession (and leasing,) repairs, foreclosure

8.23 'Ejection' of the debtor

Where the creditor wishes to exercise any of the remedies under standard condition 10, he may find that the debtor is still in occupation of the security subjects. Several cases have arisen on what is the correct procedure for 'ejecting' the debtor but the matter has now been resolved by Act of Sederunt. (There are 'effective' methods for ejecting debtors but many of them are not countenanced by the law.)

At the outset, a distinction has to be drawn between proceedings by way of a calling-up notice or notice of default on the one hand, and proceeding by way of an application to the court on the other. Although there are other remedies apart from sale, it has been in the context of an attempt by the creditor to sell that these issues have been raised. In the following paragraph, unless the context indicates otherwise 'sale' means sale and the other remedies under standard condition 10.

If a calling-up notice has been served and not complied with, the creditor has all the remedies in standard condition 10[1]. If he has served a notice of default and it has not been complied with, he can sell, carry out repairs and apply for a decree of foreclosure, but if he wishes to enter into possession, he has to apply to the court[2].

Where the creditor has the power to sell without any need to apply to the court, the debtor can be ejected only by an ordinary action of ejection[3]. The Heritable Securities (Scotland) Act 1894 provides that a creditor may bring an action of ejection against a proprietor who is in personal occupation of the security subjects, but only in two situations: (1) where there has been a failure to pay interest punctually, and (2) where he has been asked to pay the principal sum and has failed[4]. It is submitted that there is little room for argument thus far.

The difference of opinion arose in the situation where the creditor had made an application under section 24 to exercise the remedies in standard condition 10. Two issues have arisen: (a) whether it is competent to crave for ejection in such an application, and (b) whether it is competent to proceed by an ordinary action to obtain the remedies under standard condition 10 and obtain warrant to eject the debtor. There have been a large number of cases on the first issue and a few on the second[5].

The Scottish Law Commission in their Report on the Recovery of Possession of Heritable Property[6] suggested an amendment to the 1970 Act which would have resolved the problem. That has not been enacted as yet, but by an Act of Sederunt[7], the Sheriff Court Rules have been altered and the position is now as follows. If a heritable creditor applies to the court for the exercise of any of the remedies under standard condition 10 and nothing else, he must proceed by a summary application. If, however, he seeks any other remedy, for example ejection, he must proceed by an ordinary action. The Act of Sederunt repeals section 29(2) of the 1970 Act.

1 1970 Act, s 20(1) (App [48]); 1970 Act, Sch 3, standard condition 10(1) (App [105]).
2 1970 Act, s 23(2); App [62].
3 *Hill Samuel & Co Ltd v Haas* 1989 SLT (Sh Ct) 68.
4 Heritable Securities (Scotland) Act 1894, s 5.
5 The cases are listed in G Maher and D J Cusine *The Law and Practice of Diligence* para 9.92.
6 Report on Recovery of Possession of Heritable Property (Scot Law Com no 118 (1989)), recommendation 95.
7 AS (Amendment of Sheriff Court Ordinary Cause, Summary Cause, and Small Claim, Rules) 1990, SI 1990/661.

THE REMEDIES

8.24 General

The remedies available to a heritable creditor under standard condition 10 are (1) to sell the security subjects; (2) to enter into possession and while in possession to grant leases; (3) to carry out repairs and improvements; and (4) to apply for a decree of foreclosure. Undoubtedly, the most important and most frequently-used remedy is sale.

8.25 Has the creditor an unfettered right to sell?

In *United Dominions Trust Ltd v Site Preparations Ltd (No 1)*[1], Sheriff Smith held that if it is established that the debtor is in default, the court has no option but to grant warrant to the creditor to exercise the remedies in standard condition 10. That decision must be qualified to some extent in the light of the decision in *Armstrong Petitioner*[2] where a judicial factor on a bankrupt partnership estate petitioned successfully for interdict to prevent a heritable creditor in a standard security from exercising his power of sale. The security was granted over a farm which was one of the partnership assets.

Lord Jauncey granted interdict, pointing out that a heritable creditor must exercise his rights having regard to the interests of the debtor and that the heritable creditor did not have an unlimited discretion as to which of the powers in standard condition 10 he would exercise. In the course of his judgment, his Lordship said:

> 'A creditor's primary interest will normally be the recovery of the debt due to him and I do not consider that he has unlimited discretion as to which one or more of the powers he exercises. If the value of the heritage is likely to exceed the sum of his debt, his interest is to have the heritage sold and thereafter to account

for the surplus to the debtor. If in such a situation he elected to exercise the powers in condition 10 in a manner which did not result in money being available for the debtor, he might very well be restrained from so acting. A heritable creditor cannot use his powers for the primary purpose of advancing his own interests at the expense of the debtor when he has the alternative of proceeding in a more equitable manner'[3].

The case is somewhat special in that there were two people who had the power of sale and their interests to some extent were in conflict. If the decision is correct (it was under appeal but the appeal was abandoned for other reasons) it means that the creditor must not only advertise and obtain the best price but before considering advertising, he must attempt to assess what is in the debtor's best interest. It is difficult to see how a creditor can do that or reconcile these two obligations. Clearly the solicitor acting for a creditor cannot consider also the debtor's best interests, without suggesting that the debtor should be separately advised, because of the conflict.

It is submitted with respect that *Armstrong* is not correctly decided. While reference was made to some cases involving judicial factors[4], there was no reference to *Ker v Brown*[5] where the court held that a judicial factor's appointment did not prevent creditors from doing diligence. Furthermore, although mention was made of the obligation on the part of the heritable creditor not to act unfairly towards the debtor, none of the relevant authorities was referred to. For example in *Baillie v Drew*[6], Lord Justice-Clerk Moncreiff said that the court would not reduce a sale but would award damages if loss resulted from any 'reckless or inequitable use of' the heritable creditor's powers. He had expressed a similar view in *Parks v Alliance Heritable Security Co*[7]. Damages are mentioned in other cases as the appropriate remedy[8].

Bell states that the heritable creditor cannot be prevented by the debtor or those 'in his right' from exercising his power of sale[9] and in *Beveridge v Wilson*[10] an attempt by a trustee in bankruptcy to prevent a heritable creditor from selling failed. In the course of a judgment of the First Division and Permanent Lords Ordinary, it was said

> 'Our opinion, therefore is that, by law, the heritable creditor, whose right is constituted by infeftment . . . cannot be deprived of his right to sell. Still, however, it is a right subject to control. He is but an incumbrancer. Further, he is, to a certain degree, trustee for the common debtor, and of course for his representatives; and therefore, when he exercises his right, he must do so in a way beneficial, and not hurtful to those concerned. If he acted

nimiously, the Court would certainly interfere in the exercise of the right of sale.'

The following sentence is, however, of special significance.

'Now, in the present case, although neither the common debtor, nor the trustee, his legal representative, can *de jure*, deprive the creditor of his right of selling, if they can point out to the creditor that, by adopting a certain mode of sale no ways injurious to him, the highest possible price, at the least possible expense, may be obtained, it seems reasonable that the Court, *ex equitate*, may so direct[11].'

In other words, the heritable creditor may be directed in the manner of the sale but not prevented from selling.

It is submitted that there is no difference between a judicial factor and a trustee which is of such significance as would prevent a heritable creditor from selling. Furthermore, it is submitted that in *Armstrong* his Lordship was incorrect in so far as he suggested that the sale could be prevented where the sale would not result in a surplus for the debtor. In forced sales, there must be a few where there is such a surplus. In many cases, the heritable creditor may sell to minimise loss, but will realise that the sale proceeds may be insufficient to eliminate the debt.

1 1978 SLT (Sh Ct) 14.
2 1988 SLT 255.
3 1988 SLT 255 at 258.
4 *McCulloch v McCulloch* 1953 SC 189; *Ferguson v Murray* (1853) 15D 682; *Key v Cleugh* (1840) 3D 252.
5 (1902) 10 SLT 272.
6 (1884) 12 R 199.
7 (1880) 7R 546.
8 See *Kerr v McArthur's Trs* (1848) 11 D 301; *Stewart v Brown* (1882) 10 R 192; *Shrubb v Clark* (1897) 5 SLT 125; *Aberdeen Trades Council v Shipconstructors and Shipwrights Association* 1949 SC (HL) 45; *Rimmer v Thomas Usher & Co Ltd* 1967 SLT 7.
9 Bell *Comm* II, 271; see also Bell *Prin* s 891.
10 (1829) 7 S 279.
11 (1829) 7 S 279 at 281.

(1) SALE

8.26 General

The creditor will have the power of sale if a calling-up notice or a notice of default has not been complied with, or if the court has granted warrant to the creditor to sell. The power of sale is exercised in accordance with sections 25 and 27 of the 1970 Act.

The statutory duties are now to advertise the sale and to secure the best price that can reasonably be obtained. The sale may follow on a private bargain or a public roup[1]. The creditor would, of course, have to observe any relevant title conditions, for example a clause of pre-emption[2].

1 1970 Act, s 25; App [66].
2 *Cumming v Stewart* 1928 SC 296 (bond and disposition in security).

8.27 Advertisement

It should be noted that there are no set requirements as to the manner in which the creditor must advertise, nor indeed as to the period for which the advertisement must appear. There were provisions of this kind for bonds and dispositions in security, but the 1970 Act has reduced these requirements so far as pre-existing bonds are concerned. If the heritable creditor under a bond and disposition in security wishes to sell, he must advertise in at least one newspaper[1]. There is no such requirement in the case of a standard security. One problem which has been referred to the Keeper, but which so far has not been the subject of litigation, is what is meant by 'advertising'. In the *Commentary*[2] and in *Conveyancing Law and Practice in Scotland* volume III[3] Professor Halliday suggests that a creditor cannot be challenged if he complies with the requirements in the Conveyancing (Scotland) Act 1924 as amended which relate to bonds and dispositions in security. That, of course, is the counsel of perfection, but something less may satisfy the provisions of the 1970 Act. Only one case has arisen on advertising , viz: *Bank of Credit v Thompson*[4].

1 Conveyancing (Scotland) Act 1924, s 38.
2 Halliday *Commentary* para 10-38.
3 *Halliday*, vol III, para 39-41.
4 1987 GWD 10-341. The case is discussed in para 8.30.

8.28 Practical problems

The Act says no more than that it is the duty of the creditor to advertise the sale, but several problems have been raised with the Keeper, again in connection with indemnity under registration of title.

Case 1

The advertisement of the property for sale was placed in the window of
an estate agent's premises in the town in which the property itself was
located. The property was also advertised in 'The Scottish Property
Magazine' which was at that time a very new magazine of limited circu-
lation. The advertisement simply narrated the street and the town, but
did not specify the precise postal address. As the Keeper pointed out,
section 25 does not state how many times a property should be advertised, nor indeed how, and he indicated that he would accept a copy of
the advertisement from the magazine and a certificate from the estate
agent about the appearance of the advertisement in his window.

Case 2

There were certificates of advertisement from estate agents that the
property had been advertised in their window. The purchaser's agents
challenged that, referring to the passage in Professor Halliday's
Commentary[1] which is repeated in *Conveyancing Law and Practice in
Scotland* volume III[2].

> 'There is no need to adopt the conditions as to advertisement which
> the Act imposes in sales under powers contained in a bond and
> disposition in security, but it would be difficult to challenge the ade-
> quacy of advertisement which complied with statutory require-
> ments in the case of a comparable heritable security. Conveyancers,
> who are a cautious race, may tend to adopt that criterion'.

The Keeper was prepared to accept the certificates as sufficient.

Case 3

That view is illustrated by a third case where the sellers accepted that
they did not advertise the property in a newspaper. What they did was to
pass the papers to their subsidiary, Donald Storie Nationwide, in Glasgow to sell the subjects and they marketed the property under their
'low-key scheme' which involves circulating details to all clients on
their mailing list as well as advertising the property within the branch.
The Keeper's view was that that was acceptable.

1 Halliday *Commentary* para 10-38.
2 *Halliday*, vol III, para 39-41.

8.29   Comment

A solicitor acting for a purchaser will doubtless find considerable
comfort in the Keeper's approach to the issue of advertising . A heritable

creditor might not, however, be willing to risk a challenge and he might be challenged if he advertised in some of the ways described above. Section 25 of the 1970 Act requires 'the creditor to advertise the sale and to take all reasonable steps to ensure that the price at which all or any of the subjects are sold is the best that can be reasonably obtained'[1].

There are two possible constructions of that part of section 25. The first construction is that the creditor must advertise and demonstrate that the price which was obtained was the best price that could reasonably be obtained, given the form of advertising employed. The Act is silent on the meaning of 'advertise'. The Keeper will not exclude indemnity, even in the 'minimal advertising' cases above described and so on that view, the heritable creditor can choose any form of advertising he likes. On that construction, a hotel could be advertised in a shop window and that would suffice. It is submitted that that interpretation of section 25 is not what Parliament intended.

The second construction is that the duties are separate and that the heritable creditor must show that the price obtained was the best that could reasonably be obtained in the circumstances. To establish that, he must advertise, but advertising is not the end of the matter if the form of advertising was such that the best price was not obtained. On that construction, the advertisement of a hotel in a shop window would not be enough.

Although the precise construction of section 25 has never been considered, it is submitted that the second view is consistent with the cases which have arisen on 'the best price'.

1 1970 Act, s 25; App [66].

8.30 'The best price'

As has been pointed out, that is short for 'take all reasonable steps to ensure that the price at which all or any of the subjects are sold is the best that can be reasonably obtained'[1].

Three cases have arisen on this point, *The Royal Bank of Scotland v A and M Johnston*[2]; *Bank of Credit v Thompson*[3] and *Associated Displays Ltd (In Liquidation) v Turnbeam Ltd*[4]. The latter two cases were sheriff court cases.

In *Royal Bank of Scotland v A and M Johnston*, the bank had exercised their power of sale, but the defenders argued that they failed to obtain the best price that could reasonably be obtained. They claimed, as a loss, the difference between the actual sale price and the price which they said the subjects would have achieved if they had been sold properly. A proof on *quantum* was allowed. That was done in the pre-1970 case of *Rimmer v Thomas Usher & Son Ltd*[5].

In *Bank of Credit v Thompson*, guarantors claimed that the heritable creditors had failed to obtain the best price because they had advertised the subjects in the local newspaper, but not in national ones. It was averred also that they had failed to mention that the property had planning permission for use as an office as well as a shop and that they failed to take account of two valuations of £17,500 and £21,000. The property was eventually sold for £16,300. The sheriff held that the appellants had failed to establish a breach of duty on the part of the heritable creditors. There was no evidence that the premises would have been more attractive if they had been advertised as an office. So far as advertising nationally was concerned, the sheriff's view was that that would have added to the cost and that there was no evidence that persons outside the immediate locale would have been interested. Furthermore, there would have been a delay which would have resulted in further interest being due by the debtor.

Associated Displays Ltd v Turnbeam Ltd raised a procedural question which was whether the debtors could interdict the heritable creditors who were advertising the property for sale. When the subjects were advertised, only one offer was received and that offer was accepted. The price was £20,000. The debtors' attempt to interdict the sale averring that they had recently obtained a valuation of the security subjects amounting to £180,000 if they were sold in separate lots and £125,000 if sold as a whole. The Sheriff Principal in Glasgow took the view that the pursuers were laying claim to a right which the 1970 Act did not confer upon them. In his view, section 25 imposed duties upon the creditor but it did not confer any right upon a debtor to call upon the creditor to demonstrate that he had fulfilled the duties. In his opinion, the onus of proving the assertion that the price obtained by the creditor was not the best that could reasonably be obtained rested upon the debtor, but the terms of the interdict sought would effectively invert that onus. If the sheriff is right, one is left wondering what remedy is available to the debtor if he feels that the best price has not been obtained. The only remedy would appear to be damages after the event. The granting of interdict would obviously affect a purchaser who would have a concluded bargain with the heritable creditor[6].

The sheriff went on to say that there were other reasons why interim interdict in the circumstances was incompetent. The principal reason was that interim interdict can never be granted against something which has already been done and in his view the pursuers were seeking to interdict the defenders *ad interim* from disposing of the security subjects. Given that missives for the sale at £20,000 had been concluded, in his view, the price had already become part of an enforceable contract of sale.

1 1970 Act, s 25; App [66]. See also para 8.29 above.
2 1987 GWD 1–5.
3 1987 GWD 10–341.
4 1988 SCLR 220.
5 1967 SLT 7.
6 See, however, *Dick v Clydesdale Bank plc* 1990 GWD 38–2209.

8.31   The missives

The offer which is received from the purchaser's solicitors will not be different from that which would be used for any purchase of heritable property. It may be, however, that the agent acting for the heritable creditor will insert qualifications which would not be encountered in a normal domestic transaction, because the creditor is often not in a position to warrant matters which would be warranted by an ordinary seller because of his knowledge of the property. The qualifications may relate to the following: (1) moveables; (2) fittings and fixtures; (3) any central heating system; (4) maintenance of the property; (5) alterations, etc; (6) the letter of obligation; and (7) matters arising out of the Matrimonial Homes (Family Protection) (Scotland) Act 1981.

(1) Moveables

In the variation of some standard conditions, the heritable creditor takes the power to deal with any moveables which may be left on the premises by the debtor in the event of default. In other cases, the heritable creditor may appoint himself as the debtor's agent to deal with them[1]. If the heritable creditor has no power to dispose of the moveables (and he does not have any unless the standard conditions specifically conferred that power) then he will not be willing to give any warranties about the ownership of these moveables. These may be owned by the debtor, members of his household or they may be on hire purchase, etc. The purchaser should be advised of the attendant risks.

(2) Fittings and fixtures

The heritable creditor will not have seen the subjects of sale and so he will agree to sell only such fittings and fixtures as are clearly heritable. The purchaser will therefore be asked to satisfy himself about any doubt there may be. Again the purchaser should be advised of the risks.

(3) Central heating system

The purchaser should ask his surveyor to check whether there is a central heating system. There is no doubt that a central heating system is not an item of moveable property, but some debtors may nevertheless have moved it out of the property before departure. However, even if the central heating system is there, the heritable creditor will not be willing to give any warranties about its condition at the date of entry and will not undertake to effect any repairs which are necessary should the purchaser find that the system is defective. The property may have been vacant for months and so the heritable creditor should be asked to give the purchaser access to the property after the conclusion of missives in order that he can satisfy himself.

(4) Maintenance

It is usual in a domestic transaction for the seller to undertake to maintain the subjects in their existing condition until entry. In a forced sale, the heritable creditor may not be willing to give such an undertaking, again because the subjects may have been empty for some time, they may have been vandalised and may be further vandalised between the conclusion of missives and the date of entry. The purchaser would therefore have to effect insurance as 'purchaser price unpaid'.

(5) Alterations, planning, building control, etc

The heritable creditor will not be willing to warrant compliance with the legislation on planning, building control, and other matters, for example environmental health, fire regulations, etc. If he has obtained and exhibited to the purchaser the usual local authority certificates, the purchaser will be deemed to have satisfied himself, or he may be given a period in which to check matters out. If the creditor has not obtained the certificates, the purchaser will require to carry out any investigations. This may seem harsh, but since the heritable creditor may never have visited the property, whereas the purchaser has and has presumably also had it surveyed, the purchaser is in a better position to know about any problems of unauthorised alterations, than the heritable creditor. Heritable creditors will not give warranties about alterations, superior's consent etc, and will not bind themselves to produce any necessary permissions.

(6) Letter of obligation

If the missives are not qualified, the purchaser is entitled to assume as a matter of practice that the solicitors for the heritable creditor will grant a letter of obligation in normal form at settlement. The heritable creditor's solicitors may, however, qualify their undertaking in this connection in relation to the obligation to give a 'clear' search. They may not undertake to clear the record of any inhibitions which post-date the date of the standard security in their favour. Such inhibitions have no effect on the standard security and hence no effect on the title to be granted by the heritable creditor, but this qualification avoids disputes about whether the search is 'clear'[2].

(7) Matrimonial home

If consents, affidavits, etc are missing, the heritable creditors may not be willing to remedy this, but the purchaser should consider the need for an indemnity against the return of a non-entitled spouse.

It must be borne in mind in any such transaction that the debtor may redeem the security at any time prior to the conclusion of a bargain[3].

1 See para 5.25 above.
2 See para 10.04 below.
3 1970 Act, s 23(3); App [63]. See also para 10.15 below.

8.32   Implement of sale

The creditor in a standard security can sell the subjects without the concurrence of the creditors in *pari passu* ranking securities because they are protected as the selling creditor must apply the proceeds of sale according to the respective ranking of various securities. It is not necessary for the creditor to have the consent of any prior-ranking security holder, nor need the prior-ranking security be discharged, but it is unlikely that a purchaser will accept the title if any extant security is not discharged. A sale is completed by the granting of a disposition by the selling creditor to the purchaser which bears to be in implement of sale[1]. This will import an assignation to the purchaser of the warrandice in the standard security and an obligation by the granter of the security to ratify, approve and confirm the sale and the disposition[2]. Once a disposition is recorded, or registered, the subjects conveyed are disburdened of the standard security and also of all other securities and diligences which rank *pari passu* with or are postponed to the standard security[3]. The debtor and any guarantor remains liable under the personal obligation for any balance due, but the right to recover will in most cases be worthless. It is interesting to note that section 26 does not specifically state that the debtor is divested of all rights in the subjects, whereas section 40 which deals with discharges of pre-1970 securities specifically says that the subjects vest in the 'person entitled thereto'. There seems little doubt that the intention of the Act is that the purchaser should have a good title to the subjects and that the debtor's rights should be extinguished and the distinction between sections 26 and 40 is a distinction without a difference.

1 1970 Act, s 26(1); App [67].
2 Conveyancing (Scotland) Act 1924, s 41(1).
3 1970 Act, s 26(1); App [67].

8.33 The proceeds of sale

The proceeds of sale are to be held by the selling creditor in trust for those having an interest. When the proceeds of sale are received they must be applied in the following order of priority: (1) The expenses of the sale; (2) the sum due under prior securities which are being redeemed; (3) the sum due under the standard security itself and sums due under any securities ranking *pari passu* with it (proportionately if necessary); (4) sums due under postponed securities according to their ranking; and (5) any surplus is payable to the owner of the security subjects[1] at the time of the sale. Because of the delays at the Registers, it may be difficult for a creditor to know whether there are any postponed securities.

1 1970 Act, s 27(1); App [69].

8.34 Comment

On the whole, the terms of section 27 of the 1970 Act are obvious. However, at least two problems of construction arise. The first of these relates to the term 'securities' which appears in subsection 1. In a sale by a heritable creditor, it is clear that when the free proceeds are available, he holds these in trust for the persons listed at heads (1) to (4). In some instances, a creditor of the debtor will have inhibited after the heritable security has been created, but before the subjects are sold. There is authority for the view that the inhibition in such a case, is a security[1]. The matter cannot be regarded as settled in that there is at least one case which takes the opposite view[2] and it is submitted that that is the correct view. An inhibition is a personal prohibition and it does not create a *nexus* over the heritable property of the debtor[3]; it cannot therefore be a security[4]. However, even if the inhibition is not regarded as a security, there is a difference of opinion on whether the inhibiting creditor has any preference *over the free proceeds* by reason only of the inhibition. In some cases, a preference has been given[5]; in others, it has not[6]. The dilemma faced by the heritable creditor can be resolved if he raises an action of multiple-poinding, or if the debtor is sequestrated. The competing creditors may themselves reach an agreement.

One other matter arises out of section 27(1) which permits the heritable creditor to deduct 'all expenses properly incurred by him in connection with the sale, or attempted sale'. If that is construed narrowly, 'expenses' might be regarded as covering only the cost of advertising the subjects and the legal fees for the conveyancing. Taking a slightly broader approach, the term would cover the expenses of serving a calling-up notice, or notice of default (and defending any objection thereto), or petitioning the court under section 24 of the 1970 Act, and any necessary action of ejection to oust the debtor. On a slightly broader approach still, it would cover the expenses of defending any action by the debtor to prevent the sale, for example on the ground that there has been inadequate advertising, or that the best price has not been obtained[7]. It is submitted that the third approach is the correct one and on that basis, the only objection open to the debtor, or other challenger, is that the expenses were not 'properly' incurred.

1 *Hay v Durham* (1850) 12 D 676; *Mitchell v Motherwell* (1888) 16 R 122; *Halifax Building Society v Smith* 1985 SLT (Sh Ct) 25; *Abbey National Building Society v Barclays Bank PLC* 1990 SCLR 639.
2 *Scottish Waggon Co v Hamilton's Tr* (1906) 13 SLT 779; see also G L Gretton *The Law of Inhibition and Adjudication* pp 81, 82.
3 J Graham Stewart *The Law of Diligence* p 551; *Gretton* pp 71–77.
4 See *Gretton* pp 81, 82.
5 *George M Allan Ltd v Waugh's Tr* 1966 SLT (Sh Ct) 17; *Bank of Scotland v Lord Advocate* 1977 SLT 24; *Abbey National Building Society v Shaik Aziz* 1981 SLT (Sh Ct) 29; *Halifax Building Society v Smith* 1985 SLT (Sh Ct) 25; *Abbey National Building Society v Barclays Bank PLC* 1990 SCLR 639.
6 *McGowan v Middlemas* 1977 SLT (Sh Ct) 41; *Ferguson and Forster v Dalbeattie Finance Co* 1981 SLT (Sh Ct) 53.
7 Expenses were awarded in *Associated Displays Limited (In Liquidation) v Turnbeam Limited*. See para 8.30 above.

8.35 Protection of purchasers

If there has been an error in the sale procedure or it transpires that the debt has in fact been paid off before the sale is carried out, the issue which then arises is whether the purchaser is protected.

Prior to the 1970 Act, where property was being sold by a creditor under a bond and disposition in security, there was always the danger of a challenge on such a ground within five years of the sale. After that period had elapsed, however, protection was afforded by section 41 of the Conveyancing (Scotland) Act 1924. The practical effect of that was that a purchaser's solicitor had to see the most detailed evidence of compliance with the various procedures before he would allow his client to part with the money.

The protection afforded by section 41 is applied to standard securities by virtue of section 38 of the 1970 Act. Section 41(2) provides:

> (2) Where a disposition of land is duly recorded in the appropriate Register of Sasines and that disposition bears to be granted in the exercise of a power of sale contained in a deed granting a bond and disposition in security, and the exercise of that power was *ex facie* regular, the title of a *bona fide* purchaser of the land for value shall not be challengeable on the ground that the debt had ceased to exist, unless that fact appeared in the said Register, or was known to the purchaser prior to the payment of the price, or on the ground of any irregularity relating to the sale or in any preliminary procedure thereto; but nothing in the provisions of this subsection shall affect the competency of any claim for damages in respect of the sale of land against the person exercising the said power[1].

There are two conditions which must be noted (1) the exercise of the power must be *ex facie* regular; and (2) the purchaser must act in good faith. However, the purchaser no longer needs to wait for five years for the protection.

There is some doubt as to what is meant by the exercise of the power being *ex facie* regular. It is not clear whether that means just advertising and obtaining the best price, or whether it includes all the preliminaries leading to the sale as well, such as the calling-up notice, notice of default, or court decree.

Section 41(2) of the 1924 Act is therefore capable of being interpreted in three ways. The first is that if the creditor satisfies the purchaser that he has advertised the subjects and secured the best price, the purchaser will be in good faith and hence protected.

The second interpretation is that the purchaser requires to see evidence of all the preliminaries, in order to satisfy himself that the proceedings have been *ex facie* regular and only then will he be in good faith.

The third interpretation, which is a variation on the first, is that if the creditor supplies information about the advertisement, the price and the preliminaries, then the purchaser will be in good faith only if these appear to be in order. If, however, the purchaser does not receive details about the preliminary steps, he need not ask for them and will nevertheless be in good faith, provided the subjects have been advertised and the best possible price has been obtained. It is submitted that the third interpretation is the correct one because one of the objects of the 1970 Act was to simplify the procedure on sale[2].

The purchaser is also protected, despite the fact that a calling-up notice of default may have been served on someone who was legally incapax[3].

1 Conveyancing (Scotland) Act 1924, s 41(2) (substituted by the 1970 Act, s 38).
2 *Conveyancing Legislation and Practice* (the Halliday Report) (Cmnd 3118) (1966) paras 110–113.
3 Conveyancing (Scotland) Act 1924, s 41(1).

(2) ENTERING INTO POSSESSION

8.36 General

Under a bond and disposition in security, by virtue of the clause of assignation of rents, the heritable creditor could enter into possession of the security subjects and uplift the rents. This he did by an action of maills and duties. The standard security does not contain a clause of assignation of rents, but standard condition 10(3) entitles the creditor, on default by the debtor, to enter into possession of the security subjects. A warrant is not actually required from the court to enable the creditor to enter into possession. If a calling-up notice has not been complied with, he can do so right away. If however the debtor is in default within the meaning of standard condition 9(1)(b), ie failure to comply with some other requirement arising out of the security, the creditor will require to apply to the court for the exercise of this right. If the subjects are let, or are an estate of superiority, or the right to a ground annual, the creditor is also given the right to receive or recover feu duties, ground annuals or rents.

The creditor will also have to apply to the court if the ground of default is that the proprietor is involvent. In practice, the creditor may wish a court decree in order to convince feuars or tenants that it is in order for them to make payment to him.

If the property is in the personal occupation of the debtor, it may be necessary to have him dispossessed. Section 5 of the Heritable Securities (Scotland) Act 1894 would permit an action of ejection to be raised provided the debtor has failed to pay an instalment of interest or some part of the capital.

8.37 Powers of the creditor in possession

If the creditor has taken possession by arrangement with the debtor, then clearly the terms of that arrangement will regulate the creditor's powers. If, as is more likely, possession has been taken because there has been a failure to comply with a calling-up notice, then the whole powers under standard condition 10 are available, subject to any agreed variation. If the possession has been taken under a warrant from the court, then the warrant will dictate what powers the creditor has. A heritable creditor who has entered into possession may prevent a postponed creditor from exercising any of the statutory remedies[1].

In terms of standard condition 10(3) and (4) (read along with section 20(3) of the 1970 Act), a creditor in possession may, in addition to recovering feu duties, ground annuals or rents, grant leases for up to seven years, or for longer periods if he has obtained the permission from the court. Where the heritable creditor enters into possession, it has not been decided whether the heritable creditor has the right only to the rents from the date on which he enters into possession, or whether he is entitled also to the arrears. Where the creditor in a bond and disposition in security entered into possession by virtue of an action of maills and duties, he was entitled to not only future rents but also to arrears[2], the *ratio* being that he had a right to the rents assigned to him from the date of his infeftment and decree in the action of maills and duties interpelled the tenants from paying to the debtor.

The standard security does not contain a clause of assignation of rents, but, as has been noted, the standard conditions confer the rights on the creditor which he would have by virtue of such a clause. It is therefore arguable, on the analogy of the position under a bond and disposition in security that the creditor has the right to arrears of rent. Section 20(1) provides that the rights which the creditor has under the security shall be in addition to those 'conferred by any rule of law on the creditor in a heritable security'.

On the other hand, it can be contended that the creditor has no such assignation of the rents and that his entitlement to them arises only when the debtor is in default. Until that time, the debtor is entitled to the use of the property and its fruits.

The arguments are finely balanced, but possibly tilted slightly in favour of the position under the bond. The matter has never been decided upon, but it could be quite important in any competition between the heritable creditor on the one hand and say, a trustee in bankruptcy.

The creditor is also entitled to manage, reconstruct and improve the security subjects. The standard conditions as varied will almost certainly provide for the serving of a 'seven day' letter requiring the debtor to vacate the premises[3].

As a matter of practice, the remedy of entering into possession is one which a creditor should be, and is, slow to adopt. It would be used normally only if the personal obligation is of little value, and, for some reason, the property cannot be sold immediately. It involves the trouble of managing someone else's property with an obligation ultimately to account for intromissions. That entails the keeping of accurate records which must be properly vouched. The creditor may also incur certain liabilities. As an intromitter with the rents, he is liable for the feuduty, as well as tax. He may also be liable as an occupier in a question with the public, under the Occupiers Liability (Scotland) Act 1960.

1 *Skipton Building Society v Wain* 1986 SLT 96.
2 *Budge v Brown's Trs* (1872) 10 M 958.
3 For practical problems, see para 5.29 above.

8.38 In lawful possession

In section 20 of the 1970 Act, there are two references to 'a creditor who is in lawful possession of the security subjects'. The first appears in subsection 3 which provides that a creditor in a standard security who is in lawful possession of the security subjects may let the security subjects for not more than seven years, or for longer if he has warrant from the court. This amplifies standard condition 10(4) which, like standard condition 10(3), uses the phrase 'has entered into possession'. It is submitted that 'the creditor who is in lawful possession of the security subjects' is one 'who has entered into possession'.

The phrase appears also in subsection 5 which it is helpful to set out in full.

> (5) There shall be deemed to be assigned to a creditor who is in lawful possession of the security subjects all rights and obligations of the proprietor relating to—
> (a) leases, or any permission or right of occupancy, granted in respect of those subjects or any part thereof, and
> (b) the management and maintenance of the subjects and the effecting of any reconstruction, alteration or improvement reasonably required for the purpose of maintaining the market value of the subjects.

Subsection 5(a) assigns all rights and obligations under leases, etc which is a sensible concomitant of the right to uplift the rents, etc in standard condition 10(3).

Sub-section 5(b) was considered in *David Watson Property Management Ltd v Woolwich Equitable Building Society*[1]. The building society had repossessed subjects in respect of which there were outstanding charges for common repairs. The pursuers who were the factors of the property raised an action against the society for payment of the repairs. The sheriff, and on appeal the Sheriff Principal, held that section 20(5)(b) rendered the heritable creditor liable. There was some discussion by the Sheriff Principal of whether 'all rights and obligations . . . relating to . . . the management and maintenance of the subjects' might not include charges for common repairs, but it would be difficult to sustain an argument to this effect given the generality of the phraseology.

On appeal, the First Division held (reversing the lower courts)[2] that what were assigned under the subsection were the rights of the proprietor and not the debtor, and the Act draws a clear distinction between them. To have upheld the decision of the sheriffs would have meant that a heritable creditor might have to pay debts personal to the proprietor and be unable to recover from the proceeds of sale if the debtor and the proprietor were different persons.

It is worth noting in this context that local authorities have powers to require repairs to be done to houses within their areas. The principal statutes are the Civic Government (Scotland) Act 1982 and the Housing (Scotland) Act 1987. Without going into detail, the 1982 Act provides that the 'owner' may be required to carry out the repairs and failing that, may be charged by the local authority should they carry out the repairs[3]. 'Owner' is not defined, but standing the decision of the First Division in *David Watson*, it is submitted that a heritable creditor is not liable under the Act. Under the 1987 Act, it is the 'person having control of the house'[4] who is obliged to carry out the repairs and who may be charged by the local authority if the repairs are not done. Once again, there is no definition, but it is arguable that a heritable creditor who has entered into possession has 'control' and hence is liable under the 1987 Act, but a heritable creditor who is doing no more than exercising the power of sale is not in 'control' for this purpose.

The term 'owner' also appears in the Building (Scotland) Act 1959 where the local authority may recover expenses incurred by them in the exercise of their powers in respect of unauthorised works[5]. They may also serve a notice on the 'owner' of a dangerous building[6].

1 1989 SLT (Sh Ct) 74.
2 1990 SLT 764. This decision has been appealed to the House of Lords.
3 Civic Government (Scotland) Act 1982, s 87.
4 Housing (Scotland) Act 1987, s 108.
5 Building (Scotland) Act 1959, s 10.
6 Ibid, s 11.

8.39   The community charge

Some local authorities have taken the view that where a heritable creditor enters into possession, he thereby becomes liable for the community charge at the standard rate. The liability of the heritable creditor would turn, not upon an interpretation of section 20(5) of the 1970 Act, but rather of the Abolition of Domestic Rates Etc (Scotland) Act 1987.

The first point worth noting is that the 1987 Act does not contain a definition of 'owner', but the legislation on rating contained a definition of 'owner' who was someone who received the rents or other profits from the lands[1]. In *MacBain v Gordon*[2], Lord Salvesen pointed out that liability for rates was based not on title, but on entitlement to receive rents. On the other hand, in *Lanarkshire County Council v Miller*[3], it was held that it was competent to enter as the 'proprietor' someone who was described as the proprietor, even although there was a heritable creditor who was collecting rents. The case was, however, based on a provision which indicated that the person who actually received the rents was not the only person who could be entered as the proprietor[4]. There are at least two relevant sheriff court cases. In one of these, it was held that bondholders who were not in possession were not proprietors for the purposes of the same statute as was considered in the *Miller* case[5]. In the other, it was held that heritable proprietors were liable for assessments, rather than bond-holders in possession[6]. Unfortunately, the report does not make it clear which statutes were involved and so the case is of little assistance. On the basis of these cases, there is an argument that the heritable creditor who enters into possession is also liable for the community charge.

Against that, however, is the fact that these statutes did define 'proprietor' whereas, the 1987 Act does not define 'owner' and it is not acceptable to pluck the definition of a term, even the same term, from one Act in order to construe another[7]. On the basis that the 1987 Act is silent on the issue, one has to look elsewhere for assistance and it is submitted that it is to be had from a consideration of whether a heritable creditor has been treated as an owner of the subjects when the debtor has defaulted. Certainly, in the context of the bond and disposition in security, he was not[8] and the First Division followed that approach in the *David Watson* case in relation to the creditor under a standard security. It would therefore follow that a heritable creditor who enters into possession is not liable for the community charge. It is submitted that that is the preferable view and that was the decision of Sheriff McEwan in *Northern Rock Building Society v Wood*[9].

1 Poor Law (Scotland) Act 1845, s 1; Lands Valuation (Scotland) Act 1854, s 42.
2 1917 SC 185 at 195.
3 1917 SC 35.
4 Lands Valuation (Scotland) Act 1854, s 42.
5 *Connell's Trs v Glasgow Corporation* (1910) 26 Sh Ct Rep 127.
6 *Kilmore and Kilbride Parish Council v Campbell* (1917) 33 Sh Ct Rep 176.
7 Maxwell on Interpretation of Statutes (12th edn) p 58 et seq.
8 W M Gloag and J M Irvine *Rights in Security and Cautionary Obligations* p 100.
9 18 June 1990 (unreported). It is understood that this decision may have been appealed. I am grateful to Roddy Paisley of Messrs McGrigor Donald for informing me of this case and other relevant material.

8.40 Comment

In the *David Watson* case, it was admitted that the heritable creditors had entered into possession. The remedy of entering into possession is the equivalent of the remedy of an action of maills and duties which was available to a bondholder. That remedy and that of entering into possession is, it is submitted, different from exercising the power of sale, although it is possible to argue that before a heritable creditor can exercise his power of sale, he has to enter into possession of the security subjects in the sense of depriving the debtor of possession of them, or at least having them under his control, rather than the control of the debtor. It seems clear, however, that the 1970 Act envisages that when the heritable creditor enters into possession, there will be some degree of management of the subjects. That is evidenced by his right to collect the rents, enter into leases, etc. If it is correct to state that this distinction exists, it seems to follow that the heritable creditor who does no more than exercise his power of sale is not subject to the terms of section 20(5) of the 1970 Act[1], nor would he be liable for community charge, or for rates, in the case of a commercial property.

1 For a case involving a bondholder, see *Connell's Trs v Glasgow Corporation* (1910) 26 Sh Ct Rep 127.

(3) REPAIRS, RECONSTRUCTION, ETC

8.41 General

In terms of standard condition 1, the debtor is obliged to keep the security subjects in good and sufficient repair and to make good all defects within such reasonable period as the creditor may specify. The creditor can give seven days' notice in writing of his intimation to inspect the subjects. If the debtor fails to comply with standard condition 1, the creditor has power to put matters right under standard condition 7.

When the debtor is in default within the meaning of standard condition 9, the creditor has the power not only to carry out repairs and make good any defects, but in addition, he may effect 'such reconstruction, alteration and improvement on the subjects as would be expected of a prudent proprietor' in order to maintain the market value. To this end, the creditor may enter on the security subjects at all reasonable times[1].

Thus when the debtor is not in default, but has not kept the subjects in good and sufficient repair, the creditor may do so, but he has to give the debtor seven days' notice in writing. Where the debtor is in default, the creditor has the same power, but no notice is required and the creditor has the additional powers of reconstruction, etc.

The powers exerciseable on default will usually be exercised prior to a sale or let of the security subjects. In cases where the state of repair would have only a minimal effect on the sale price, the creditor will probably not carry out the repairs in case the cost is not recovered from the sale price.

1 1970 Act, Sch 3, standard condition 10(6); App [105].

(4) FORECLOSURE

8.42   General

The right of foreclosure[1] enables a creditor who has failed to find a purchaser for the security subjects at a price sufficient to cover the amount due to the creditor, to take over the security subjects as his own, rather than sell them at a lower figure. The right is available only (1) where the creditor has exposed the security subjects for sale by public roup at a price not exceeding the sum due under the security and any prior ranking security or one ranking *pari passu*, and has failed to find a purchaser, or (2) where he has failed to secure that price but has managed to sell a part of the subjects at a price which is less than the amounts due to him and any prior ranking, or *pari passu* ranking security holder[2]. The standard conditions relating to foreclosure cannot be altered[3]. It is important to emphasise that the exposure must have been by public roup which, in most instances, would be unusual. An unsuccessful attempt to sell by private bargain does not produce the same result. It is also necessary for a period of two months to have elapsed from the date of the first exposure to sale.

1 See Halliday *Commentary* paras 10-71–10-86; *Halliday* vol III paras 39-70–39-85.
2 1970 Act, s 28; App [72]–[79].
3 1970 Act, s 11(3); App [15].

8.43 Procedure

The procedure is similar to but slightly more flexible than that which applies to a bond in disposition in security; in particular, the court is given a wide discretion under section 28.

The creditor must lodge in court a statement setting out the whole amount due under the security and the court must be satisfied that the amount stated is not less than the price at which the property has been exposed or part of it has been sold[1]. The application must be served on a number of people. These are (1) the debtor; (2) the proprietor, if he is not the debtor; and (3) any other heritable creditor who is disclosed by a 20-year search[2], or on examination of the Title Sheet in the Land Register.

The court may order such intimation and enquiry as it thinks fit. It may allow the debtor or proprietor a period not exceeding three months in which to pay the whole amount due. It may order the exposure of the subjects at a price to be fixed by the court, and in that event, the creditor may bid and purchase, or it may grant a decree of foreclosure without the need for further advertisement[3].

1 1970 Act, s 28(2); App [73].
2 1970 Act, s 28(3); App [74].
3 1970 Act, s 28(4); App [75].

8.44 Contents of the decree

The decree will contain a declaration that on recording of the extract decree, any right to redeem the standard security has been extinguished and that the creditor has the right to the security subjects or the unsold part, at the price at which the subjects were last exposed under deduction of the price received for any parts sold[1]. The security subjects or the unsold part will be described by means of a particular description or a statutory description by reference[1], and in addition, there will be a reference to burdens affecting the subjects. The decree of foreclosure contains a warrant for recording the extract in the Register of Sasines. Where the subjects are in an area to which registration of title applies, then an application to the Keeper replaces the warrant.

1 1970 Act, s 28(5); App [76].

8.45   Effect of the decree

The recording or registration of the extract decree has three consequences. Firstly, it extinguishes any right of redemption and vests the
security subjects in the creditor, as if he has a recorded title to them
granted by proprietor. Secondly, it disburdens the subjects of any
standard security and all postponed securities and diligences, and
thirdly, it gives the creditor the same right as the debtor to redeem
prior or *pari passu* ranking securities[1].

As in the case of the bond and disposition in security, the personal
obligation of the debtor remains in full force to the extent of any excess
still owing over and above the value at which the property is deemed to
be taken over[2].

Once the extract decree has been recorded or registration takes
place, the creditor's title is not challengeable on the ground of any
irregularity in the proceedings for foreclosure, or calling-up or default
which preceded it, but that is without prejudice to any claims for
damages which may be competent to the debtor against the creditor in
respect of that irregularity[3]. Stamp Duty is due *ad valorem* on the
decree as a conveyance on sale[4].

1 1970 Act, s 28(6); App [77].
2 1970 Act, s 28(7); App [78].
3 1970 Act, s 28(6); App [77].
4 Stamp Act 1891, s 54 (expld Finance Act 1898, s 6).

CHAPTER 9

Other remedies

9.01 Introduction

The remedies available to the heritable creditor under the standard security have been dealt with in chapter 8. However, the 1970 Act preserves to the creditor any contractual remedies[1] and remedies which were available to the creditor in a bond and disposition in security in so far as they are not inconsistent with the 1970 Act[2]. These remedies are (1) enforcement of the personal obligation; (2) poinding of the ground; and (3) adjudication.

1 1970 Act, s 20(1); App [48].
2 1970 Act, s 32 (App [86]); 1970 Act, Sch 8.

(1) THE PERSONAL OBLIGATION

9.02 General

The personal obligation under a Form A standard security may, unless otherwise provided, be enforced on demand[1]. That is so, despite the requirements for notice to the debtor for enforcing the security[2]. In a Form B standard security, the personal obligation is contained in separate documentation, but as there is no statutory provision to the effect that performance is due on demand[3], that has to be provided for expressly if the creditor wishes. As has already been noted, the right to enforce that personal obligation is additional to any rights under the security[4] and both sets of rights may be pursued concurrently[5]. Where the obligation is contained in separate documents, it is important to ensure that on assignation of the security, the personal obligation transmits also[6].

The personal obligation will normally be an obligation to pay the amount which has been borrowed, and interest thereon. The obligation, however, may be one *ad factum praestandum*, or it may be an

148

undertaking not to do something. The personal obligation may consist of a combination of these. For example, in a loan transaction in respect of a garage, or licensed premises, the personal obligation will consist not only of the obligation to repay what has been lent, but there may also be an obligation to purchase the lender's goods, for example petrol or beer, and an obligation not to purchase similar products from anyone other than the lender. The obligation to repay the amount lent may be enforced by an action for payment, but if there is a clause of consent to registration for execution, as there almost certainly will be, the obligation can be enforced by summary diligence. Where the obligation is *ad factum praestandum*, it is enforceable by an action for specific implement and where the obligation is an undertaking not to do something, the appropriate remedy is interdict[7].

1 1970 Act, s 10(1); App [9].
2 1970 Act, ss 19, 21 (calling-up; notice of default) (App [37]–[47]; [53]–[56]).
3 1970 Act, s 10 deals only with Form A.
4 1970 Act, ss 20(1), 21(1) (App [48], [53]).
5 *McWhirter v McCulloch's Trs* (1887) 14 R 918; *McNab v Clarke* (1889) 16 R 610.
6 See Halliday *Commentary* para 9-02; *Halliday* vol III, para 40-14.
7 For the circumstances in which specific implement will not be granted, see W M Gloag and R C Henderson *Introduction to the Law of Scotland* (9th edn) para 13-2.

9.03 Summary diligence

There is a clause of consent to registration for preservation and execution in the Form A standard security[1], but not in the Form B, and it would therefore have to be incorporated into the separate personal bond or minute of agreement. If the debt is for a fluctuating or uncertain amount, a certificate from the creditor or someone authorised on his behalf will be needed to ascertain the sum due for the purposes of enforcing the obligation by using summary diligence[2]. It is, of course, common for the standard conditions to deal with this by providing that the certificate will be conclusive as to the amount due[3]. Summary diligence would not be available against an assignee or other successor of the debtor unless he has agreed to that[4]. In order to be enforceable by summary diligence, the debt or obligation must be precise[5].

1 1970 Act, Sch 2; App [87]–[95].
2 *Halliday* vol 1, para 4-65; G Maher and D J Cusine *The Law and Practice of Diligence* paras 2.16-2.26.
3 See para 4-30 above.
4 Conveyancing (Scotland) Act 1874, s 47 as amended by the Conveyancing (Scotland) Act 1924, s 15.
5 *Hendry v Marshall* (1878) 5 R 687.

9.04 When will the personal obligation be enforced?

Given the extensive and effective remedies available under the security, it is obvious that a creditor will attempt to use these first. It seems, therefore, that the personal obligation will be enforced only where the security subjects, if sold, would not realise the full amount due, but the personal obligation is still worth enforcing. There are, of course, many cases where the security subjects do not realise the full amount due, but in almost all these cases, the personal obligation is worthless also.

9.05 Effect of transfer or transmission of the security subjects

Although the security right will continue to affect the property after its transfer or transmission, the same does not apply to the personal obligation. The transferee does not *ipso facto* become liable under the personal obligation. The matter is dealt with in section 47 of the 1874 Act as amended by section 15 of the 1924 Act.

Where a person acquires right to a heritable property by a conveyance, the personal obligation in any security over the property will not be enforceable against the transferee unless there is an agreement *in gremio* of the conveyance to that effect and the transferee signs the conveyance. If there is that agreement and the transferee signs the conveyance, the personal obligation may be enforced against him in any competent way, including the use of summary diligence. Such a transfer does not terminate the liability of the original debtor[1].

Where a person acquires such a right by succession, gift or bequest, the transferee will be liable under the personal obligation up to the value of the subjects, but summary diligence cannot be done against him unless he signs an agreement to that effect.

It should be noted that sections 47 and 15 above referred to apply only to the obligations contained in the deed constituting the heritable security. That clearly covers a Form A standard security, but it may not cover the personal obligation contained in the separate documentation under a Form B standard security and so, in that case, a bond of corroboration by the transferee is desirable[2].

1 *University of Glasgow v Yuille's Tr* (1882) 9 R 643.
2 For further details, see Halliday *Commentary* para 9.29; *Halliday* vol III paras 33-52–33-57.

(2) POINDING OF THE GROUND

9.06   General

Poinding of the ground is the method by which a heritable creditor attaches moveables on the security subjects[1]. It depends upon the existence of a *debitum fundi*. The 1970 Act does not say so, but the standard security will clearly create a *debitum fundi*, and so, the remedy is available to the creditor.

For the reason just mentioned, it is unlikely that a creditor will pursue the remedy of poinding of the ground. In one situation, however, this remedy may be preferable to enforcing the personal obligation. If the heritable property has declined so much in value that the creditor's remedy of sale is virtually useless, poinding of the ground might be used to attach any moveables of value, for example plant, machinery and stock. The creditor may, however, have taken power in the standard conditions to deal with these[2] and so a poinding of the ground will not be necessary.

1 See J Graham Stewart *The Law of Diligence* pp 491–510; G Maher and D J Cusine *The Law and Practice of Diligence* paras 8-56–8-64; J Burns on *Conveyancing Practice* pp 512 *et seq.*
2 See para 5.25 above.

(3) ADJUDICATION

9.07   General

The 1970 Act does not make any reference to adjudication, but the remedy still exists for heritable creditors. It is fully explained elsewhere[1] but its principal drawback is that the heritable creditor has to wait for ten years until the 'expiry of the legal' before he can obtain a good title. At present therefore, a creditor would have to be in a situation where the remedies under the Act were not worth pursuing, the debtor was a man of straw and there were no moveables of value on the subjects. (In other words, the heritable creditor is clutching at some of the straw which the debtor is made of.) The Scottish Law Commission have produced a consultation paper which recommends modernising the law[2].

1 See *Graham Stewart* pp 576–667; *Gretton* pp 156–168; Maher and Cusine *The Law and Practice of Diligence* paras 9.37–9.50.
2 *Adjudications for Debt and Related Matters* Consultation Memoranda 78 (Nov 1988).

CHAPTER 10

Extinction of standard securities

10.01 Introduction

Standard Securities may be extinguished by (1) discharge; (2) payment or performance; (3) compensation; (4) *confusio*; (5) redemption; and (6) on compulsory acquisition.

(1) DISCHARGE

10.02 General

Section 17 of the 1970 Act authorises the discharge of a standard security and disburdenment of the security subjects. This can be done by a discharge in accordance with Schedule 4, Form F.

A discharge is a formal document which may be either separate from the standard security or endorsed on it. In building society transactions, a discharge may be printed at the back of the standard security, but whether that is so or not, as a matter of practice, a formal discharge should always be obtained and recorded or registered. In a Sasine transaction this may be necessary in order to satisfy the requirement to produce a clear search. It is worth noting that some lenders, particularly building societies, expressly provide in their Deeds of Variation that a solicitor in their employment may prepare the discharge and arrange for it to be recorded or registered (for example Bradford and Bingley; Newcastle; Century; National-Provincial). That practice does not offend against the provisions in the Titles to Land Consolidation (Scotland) Act 1868 dealing with warrants of registration[1].

A question which arises is the extent to which the purchaser can rely on a discharge. Can he, for example, rely on it if it appears to be signed by the creditor, or each of them if there is more than one? In that connection, section 41 of the 1970 Act gives protection to purchasers of subjects which have at one time been the subject of a security.

41. Restriction on effect of reduction of certain discharges of securities

(1) Where the discharge, in whole or in part, of a security over land is duly recorded, whether before or after the commencement of this Act, and that discharge bears to be granted by a person entitled so to do, the title of a person to any subsequent interest in the land, acquired *bona fide* and for value, shall not be challengeable, after the expiration of a period of five years commencing with the date of the recording of the discharge, by reason only of the recording of an extract of a decree of reduction of the discharge, whether or not the date of that decree was before or after the date on which the acquisition of the interest was duly recorded.

(2) Section 46 of the Act of 1924 (which requires extract decrees of reduction of certain deeds to be recorded) shall cease to apply in relation to a decree of reduction of a discharge of a security where that discharge has been duly recorded for a period of five years or more, but the provision of this subsection shall not preclude the recording of such a decree of reduction as provided for in the said section 46.

(3) Nothing in the provisions of this section shall affect any rights of a creditor in a security as against the debtor therein.

(4) The provisions of this section shall not be pleadable to any effect in any action begun, whether before or after the date of the commencement of this Act, before the expiry of a period of two years beginning with that date.

(5) This section shall apply to an order under section 8 of the Law Reform (Miscellaneous Provisions) (Scotland) Act 1985 rectifying a discharge as it applies to a decree of reduction of a discharge.

(In this context, the term 'security' covers both standard securities and pre-1970 securities.)

It also gives future lenders a degree of protection against the possibility of a discharge of a previous standard security being reduced. An action of reduction could be raised if the discharge was not granted by the creditor or person acquiring right from him and because of the possibility of assignations and transmissions, it might not always be clear who is entitled to the creditor's interest.

Section 41 provides that the title of a *bona fide* purchaser for value or lender, will be protected against the reduction of a discharge recorded more than five years prior to the decree of reduction. That protection will exist provided the discharge bears to be granted by the person entitled to grant it. The practical effect of this is that when one is examining a title to make sure that it is not encumbered by any security, if there is a discharge of a security which has been recorded more than five years ago, it is not necessary to examine all the relevant documents of transmission, etc. If, however, the discharge has been granted within the five year period, then it will still be necessary to carry out these various checks. There may be a tendency amongst some agents to accept all discharges at face value, but it is important to note that the provisions of the section apply only to discharges granted more than five years previously.

While section 41 seems to be aimed primarily at affording protection against reduction of a discharge because the wrong *creditor* may have granted it, its terms may be wide enough to cover the reduction of a discharge which is granted in favour of the wrong *debtor*. For example, a property may be purchased by two persons who are partners, but the conveyance might have been granted in their favour as individuals and a standard security granted by them as individuals. If the discharge was granted in their favour as partners of the firm, the terms of section 41 seem to be wide enough to cover that situation. It seems unlikely that that was the intention of the legislature and so it would be wise to assume that it applies only to a mistake in the creditor.

Various styles are contained in Professor Halliday's books[2], but a simple form for a Sasine transaction is as follows:

WE, the Left Bank of the Clyde plc having our Head Office at Clyde House, Clyde Square, Glasgow IN CONSIDERATION of the sum of Forty Thousand Pounds £40,000 paid to us by Charles Chancer, company director, residing at Four hundred and Forty Moncur Crescent Glasgow, hereby DISCHARGE a standard security [the foregoing standard security] for Forty Thousand Pounds granted by the said Charles Chancer in our favour recorded in the Division of the General Register of Sasines applicable to the County of Erewhom on Ninth February Nineteen hundred and Eighty IN WITNESS WHEREOF

Where the interest is registered, a simple style is as follows:

WE, the left Bank of the Clyde plc having our Head Office at Clyde House, Clyde Square, Glasgow IN CONSIDERATION of the sum of Forty Thousand pounds paid to us by Charles Chancer, a company director, residing at Four hundred and forty Moncur Crescent, Glasgow, hereby DISCHARGE a standard security [the foregoing standard security] for Forty Thousand pounds granted by the said Charles Chancer in our favour registered on 28 February, Nineteen hundred and eight-four over the subjects in Title Number REN 123456789 IN WITNESS WHEREOF

1 Titles to Land Consolidation (Scotland) Act 1868, s 141.
2 Halliday *Commentary* paras 9-52–9-59; *Halliday* vol III, paras 40-65–40-72.

(2) PAYMENT; PERFORMANCE

10.03   General

Unless the documentation provides otherwise and it is unlikely that it will, a standard security will always be extinguished by payment in full[1] but a formal discharge should be obtained and recorded for the reason give above. Where the obligation is *ad factum praestandum*, performance will discharge the obligation, but again a formal discharge should be obtained.

1 *Cameron v Williamson* (1895) 22R 393.

10.04   Procedures on discharge

It should be noted that on payment of the amount due and/or performance of the obligations, the debt is discharged[1] but in terms of the 1970 Act, the creditor is bound to grant a discharge in statutory form[2]. Almost certainly, the seller of subjects affected by a standard security will have bound himself in the missives to exhibit or deliver a clear search, or one which shows nothing prejudicial to the right of the debtor to grant a valid security, or a Land Certificate which does not disclose the standard security as being undischarged. As has been said, an undischarged standard security would result in the search not being clear or showing something prejudicial[3], despite the fact that the debt had been discharged.

When the purchaser settles the transaction, he is entitled to insist on the seller discharging any standard security. There are two practices which require comment.

The first relates to the method by which the seller's loan is discharged. In most transactions, the purchaser's solicitor will pay over his firm's cheque in settlement and the seller's solicitor will then attend to the redemption of the seller's loan. There is a risk (hopefully remote) that the seller's solicitor may not redeem the loan and while the purchaser will be protected under the Master Policy and the Guarantee Fund, some solicitors insist on settling by two cheques. One is for the amount of the outstanding loan payable to the seller's heritable creditor and the other is for the balance of the purchase price. While that has the advantage of ensuring that the loan is discharged, it does involve the selling solicitor revealing the amount of his client's loan which should not be done without his client's authority. The other method involves the executed discharge. As Professor Halliday points out, the better practice is for the selling solicitor to deliver an executed discharge at settlement along with the requisite forms for recording or registration[4]. The purchaser's solicitor will then record the disposition in his client's favour, the discharge and the standard security all of even date. The advantage is that the purchaser's solicitor ensures that the discharge will be recorded/registered and the subjects disencumbered. The selling solicitor will still add to his letter of obligation in a sasine transaction an undertaking to deliver a recorded discharge within say six months. The other practice is for the seller's solicitor to retain the discharge and record or register it, and grant an obligation to deliver it.

Although the result in both cases is the same, it is preferable that the discharge of the seller's standard security should be recorded or registered either before the purchaser's standard security or at least of even date. It is not desirable that it should be recorded or registered later. It is obviously in the purchaser's interest to ensure that the discharge is recorded or registered and there should be little risk that the purchaser's solicitors will fail to ensure that this is done.

1 *Cameron v Williamson* (1895) 22R 393.
2 1970 Act, Sch 3, standard condition 11(5); App [106].
3 *Newcastle Building Society v White* 1987 SLT (Sh Ct) 81; G L Gretton *The Law of Inhibition and Adjudication* pp 143–1435; K G C Reid 'Good and Marketable Title' (1988) 33 JLSS 162.
4 *Halliday* vol II, para 23-10.

10.05 No discharge granted

What happens if the creditor does not or cannot grant a discharge? If owing to the death or absence of the creditor or from any other cause, the debtor or proprietor is unable to obtain a discharge, the 1970 Act permits him to consign the sum in any Scottish bank or where the debt consists of an obligation *ad factum praestandum* to apply to the court for declarator of performance[1]. The consignation, or where appropriate, the decree enables a certificate to be prepared in accordance with section 18(3) and Form D of Schedule 5. When that certificate is recorded or registered, that has the effect of disburdening the security subjects in the same as if a formal discharge has been granted.

1 1970 Act, s 18(2); App [33].

10.06 'Discount' standard securities

A 'discount' standard security secures only the repayment due to the creditor in the event of the debtor disposing of the property except in the circumstances provided for in the legislation[1]. No repayment is due on the expiry of the three-year period and the Keeper's view which it is submitted is correct, is that no discharge requires to be put on the record.

1 See para 4.41 above.

10.07 Discharge of collateral obligations and securities

While any collateral or additional obligations granted as security for payment of the amount due will cease to be exigible when the amount due is paid, it is nevertheless desirable to ensure that the documentation securing the personal obligation is discharged. If, for example, shares have been assigned in security, they should be retrocessed to the debtor. A very common form of collateral security is an insurance policy, usually on the life of the debtor. The following is a simple style of retrocession.

We, the REST ASSURED BUILDING SOCIETY incorporated under the Building Societies Acts and having our Chief office at Hudribas House, Erewhon: CONSIDERING that Charles Dickens, Novelist, residing at Four Pickwick Place, Erewhon assigned to us a Policy of Assurance of the Failsafe Assurance Company effected on his own life for the sum of Forty thousand pounds, number DJC 123456789, dated Twenty Fifth December, Nineteen Hundred and Seventy-four, which policy was assigned to us in security of an advance of Thirty-eight Thousand Pounds made by us to the said Charles Dickens; which advance together with all interest and consequents due thereon has now been repaid to us: THEREFORE WE do hereby ASSIGN, RETROCESS AND MAKE OVER to the said Charles Dickens the said Policy of Assurance together with all bonuses, accrued or which may accrue thereon and the whole present and future benefit thereof; And we warrant the foregoing reassignation from our own facts and deeds only IN WITNESS WHEREOF.

10.08 Retention of titles by creditor

When the loan is repaid, the creditor is required to grant a discharge and the titles should be returned to the debtor. Some heritable cresitors try to persuade debtors to leave the titles with them for safe custody while others may suggest that a minimal amount of the loan, for example £5, be left outstanding to facilitate the granting of a further loan. There can be no objection to either of these practices, provided the lender makes it clear that the security is not discharged, that the object is to facilitate a further loan and that the debtor need not make use of the 'service'. Borrowers should, however, be encouraged to obtain a discharge and have it recorded or registered and ignore such 'kind' offers.

(3) COMPENSATION OR SET-OFF

10.09 General

If one debt is set-off against another, this will extinguish the debt and will also extinguish a standard security, but a formal discharge once again should be obtained.

(4) CONFUSIO

10.10 General

The same applies as in compensation or set-off. While it may not be common for the debtor's and creditor's interests to become vested in the one party, this may happen in company reconstructions. If there is a standard security by company A to an associated company B and the loan is to remain after the reconstruction of the companies, it will be necessary to ensure that the assets and liabilities of the companies are not merged. If that happens at any point, the loan will be extinguished *confusione*[1]. In this context, the following comment should be noted. 'There is some doubt as to the exact circumstances which will result in the extinction of a bond and disposition, or other heritable security, *confusione*[2].

1 W M Gloag *The Law of Contract* (2nd edn) p 725; Halliday *Commentary* para 9–08; *Halliday* vol III, para 40.29.
2 W M Gloag and J M Irvine *Rights in Security and Cautionary Obligations* p 137 *et seq.*

(5) REDEMPTION

10.11 General

The debtor may redeem the standard security in accordance with section 18 of the 1970 Act and standard condition 11. Under the 1970

Act in its original form, this right and the manner of its exercise, could not be varied, but the Redemption of Standard Securities (Scotland) Act 1971 permits variation[1]. The parties may therefore agree that the loan will subsist for a fixed period, or they may agree that there should be a different period of notice of redemption. However, the procedure for redemption cannot be varied. Where the debtor is not the proprietor, it is the proprietor who has the right to redeem. This covers the case where there is a guarantor and the situation, which is not uncommon under the 'right to buy' legislation, where the repayments of the loan may be undertaken by a relative of the proprietor (the former tenant). On the analogy of a bond and disposition in security, the creditor in a postponed standard security may redeem an earlier one[2].

1 Redemption of Standard Securities (Scotland) Act 1971, s 1.
2 *Adair's Tr v Rankin* (1895) 22 R 975.

10.12 Procedure for redemption

The procedure is identical in each case. Unless the parties have agreed otherwise, the person exercising his right to redeem has to give the creditor two months' notice in accordance with Schedule 5, Form A[1]. The period of notice may be shortened by agreement with the creditor, or the creditor may waive the period of notice[2]. If the creditor has not waived notice, or agreed to a shorter period, he cannot be compelled to accept redemption other than in terms of the agreement. In *Ashburton v Escombe*[3] a creditor in a bond and disposition in security entered into an agreement with the debtor, whereby the creditor agreed to be bound to accept payment only by instalments over a period of years. That agreement was unrecorded. The debtor conveyed the property to others in security of a further advance and bound himself to pay off the first loan. It was held that the first creditor could not be compelled to accept payment otherwise than in terms of the original agreement.

1 The debtor in default need not give notice. See para 10.15 below.
2 1970 Act, Sch 3, standard condition 11(2); App [106].
3 (1893) 20 R 107.

10.13 Restrictions on the excercise of the right of redemption

As a result of the Redemption of Standard Securities (Scotland) Act 1971, a debtor may forfeit his right of redemption if there is a contracting-out clause in the security documentation. In other words, he might find that he is not able to exercise his right of redemption for a number of years for example, because he had been given a favourable rate of interest. Section 11 of the Land Tenure Reform (Scotland) Act 1974 permits the redemption of heritable securities over private dwelling-houses, even where there is such a 'time bargain' which prevents earlier redemption. The Act applies only to heritable securities executed after 1 September 1974 and provides that if the security has endured for 20 years, then it can be redeemed. The provision for notice is the same as that under the 1971 Act.

The 1974 Act does not define the term 'private dwelling-house'. In one case[1], involving water rates, Lord Low said 'I take it that the expression "private dwelling-house" denotes according to the ordinary use of language, the house in which a man lives as his home, as distinguished from a house which he used for business purposes'. As that opinion was expressed in attempting to construe another and unrelated statutory provision, there is no guarantee that the definition is acceptable for the purposes of the 1974 Act.

1 *Airdrie, Coatbridge and District Water Trs v Flanagan* (1906) 8F 942 at 946. In *Gordon v Kirkcaldy District Council* 1990 SLT 644 reference was made to dictionary definitions to determine whether a caravan was a dwelling-house for the purposes of refuse collection.

10.14   Penalty for early redemption

If the creditor has imposed a penalty for early redemption, there is an argument that this contravenes section 11(3) of the 1970 Act which provides that standard condition 11 which deals with redemption cannot be varied. The contention would be that the penalty restricts the debtor's right to redeem and hence is invalid.

On the other hand, it may be argued that the debtor is bound to repay all sums due to the creditor before a discharge can be granted. If the debtor has obliged himself to repay all such sums, then the creditor is entitled to withhold a discharge until the penalty for early redemption is paid.

This issue has not been the subject of litigation. A court might adopt a strict interpretation of the subsection and outlaw any penalty provision. It might, however, hold that if the penalty was reasonable, it would not restrict the right to redeem and hence would be enforceable.

The writer's view is that the penalty is unenforceable unless it is reasonable.

10.15   Right to redeem where debtor is in default

Where a notice of default has been served and has not been complied with, the creditor may proceed to exercise the power of sale. In that event, the debtor or proprietor may redeem the security without notice and that may be done at any time before an enforceable bargain for sale is concluded[1]. It is not enough to purge the default, the security must be redeemed. It seems a little odd that the heritable creditor may advertise the subjects, arrange viewing and accept offers, but may find that the debtor or proprietor redeems the security at some time before the final acceptance. Furthermore, if the debtor and the family are still in possession, they may use various devices to dissuade potential purchasers, for example by telling purchasers that they are being 'ejected' or by pointing out real or imaginary defects. The same problem might face a trustee in bankruptcy but while there is a provision in the Bankruptcy (Scotland) Act 1985 which the trustee may use[2], there is no corresponding provision in the 1970 Act.

While it may be unusual for the debtor to redeem the security at this 'eleventh hour', the fact that he may do so, raises two issues relating to expenses. The first is the expenses of the purchaser whose attempts to buy the property have been thwarted by the redemption, and the second is the expenses of the creditor. So far as the potential purchaser is concerned, it is submitted that he is not in a different position from any other purchaser, who, while he may be the only person offering for the property, cannot force the creditor to sell. Accordingly, he would not have any claim against either the creditor or the debtor for any expenses he had incurred.

So far as the creditor is concerned, standard condition 12 provides that the debtor shall be personally liable for the whole expenses incurred by the creditor in 'realising or attempting to realise the security subjects'. Accordingly, he would be entitled to insist that these expenses were included in the redemption monies being proferred by the debtor. While standard condition 12 may be altered, it is unlikely that the part quoted above would be deleted.

It is submitted that this right to redeem cannot be varied by the standard conditions, even although the normal right to redeem can[3]. The right of the debtor in default to redeem prior to the conclusion of a contract for the sale of the subjects is related to the power of sale which in terms of section 11(3) means that the right cannot be varied.

1 1970 Act, s 23(3); App [63].
2 1970 Act, s 40(3)(b).
3 1970 Act, s 18(1A); App [33].

(6) COMPULSORY ACQUISITION

10.16   General

Where the land over which the security has been granted is compulsorily acquired, the acquiring authority may either redeem the security at once, or give six months' notice of the intention to redeem. Where the security is redeemed immediately, the acquiring authority is obliged to pay the principal sum, plus interest and expenses, but, in addition, it must also pay a further six months' interest. Where the acquiring authority gives six months' notice, it is required to pay the principal sum plus interest and expenses to the date of expiry of the notice[1]. There are special provisions which apply where the security subjects are worth less than the amount due under the security and where what is being compulsorily acquired is only part of the subjects covered by the security[2].

1 Lands Clauses Consolidation (Scotland) Act 1845, ss 99, 100.
2 Ibid, ss 101–104; for further details, see W M Gordon *Scottish Land Law* para 29-47; *Halliday* vol IV, paras 52-25, 52-26.

CHAPTER 11

Other transactions

11.01 Introduction

In this chapter, it is proposed to examine some transactions using standard securities which are more specialised than the usual transaction involving a domestic property. Some of the features mentioned may be encountered in the course of a domestic transaction, but others will be encountered only by those who do commercial conveyancing. The transactions considered here are (1) standard securities by companies; (2) standard securities over leases; (3) standard securities over subjects which are business premises; (4) discount standard securities; and (5) standard securities under the Consumer Credit Act 1974.

(1) COMPANIES

11.02 General

In the normal case, all that is required to give the creditor a real right in a standard security is that it should be recorded in the Register of Sasines or registered in the Land Register. In the case of a limited company, there is more to do than that because standard securities granted by limited companies raise questions of capacity, ranking and registration in the Register of Charges. The position will be altered by the Companies Act 1989.

11.03 Capacity

In this connection three questions have to be asked: (1) does the company have the power to borrow and the power to grant a standard security? It is important to check the company's Memorandum of Association on this point, and to bear in mind that a pre-existing floating charge or standard security may prohibit or restrict the creation of other securities. (2) If these powers do exist, is there any limit on the amount which may be borrowed? Where this is so, it would be necessary to enquire into any existing borrowing. (3) Do the Board of Directors have vested in them the company's powers to borrow? The powers of directors are not necessarily co-extensive with those of the company in general meeting. If the answer to any of these questions is 'no' or the answer to question (2) is that there is a limitation on the amount which the company may borrow, it may be that the Memorandum of Association should be altered by a special resolution of the company in order to avoid the risk of the directors being liable. In making this point, section 35 of the Companies Act 1985 affords protection for third parties dealing with limited companies if the third party acts in good faith, and there is a presumption that the third party has acted in good faith. If, of course, the Memorandum and Articles are examined, it may not be possible to claim 'good faith' if the Memorandum and Articles demonstrate that there are limitations. It is common for heritable creditors to require exhibition of a minute of a meeting of directors authorising the granting of the security and naming those who are authorised to execute the deed.

11.04 The Companies Act 1989

The new section 35 of the Companies Act 1985[1] provides that the validity of any act done by the company cannot be challenged on the ground of lack of capacity by reason of the Memorandum. Thus, someone dealing with the company need not concern himself with the company's objects and need not be in good faith. That being so, a lender will concentrate on the capacity of the directors. The new section 35A(4)[2] provides that if a person dealing with the company is in good faith, he need not concern himself with any limitation in the Memorandum. Section 35(2)(b) adds to this by stating that a person shall not be regarded as acting in bad faith by reason only that he knows that the act is beyond the powers of the directors. (Anyone who wishes to act in bad faith will have to try hard to achieve this). Even if there is bad faith, it would still be open to the company to ratify the actions by special resolution[3].

1 Companies Act 1985, s 35 (substituted by the Companies Act 1989, s 108).
2 Companies Act 1985, s 35A (inserted by the Companies Act 1989, s 108).
3 Companies Act 1985, s 35(2) (substituted by the Companies Act 1989, s 108).

11.05 Registration

So far as registration is concerned, sections 395–424 of the Companies Act 1985 require registration of all charges granted by incorporated companies. That registration is in the Register of Charges and that has to be done within 21 days of the right becoming real which in the case of a fixed (heritable) security (charge) is within 21 days of it being recorded in the Register of Sasines or registered in the Land Register[1]. It is vital to bear this in mind when the company is granting a standard security. Failure to register within the 21 days leaves the charge void as against the liquidator and other competing creditors. It is not possible to register late but in certain cases the creditor can petition the court to extend the period for registration[2]. When the standard security is sent off for recording or registering as the case may be the Keeper of the Registers of Scotland should be asked to confirm the date of recording or registration. This is one of the few instances in which the Keeper is willing to do this. He is not obliged to do it but he is prepared to do it in these circumstances to ensure the validity and enforceability of the security. The charge must therefore be registered in the Register of Charges within 21 days of the date confirmed by the Keeper as the date of recording/registering.

Registration is effected by lodging with the Registrar of Companies a completed official form (410) which has to be signed by an official of the borrowing company, or by the solicitor for the creditor, or the solicitor for the borrower and the form must contain particulars of the security together with a certified copy of it. Thereafter a certificate of registration is issued by the Registrar.

1 Companies Act 1985, s 410.
2 Ibid, s 420; *Allan, Black and McCaskie Petitioner* 1987 GWD 17–709; *Price Petitioner* 1989 SLT 840.

11.06   The Companies Act 1989 and registration

The 1989 Act does not make any changes to the requirements for registration in the Register of Charges, nor to the 21 day period[1], but it is now possible to register late[2]. However, in the case of late registration, the charge will be void against (1) a liquidator, or administrator appointed under insolvency proceedings commenced in the period between the date of execution of the charge and the actual date on which it was registered and (2) anyone who acquired an interest in, a right over the charged property in that period[3]. The charge is also void in respect of any error or omission in the registered particulars[4].

1 Companies Act 1985, s 141.
2 Companies Act 1985, s 400 (substituted by the Companies Act 1989, s 95).
3 Companies Act 1985, s 399 (as so substituted).
4 Ibid, s 402 (substituted by the Companies Act 1989, s 97).

11.07 Company registered in England

Where the company is registered in England but is borrowing on the security of property owned in Scotland, the security must be registered with the Registrar of Companies in England within 21 days of its creation, but it is not necessary to register the security in the Scottish Register of Charges also[1].

1 Companies Act 1985, ss 395–398.

11.08 Ranking

In addition to questions of capacity, the possible existence of a floating charge must be borne in mind when taking a heritable security from a company. The lender will be interested to know whether any floating charge exists as an indicator of the company's financial position and, more importantly, because the existence of the charge may be prejudicial to the proposed security. It is common for the floating charge to prohibit or restrict the granting of any other security which would rank prior to or *pari passu* with the floating charge. If this prohibition is ignored, further charges (whether fixed or floating) will rank after the floating charge, unless the holder of that charge agrees otherwise.

(2) LEASES

11.09 General

A standard security can be created over a lease only if the lease is registrable. To be registrable, the lease must (1) be probative (and if it is not, the defect cannot be cured by *rei interventus* or homologation); and (2) it must be for a period of 20 years or more, or oblige the landlord to renew the lease in such a way that it will endure for 20 years or more[1]. That second requirement excludes leases of subjects or part of subjects which may be used as a dwelling-house[2]. In considering whether to lend on the security of a lease, the landlord may consider the matters raised in the following paragraphs.

1 Registration of Leases (Scotland) Act 1857, s 1.
2 Land Tenure Reform (Scotland) Act 1974, s 8; see para 10.13 above.

11.10   The tenant's right to assign

From the creditor's point of view, the tenant's right to assign should be either unrestricted, or if the landlord's consent is required, the lease should provide that the consent should not be unreasonably withheld or delayed, or granted subject to unreasonable conditions. If the right to assign is more restricted than that, the heritable creditor may find it difficult to assign the lease, if he exercises his right to sell on the tenant/debtor's default.

11.11   User clause

The user clause in modern commercial leases is usually expressed in wide terms, so that the landlord can attract a variety of persons as potential lessees and also so that the tenant has a wide group of potential users from which to draw an assignee. This is not the case in older commercial leases. If there is a restriction on use, that could adversely affect the marketability of the subjects. In some shopping developments, the landlord may have inserted a provision which is designed to ensure that there cannot be two or more shops of the same type. Even if there is an express provision to this effect, that would not normally be regarded as operating to the disadvantage of the lender, since it operates to prevent unnecessary competition for all the tenants.

11.12   Irritancy provisions

The lender should ensure that the lease, or sublease, gives him the power to perform any obligations incumbent upon, but not implemented by the debtor, and that where the tenant is bankrupt, or in liquidation, or in receivership or where an administrator is appointed, the lender is given an opportunity to sell the subjects, provided he performs the debtor's outstanding obligations. A lease will normally have an irritancy provision whereby the lease will come to an end in the event that the tenant fails to perform any of his obligations, or becomes bankrupt, etc. The Law Reform (Miscellaneous Provisions) (Scotland) Act 1985 has afforded some protection to the tenant against irritancy provisions[1], but that protection is not extended to other than the tenant. It is normal for the heritable creditor to obtain a period of grace to allow him to perform the debtor's obligations, and for the lease to provide that any irritancy notice must be served on the heritable creditor where the landlord has notice of his existence.

1 Law Reform (Miscellaneous Provisions) (Scotland) Act 1985, ss 3–6.

11.13 Prohibition on leasing in standard security by landlord

In the light of the *Trade Development Bank* cases[1], anyone contemplating taking a standard security over a lease or a sub-lease should ensure that the consent of the landlord's heritable creditor, or in the case of a sub-lease, both that creditor and any heritable creditor of the midtenant has consented to the proposed lease, or sublease.

1 See paras 5.31 *et seq.*

11.14 Interposed leases

Prior to the passing of the Land Tenure Reform (Scotland) Act 1974, it was thought to be incompetent for a person who had already granted a lease to interpose another party as the tenant and thus make the existing tenant into a sub-tenant. The 1974 Act now permits this to be done[1] and the effect is that the interposed tenant becomes the landlord under the leases as if the leases had been assigned to him. A potential heritable creditor of the tenant will wish to ascertain whether the landlord has power to create interposed leases.

1 Land Tenure Reform (Scotland) Act 1974, s 17.

(3) STANDARD SECURITIES OVER BUSINESS PREMISES

11.15 General[1]

Where a lender is contemplating taking a security over subjects used in connection with a business, the standard security will usually be in Form B and if the borrower is a company, it may be asked to grant a floating charge as well as the fixed charge. Apart from considering the usual title questions, there are a number of other matters to which the creditor should address himself and these are dealt with in the following paragraphs[2].

1 For further details, see Linda Urquhart 'Heritable Securities I' in PQLE Commercial Conveyancing Course April 1990 pp 97–118.
2 I am grateful to Hugh Henderson of Messrs Morton Fraser and Milligan for information about brewers' loans and to James Campbell of Messrs Bird Senper Fyfe Ireland for information about petrol company loans.

11.16   Goodwill

As the goodwill may be valuable, the standard security should include the goodwill in so far as it is heritable. However, it has been held in England that a failure to include goodwill in a mortgage does not amount to negligence[1].

1 *Palmer v Barclays Bank Ltd* (1971) 23 P&CR 30.

11.17   Fittings and fixtures

The standard security should expressly cover fittings and fixtures since the business cannot be run successfully without them.

11.18   Stock

If the borrower is not already obliged by another creditor to do so, the security documentation should require the borrower to maintain stocks at a sufficient level. In the case of licensed premises where the loan comes from brewers, and in the case of a filling station or garage where the loan comes from a petrol company, there will almost invariably be a 'trade tie agreement' or some other agreement requiring the borrower to buy the brewers' or petrol company's products and not to buy others. These must comply with the Commission Regulation[1]. The personal obligation covered by the standard security will also cover any balance due to the brewer or the petrol company on the trading account.

1 EC Commission Regulation 1984/83.

11.19   Other moveables

Although the standard security cannot extend to items which are truly moveable, for example table, chairs, crockery, office equipment, the security documentation should permit the heritable creditor to deal with these as if he were the owner in the event of the debtor being in default. This is frequently provided for in the security documentation in respect of domestic property[1]. In such a case, the moveables may not add very much to the value but if the creditor has no power to dispose of them, they must be stored and become, bluntly, a nuisance. In the case of a business, the moveables may be valuable in a monetary sense but they are obviously essential for the business and that is why the heritable creditor should have full powers to dispose of them.

1 See para 5.25 above.

11.20 Licences

The valuation of a property will be based on the assumption that there is a valid licence in existence where one is required, as it would be for licensed premises. The heritable creditor must therefore ensure that the licence exists and that it is valid for all the activities carried on in the premises, for example regular extensions, entertainment, etc. The creditor should also seek an undertaking from the debtor to keep the licence in existence and not to do anything which might prejudice its existence. Furthermore, in the event of default by the debtor, the creditor may wish powers to deal with the licence as agent of the licence holder. That does not permit the heritable creditor to operate the licence, but only to ensure its continuation by making applications in the debtor's name.

11.21 Planning legislation, etc

The planning position will have been checked at the time of the acquisition by the debtor but the requirements in standard condition 4[1] (perhaps in a varied form) are designed to ensure that the planning authorities do not take an action, the effect of which may be to close the business down even on a temporary basis. Standard condition 4 requires the debtor to notify the heritable creditor of any notices which he receives. The standard condition will probably be varied to take account of other relevant legislation, or regulations such as those dealing with environmental health, fire, health and safety at work, office shops and railway premises[1].

1 See para 5.06 above.

(4) 'DISCOUNT' STANDARD SECURITIES

11.22 General

A 'discount' standard security is one which secures the discount at which a tenant of a local authority house, (or a tenant of a house belonging to one of the other recognised bodies) has purchased the house under the 'right to buy' legislation. This was formerly the Tenants' Rights Etc (Scotland) Act 1980 as amended, and is now the Housing (Scotland) Act 1987[1].

Under that legislation, the tenant agrees to repay a proportion of the discount to the relevant authority if he disposes of the property within three years of the date of entry[2], unless the disposal comes within one of the exceptions specified in the Act[3], which may include a property transfer order[4]. The tenant/purchaser grants a standard security in favour of the local authority, or other body, but the 1987 Act provides in section 72(5) that any standard security granted in respect of the purchase of the house, or one for the improvement of the house (what I shall refer to as 'the first security') will rank prior to the 'discount' security. It is difficult to reconcile the terms of section 72 with section 13 of the 1970 Act which also deals with ranking of standard securities. In terms of section 72, the first security ranks for the principal sum 'and any interest present or future thereon . . . and any expenses or outlays . . .'. The subsection then states that 'if the landlord consents' a standard security granted 'in security of any other loan . . . and any interest, expenses or outlays' will also rank prior to the 'discount' standard security. However, section 13 of the 1970 Act gives the holder of the first security a preference also in respect of 'future advances which he may be required to make under the contract'. The normal rule of statutory construction is that the later provision prevails[5] and so the conclusion must be that the first standard security holder does not rank prior to the holder of the 'discount' standard security in respect of such future advances and he will have a preferential ranking for these only if the holder of the 'discount' standard security consents. In most instances, there will be no problem because there will be sufficient reversionary value in the property to cover other advances as well as the amount of the discount.

After the three year period expires, the security comes to an end and no discharge is required[6].

1 See the Housing (Scotland) Act 1987, ss 61–84.
2 Ibid, s 72.
3 Ibid, s 73.
4 See D J Cusine 'Property Transfer Orders: Some Conveyancing Imponderables' (1990) 35 JLSS 52; E M Clive (1990) 35 JLSS 188.
5 Maxwell on Interpretation of Statutes 12ed p 161 *et seq*.
6 See para 10.06 above.

THE CONSUMER CREDIT ACT 1974

11.23 General

The loan to be secured may be less than £15,000 in which event it is a regulated debtor-creditor agreement governed by the Consumer Credit Act 1974, unless the creditor is an exempt body. Local authorities and building societies are exempt from the Regulations mentioned below, but banks are not[1]. If the agreement is a regulated debtor-creditor agreement, it is governed by Regulations made under the Act[2] and by the Act itself in relation to mortgages[3]. The provisions are complex and it is not necessary here to do more than refer to other sources which give the details[4].

1 Building Societies will not be exempt if they are granting personal loans.
2 The Consumer Credit (Agreements) Regulations 1983, SI 1983/1553.
3 Consumer Credit Act 1974, ss 58(1), 189(1).
4 R B Wood 'The Consumer Credit Act and its Implications for Conveyancers' PQLE General Conveyancing Course, December 1986, pp 136–163; 'The Consumer Credit Act 1974' (1985) 30 JLSS 130; cf L W Foley 'The Consumer Credit Act 1974: Loan Agreements and Standard Securities' (1985) 30 JLSS 222.

APPENDIX

Conveyancing and Feudal Reform (Scotland) Act 1970 (c 35)

PART II   THE STANDARD SECURITY

Schedule 3

Standard conditions

1 Maintenance and repair.
2 Completion of buildings, etc and prohibition of alterations, etc.
3 Observance of conditions in title, payment of duties, charges, etc, and general compliance with requirements of law relating to security subjects.
4 Planning notices, etc.
5 Insurance.
6 Restriction on letting.
7 General power of creditor to perform obligations, etc, on failure of debtor and power to charge debtor.
8 Calling-up.
9 Default.
10 Rights of creditor on default.
11, 12 Exercise of right of redemption.

Schedule 4

Forms of deeds of Assignation, Restriction, and others.
Forms A, B: Assignation of standard security.
Form C: Restriction of standard security.
Form D: Combined partial discharge and deed of restriction of standard security.
Form E: Variation of standard security.
Form F: Discharge of standard security.
Notes to Schedule 4.

Schedule 5

Procedures as to redemption.
Forms A, B and C: Notice of redemption of standard security.
Form D: 1 Certificate of consignation on redemption of standard security where discharge cannot be obtained.
        2 Certificate of Declarator of Performance of debtor's obligations under standard security where discharge cannot be obtained.

Schedule 6

Procedures as to calling-up and default.
Form A: Notice of calling-up of standard security.
Forms B, C, D: Notice of default under standard security.

Schedule 7

Contents of certificate stating a default.

THE STANDARD CONDITIONS

9. The standard security

(1) The provisions of this Part of this Act shall have effect for the purpose of enabling a new form of heritable security to be created to be known as a standard security. [1]

(2) It shall be competent to grant and record in the Register of Sasines a standard security over any interest in land to be expressed in conformity with one of the forms prescribed in Schedule 2 to this Act. [2]

(3) A grant of any right over an interest in land for the purpose of securing any debt by way of a heritable security shall only be capable of being effected at law if it is embodied in a standard security. [3]

(4) Where for the purpose last-mentioned any deed which is not in the form of a standard security contains a disposition or assignation of an interest in land, it shall to that extent be void and unenforceable, and where that deed has been duly recorded the creditor in the purported security may be required, by any person having an interest, to grant any deed which may be appropriate to clear the Register of Sasines of that security. [4]

(5) A standard security may be used for any other purpose for which a heritable security may be used if any of the said forms is appropriate to that purpose, and for the purpose of any enactment affecting heritable securities a standard security, if so used, or if used as is required by this Act instead of a heritable security as defined therein, shall be a heritable security for the purposes of that enactment. [5]

(6) The Bankruptcy Act 1696, in so far as it renders a heritable security of no effect in relation to a debt contracted after the recording of that security, and any rule of law which requires that a real burden for money may only be created in respect of a sum specified in the deed of creation, shall not apply in relation to a standard security. [6]

(7) [*Repealed by the Tenants' Rights, etc (Scotland) Act 1980 (c 52), s 84, Sch 5*].
[7]

(8) For the purposes of this Part of this Act—
  [1](a) 'heritable security' (except in subsection (5) of this section if the context otherwise requires) means any security capable of being constituted over any interest in land by disposition or assignation of that interest in security of any debt and of being recorded in the Register of Sasines;
  (b) 'interest in land' means any estate or interest in land, other than an entailed estate or any interest therein, which is capable of being owned or held as a separate interest and to which a title may be recorded in the Register of Sasines;
  (c) 'debt' means any obligation due, or which will or may become due, to repay or pay money, including any such obligation arising from a transaction or part of a transaction in the course of any trade, business or profession, and any obligation to pay an annuity or *ad factum praestandum*, but does not include an obligation to pay any feuduty,

ground annual, rent or other periodical sum payable in respect of land, and 'creditor' and 'debtor', in relation to a standard security, shall be construed accordingly. [8]

10. Import of forms of, and certain clauses in, standard security

(1) The import of the clause relating to the personal obligation contained in Form A of Schedule 2 to this Act expressed in any standard security shall, unless specially qualified, be as follows—

  (a) where the security is for a fixed amount advanced or payable at, or prior to, the delivery of the deed, the clause undertaking to make payment to the creditor shall import an acknowledgment of receipt by the debtor of the principal sum advanced or an acknowledgment by the debtor of liability to pay that sum and a personal obligation undertaken by the debtor to repay or pay to the creditor on demand in writing at any time after the date of delivery of the standard security the said sum, with interest at the rate stated payable on the dates specified, together with all expenses for which the debtor is liable by virtue of the deed or of this Part of this Act;

  (b) where the security is for a fluctuating amount, whether subject to a maximum amount or not and whether advanced or due partly before and partly after delivery of the deed or whether to be advanced or to become due wholly after such delivery, the clause undertaking to make payment to the creditor shall import a personal obligation by the debtor to repay or pay to the creditor on demand in writing the amount, not being greater than the maximum amount, if any, specified in the deed, advanced or due and outstanding at the time of demand, with interest on each advance from the date when it was made until repayment thereof, or on each sum payable from the date on which it became due until payment thereof, and at the rate stated payable on the dates specified, together with all expenses for which the debtor is liable by virtue of the deed or of this Part of this Act. [9]

(2) The clause of warrandice in the forms of standard security contained in Schedule 2 to this Act expressed in any standard security shall, unless specially qualified, import absolute warrandice as regards the interest in land over which the security is granted and the title deeds thereof, and warrandice from fact and deed as regards the rents thereof. [10]

(3) The clause relating to consent to registration for execution contained in Form A of Schedule 2 to this Act, expressed in any standard security shall, unless specially qualified, import a consent to registration in the Books of Council and Session, or, as the case may be, in the books of the appropriate sheriff court, for execution. [11]

(4) The forms of standard security contained in Schedule 2 to this Act shall, unless specially qualified, import an assignation to the creditor of the title deeds, including searches, and all conveyances not duly recorded, affecting the security subjects or any part thereof, with power to the creditor in the event of a sale under the powers conferred by the security, but subject to the rights of

any person holding prior rights to possession of those title deeds, to deliver them, so far as in the creditor's possession, to the purchaser, and to assign to the purchaser any right he may possess to have the title deeds made forthcoming.   [12]

11. Effect of recorded standard security, and incorporation of standard conditions

(1) Where a standard security is duly recorded, it shall operate to vest the interest over which it is granted in the grantee as a security for the performance of the contract to which the security relates.   [13]

(2) Subject to the provisions of this Part of this Act, the conditions set out in Schedule 3 to this Act, either as so set out or with such variations as have been agreed by the parties in the exercise of the powers conferred by the said Part (which conditions are hereinafter in this Act referred to as 'the standard conditions'), shall regulate every standard security.   [14]

(3) Subject to the provisions of this Part of this Act, the creditor and debtor in a standard security may vary any of the standard conditions, other than [¹standard condition 11 (procedure on redemption) and] the provisions of Schedule 3 to this Act relating to the powers of sale [². . .] and foreclosure and to the exercise of those powers, but no condition capable of being varied shall be varied in a manner inconsistent with any condition which may not be varied by virtue of this subsection.   [15]

(4) In this Part of this Act—
  (a) any reference to a variation of the standard conditions shall include a reference to the inclusion of an additional condition and to the exclusion of a standard condition;
  (b) any purported variation of a standard condition which contravenes the provisions of subsection (3) of this section shall be void and unenforceable.   [16]

Notes.—1 Words in sub-s (3) added by the Redemption of Standard Securities (Scotland) Act 1971 (c 45), s 1(a).
2 Words in sub-s (3) repealed by ibid, s 1(a).

---

12. Standard security may be granted by person uninfeft

¹(1) Notwithstanding any rule of law, a standard security may be granted over an interest in land by a person having right to that interest, but whose title thereto has not been completed by being duly recorded, if in the deed expressing that security the grantor deduces his title to that interest from the person who appears in the Register of Sasines as having the last recorded title thereto.   [17]

(2) A deduction of title in a deed for the purposes of the foregoing subsection shall be expressed in the form prescribed by Note 2 or 3 of Schedule 2 to this Act, and on such a deed being recorded as aforesaid the title of the grantee

shall, for the purposes of the rights and obligations between the grantor and the grantee thereof, and those deriving right from them, but for no other purpose, in all respects be of the same effect as if the title of the grantor of the deed to the interest to which he has deduced title therein had been duly completed; and any references to a proprietor or to a person last infeft shall in this Part of this Act be construed accordingly.   [18]

(3) There may be specified for the purposes of any deduction of title in pursuance of any provision of this Part of this Act any writing which it is competent to specify as a title, midcouple, or link in title for the purposes of section 5 of the Conveyancing (Scotland) Act 1924 (deduction of title). [19]

Note.—1 Section 12 excluded by the Land Registration (Scotland) Act 1979 (c 33), s 15(3).

13. Ranking of standard securities

(1) Where the creditor in a standard security duly recorded has received notice of the creation of a subsequent security over the same interest in land or any part thereof, or of the subsequent assignation or conveyance of that interest in whole or in part, being a security, assignation or conveyance so recorded, the preference in ranking of the security of that creditor shall be restricted to security for his present advances and future advances which he may be required to make under the contract to which the security relates and interest present or future due thereon (including any such interest which has accrued or may accrue) and for any expenses or outlays (including interest thereon) which may be, or may have been, reasonably incurred in the exercise of any power conferred on any creditor by the deed expressing the existing security.   [20]

(2) For the purposes of the foregoing subsection—
   (a) a creditor in an existing standard security duly recorded shall not be held to have had any notice referred to in that subsection, by reason only of the subsequent recording of the relevant deed in the Register of Sasines;
   (b) any assignation, conveyance or vesting in favour of or in any other person of the interest of the debtor in the security subjects or in any part thereof resulting from any judicial decree, or otherwise by operation of law, shall constitute sufficient notice thereof to the creditor.   [21]

(3) Nothing in the foregoing provisions of this section shall affect—
   (a) any preference in ranking enjoyed by the Crown; and
   (b) any powers of the creditor and debtor in any heritable security to regulate the preference to be enjoyed by creditors in such manner as they may think fit.   [22]

Note.—1 Section 13 excluded by the Tenants' Rights Etc (Scotland) Act 1980 (c 52), s 6(5).

14.   Assignation of standard security

(1) Any standard security duly recorded may be transferred, in whole or in part, by the creditor by an assignation in conformity with Form A or B of Schedule 4 to this Act, and upon such an assignation being duly recorded, the security, or, as the case may be, part thereof, shall be vested in the assignee as effectually as if the security or the part had been granted in his favour. [23]

(2) An assignation of a standard security shall, except so far as otherwise therein stated, be deemed to convey to the grantee all rights competent to the grantor to the writs, and shall have the effect *inter alia* of vesting in the assignee—

- (a) the full benefit of all corroborative or substitutional obligations for the debt, or any part thereof, whether those obligations are contained in any deed or arise by operation of law or otherwise,
- (b) the right to recover payment from the debtor of all expenses properly incurred by the creditor in connection with the security, and
- (c) the entitlement to the benefit of any notices served and of all procedure instituted by the creditor in respect of the security to the effect that the grantee may proceed as if he had originally served or instituted such notices or procedure.   [24]

15.   Restriction of standard security

(1) The security constituted by any standard security duly recorded may be restricted, as regards any part of the interest in land burdened by the security, by a deed of restriction in conformity with Form C of Schedule 4 to this Act, and, upon that deed being duly recorded, the security shall be restricted to the interest in land contained in the standard security other than the part of that interest disburdened by the deed; and the interest in land thereby disburdened shall be released from the security wholly or to the extent specified in the deed.   [25]

(2) A partial discharge and deed of restriction of a standard security, which has been duly recorded, may be combined in one deed, which shall be in conformity with Form D of the said Schedule 4.   [26]

16.   Variation of standard security

(1) Any alteration in the provisions (including any standard condition) of a standard security duly recorded, other than an alteration which may appropriately be effected by an assignation, discharge or restriction of that standard security, or an alteration which involves an addition to, or an extension of, the interest in land mentioned therein, may be effected by a variation endorsed on the standard security in conformity with Form E of Schedule 4 to this Act, or by a variation contained in a separate deed in a form appropriate for that purpose, duly recorded in either case.   [27]

(2) Where a standard security has been duly recorded, but the personal obligation or any other provision (including any standard condition) relating to the security has been created or specified in a deed which has not been so recorded, nothing contained in this section shall prevent any alteration in that

personal obligation or provision, other than an alteration which may be appropriately effected by an assignation, discharge or restriction of the standard security, or an alteration which involves an addition to, or an extension of, the interest in land mentioned therein, by a variation contained in any form of deed appropriate for that purpose, and such a variation shall not require to be recorded in the Register of Sasines.   [28]

(3) [*Repealed by the Finance Act 1971 (c 68), s 69(7), Sch 14, Pt VI.*]   [29]

(4) Any variation effected in accordance with this section shall not prejudice any other security or right over the same interest in land, or any part thereof, effectively constituted before the variation is recorded, or, where the variation is effected by an unrecorded deed, before that deed is executed, as the case may be.   [30]

17. Discharge of standard security

A standard security duly recorded may be discharged, and the interest in land burdened by that security may be disburdened thereof, in whole or in part, by a discharge in conformity with Form F of Schedule 4 to this Act, duly recorded.
                                                                                                                                    [31]

18. Redemption of standard security

(1) [¹Subject to the provisions of subsection (1A) of this section] the debtor in a standard security or, where the debtor is not the proprietor, the proprietor of the security subjects shall be entitled to redeem the security [¹on giving two months' notice of his intention so to do and] in conformity with the terms of standard condition 11 and the appropriate Forms of Schedule 5 to this Act.
                                                                                                                                    [32]

[²(1A) [³Without prejudice to section 11 of the Land Tenure Reform (Scotland) Act 1974,] the provisions of the foregoing subsection shall be subject to any agreement to the contrary, but any right to redeem the security shall be exercisable in conformity with the terms and Forms referred to in that subsection.]   [33]

(2) Where owing to the death or absence of the creditor, or to any other cause, the debtor in a standard security or, as the case may be, the proprietor of the security subjects [⁴(being in either case a person entitled to redeem the security)] is unable to obtain a discharge under the [⁵foregoing provisions of this section], he may—

    (a) where the security was granted in respect of any obligation to repay or pay money, consign in any bank in Scotland, incorporated by or under Act of Parliament or by Royal Charter, the whole amount due to the creditor on redemption, other than any unascertained expenses of the creditor, for the person appearing to have the best right thereto, and

    (b) in any other case, apply to the court for declarator that the whole obligations under the contract to which the security relates have been performed.   [34]

(3) On consignation, or on the court granting declarator as aforesaid, a certificate to that effect may be expede by a solicitor in the appropriate form

prescribed by Form D of Schedule 5 to this Act, which on being duly recorded shall disburden the interest in land, to which the standard security relates, of that security. [35]

(4) For the purposes of this section, 'whole amount due' means the debt to which the security relates, so far as outstanding, and any other sums due thereunder by way of interest or otherwise. [36]

Notes.—1 Words in sub-s (1) added by the Redemption of Standard Securities (Scotland) Act 1971 (c 45), s 1(b).

2 Subs-s 1A added by ibid, s 1(c).

3 Words in sub-s (1A) added by the Land Tenure Reform (Scotland) Act 1974 (c 38), s 11(6).

4 Words in sub-s (2) added by the Redemption of Standard Securities (Scotland) Act 1971, s 1(d).

5 Words in sub-s (2) substituted by ibid, s 1(d).

---

19. Calling-up of standard security

(1) Where a creditor in a standard security intends to require discharge of the debt thereby secured and, failing that discharge, to exercise any power conferred by the security to sell any subjects of the security or any other power which he may appropriately exercise on the default of the debtor within the meaning of standard condition 9(1)(a), he shall serve a notice calling-up the security in conformity with Form A of Schedule 6 to this Act (hereinafter in this Act referred to as a 'calling-up notice'), in accordance with the following provisions of this section. [37]

(2) Subject to the following provisions of this section, a calling-up notice shall be served on the person last infeft in the security subjects and appearing on the record as the proprietor and, should the proprietor of those subjects, or any part thereof, be dead then on his representative or the person entitled to the subjects in terms of the last recorded title thereto, notwithstanding any alteration of the succession not appearing in the Register of Sasines. [38]

(3) Where the person last infeft in the security subjects was an incorporated company which has been removed from the Register of Companies, or a person deceased who has left no representatives, a calling-up notice shall be served on the Lord Advocate and, where the estates of the person last infeft have been sequestrated under the Bankruptcy (Scotland) Act 1913, the notice shall be served on the trustee in the sequestration (unless such trustee has been discharged) as well as on the bankrupt. [39]

(4) If the proprietor be a body of trustees, it shall be sufficient if the notice is served on a majority of the trustees infeft in the security subjects. [40]

(5) It shall be an obligation on the creditor to serve a copy of the calling-up notice on any other person against whom he wishes to preserve any right of recourse in respect of the debt. [41]

(6) For the purposes of the foregoing provisions of this section, the service of a

calling-up notice may be made by delivery to the person on whom it is desired to be served or the notice may be sent by registered post or by the recorded delivery service to him at his last known address, or, in the case of the Lord Advocate, at the Crown Office, Edinburgh, and an acknowledgment, signed by the person on whom service has been made, in conformity with Form C of Schedule 6 to this Act, or, as the case may be, a certificate in conformity with Form D of that Schedule, accompanied by the postal receipt shall be sufficient evidence of the service of that notice; and if the address of the person on whom the notice is desired to be served is not known, or if it is not known whether that person is still alive, or if the packet containing a calling-up notice is returned to the creditor with an intimation that it could not be delivered, that notice shall be sent to the Extractor of the Court of Session, and shall be equivalent to the service of a calling-up notice on the person on whom it is desired to be served.   [42]

(7) For the purposes of the last foregoing subsection, an acknowledgment of receipt by the said Extractor on a copy of a calling-up notice shall be sufficient evidence of the receipt by him of that notice.   [43]

(8) A calling-up notice served by post shall be held to have been served on the next day after the day of posting.   [44]

(9) Where a creditor in a standard security has indicated in a calling-up notice that any sum and any interest thereon due under the contract may be subject to adjustment in amount, he shall, if the person on whom notice has been served so requests, furnish the debtor with a statement of the amount as finally determined within a period of one month from the date of service of the calling-up notice, and a failure by the creditor to comply with the provisions of this subsection shall cause the calling-up notice to be of no effect.   [45]

(10) The period of notice mentioned in the calling-up notice may be effectively dispensed with or shortened by the person on whom it is served, with the consent of the creditors, if any, holding securities *pari passu* with, or postponed to, the security held by the creditor serving the calling-up notice, by a minute written or endorsed upon the said notice, or a copy thereof, in conformity with Form C of Schedule 6 to this Act.

[1Provided that, without prejudice to the foregoing generality, if the standard security is over a matrimonial home as defined in section 22 of the Matrimonial Homes (Family Protection) (Scotland) Act 1981, the spouse on whom the calling-up notice has been served may not dispense with or shorten the said period without the consent in writing of the other spouse.]   [46]

(11) A calling-up notice shall cease to have effect for the purpose of a sale in the exercise of any power conferred by the security on the expiration of a period of five years, which period shall run—

  (a) in the case where the subjects of the security, or any part thereof, have not been offered for or exposed to sale, from the date of the notice.

  (b) in the case where there has been such an offer or exposure, from the date of the last offer or exposure.   [47]

Note.—1 Proviso to sub-s (10) added by the Matrimonial Homes (Family Protection) (Scotland) Act 1981 (c 59), s 20.

20. Exercise of rights of creditor on default of debtor in complying with a calling-up notice

(1) Where the debtor in a standard security is in default within the meaning of standard condition 9(1)(a), the creditor may exercise such of his rights under the security as he may consider appropriate, and any such right shall be in addition to and not in derogation from any other remedy arising from the contract to which the security relates or from any right conferred by any enactment or by any rule of law on the creditor in a heritable security. [48]

(2) Where the debtor is in default as aforesaid, the creditor shall have the right to sell the security subjects, or any part thereof, in accordance with the provisions of this Part of this Act. [49]

(3) A creditor in a standard security who is in lawful possession of the security subjects may let the security subjects, or any part thereof, for any period not exceeding seven years, or may make application to the court for warrant to let those subjects, or any part thereof, for a period exceeding seven years, and the application shall state the proposed tenant, and the duration and conditions of the proposed lease, and shall be served on the proprietor of the subjects and on any other heritable creditor having interest as such a creditor in the subjects. [50]

(4) The court, on such an application as aforesaid and after such inquiry and such further intimation of the application as it may think fit, may grant the application as submitted, or subject to such variation as it may consider reasonable in all the circumstances of the case, or may refuse the application. [51]

(5) There shall be deemed to be assigned to a creditor who is in lawful possession of the security subjects all rights and obligations of the proprietor relating to—
  (a) leases, or any permission or right of occupancy, granted in respect of those subjects or any part thereof, and
  (b) the management and maintenance of the subjects and the effecting of any reconstruction, alteration or improvement reasonably required for the purpose of maintaining the market value of the subjects. [52]

21. Notice of default

(1) Where the debtor in a standard security is in default within the meaning of standard condition 9(1)(b), and the default is remediable, the creditor may, without prejudice to any other powers he may have by virtue of this Act or otherwise, proceed in accordance with the provisions of this section to call on the debtor and on the proprietor, where he is not the debtor, to purge the default. [53]

(2) For the aforesaid purpose the creditor may serve on the debtor and, as the case may be, on the proprietor a notice in conformity with Form B of Schedule 6 to this Act (hereinafter in this Act referred to as a 'notice of default') which shall be served in the like manner and with the like requirements as to proof of service as a calling-up notice. [54]

(3) For the purpose of dispensing with, or shortening, the period of notice mentioned in a notice of default, section 19(10) of this Act shall apply as it applies in relation to a calling-up notice.   [55]

(4) Notwithstanding the failure to comply with any requirement contained in the notice, a notice of default shall cease to be authority for the exercise of the rights mentioned in section 23(2) of this Act on the expiration of a period of five years from the date of the notice.   [56]

22. Objections to notice of default

(1) Where a person on whom a notice of default has been served considers himself aggrieved by any requirement of that notice he may, within a period of fourteen days of the service of the notice, object to the notice by way of application to the court; and the applicant shall, not later than the lodging of that application, serve a copy of his application on the creditor, and on any other party on whom the notice has been served by the creditor.   [57]

(2) On any such application the court, after hearing the parties and making such inquiry as it may think fit, may order the notice appealed against to be set aside, in whole or in part, or otherwise to be varied, or to be upheld.   [58]

(3) The respondent in any such application may make a counter-application craving for any of the remedies conferred on him by this Act or by any other enactment relating to heritable securities, and the court may grant any such remedy as aforesaid as it may think proper.   [59]

(4) For the purposes of such a counter-application as aforesaid, a certificate which conforms with the requirements of Schedule 7 to this Act may be lodged in court by the creditor, and that certificate shall be *prima facie* evidence of the facts directed by the said Schedule to be contained therein.
                                    [60]

23. Rights and duties of parties after service of notice of default to which objection is not taken, or where the notice is not set aside

(1) Where a person does not object to a notice of default in accordance with the provisions of the last foregoing section, or where he has so objected and the notice has been upheld or varied under that section, it shall be his duty to comply with any requirement, due to be performed or fulfilled by him, contained in the notice or, as the case may be, in the notice as so varied.   [61]

(2) Subject to the provisions of section 21(4) of this Act, where a person fails to comply as aforesaid, the creditor, subject to the next following subsection, may proceed to exercise such of his rights on default under standard condition 10(2), (6) and (7) as he may consider appropriate.   [62]

(3) At any time after the expiry of the period stated in a notice of default, or in a notice varied as aforesaid, but before the conclusion of any enforceable contract to sell the security subjects, or any part thereof, by virtue of the last foregoing subsection, the debtor or proprietor [1(being in either case a person entitled to redeem the security)] may, subject to any agreement to the contrary, redeem the security without the necessity of observance of any requirement as to notice.   [63]

Note.—1 Words in sub-s (3) added by the Redemption of Standard Securities (Scotland) Act 1971 (c 45), s 1(e).

24. Application by creditor to court for remedies on default

(1) Without prejudice to his proceeding by way of notice of default in respect of a default within the meaning of standard condition 9(1)(b), a creditor in a standard security, where the debtor is in default within the meaning of that standard condition or standard condition 9(1)(c), may apply to the court for warrant to exercise any of the remedies which he is entitled to exercise on a default within the meaning of standard condition 9(1)(a). [64]

(2) For the purposes of such an application as aforesaid in respect of a default within the meaning of standard condition 9(1)(b), a certificate which conforms with the requirements of Schedule 7 to this Act may be lodged in court by the creditor, and that certificate shall be *prima facie* evidence of the facts directed by the said Schedule to be contained therein. [65]

25. Exercise of power of sale

A creditor in a standard security having right to sell the security subjects may exercise that right either by private bargain or by exposure to sale, and in either event it shall be the duty of the creditor to advertise the sale and to take all reasonable steps to ensure that the price at which all or any of the subjects are sold is the best that can be reasonably obtained. [66]

26. Disposition by creditor on sale

(1) Where a creditor in a standard security has effected a sale of the security subjects, or any part thereof, and grants to the purchaser or his nominee a disposition of the subjects sold thereby, which bears to be in implement of the sale, then, on that disposition being duly recorded, those subjects shall be disburdened of the standard security and of all other heritable securities and diligences ranking *pari passu* with, or postponed to, that security. [67]

(2) Where on a sale as aforesaid the security subjects remain subject to a prior security, the recording of a disposition under the foregoing subsection shall not affect the rights of the creditor in that security, but the creditor who has effected the sale shall have the like right as the debtor to redeem the security.

[68]

27. Application of proceeds of sale

(1) The money which is received by the creditor in a standard security, arising from any sale by him of the security subjects, shall be held by him in trust to be applied by him in accordance with the following order of priority—

   (a) first, in payment of all expenses properly incurred by him in connection with the sale, or any attempted sale;

   (b) secondly, in payment of the whole amount due under any prior security to which the sale is not made subject;

   (c) thirdly, in payment of the whole amount due under the standard security, and in payment, in due proportion, of the whole amount due under a security, if any, ranking *pari passu* with his own security, which has been duly recorded;

    (d) fourthly, in payment of any amounts due under any securities with a ranking postponed to that of his own security, according to their ranking,

and any residue of the money so received shall be paid to the person entitled to the security subjects at the time of sale, or to any person authorised to give receipts for the proceeds of the sale thereof.   [69]

(2) Where owing to the death or absence of any other creditor, or to any other cause, a creditor is unable to obtain a receipt or discharge for any payment he is required to make under the provisions of the foregoing subsection, he may, without prejudice to his liability to account therefor, consign the amount due (so far as ascertainable) in the sheriff court for the person appearing to have the best right thereto; and where consignation is so made, the creditor shall lodge in court a statement of the amount consigned.   [70]

(3) A consignation made in pursuance of the last foregoing subsection shall operate as a discharge of the payment of the amount due, and a certificate under the hand of the sheriff clerk shall be sufficient evidence thereof. [71]

28. Foreclosure

(1) Where the creditor in a standard security has exposed the security subjects to sale at a price not exceeding the amount due under the security and under any security ranking prior to, or *pari passu* with, the security, and has failed to find a purchaser, or where, having so failed, he has succeeded in selling only a part of the subjects at a price which is less than the amount due as aforesaid, he may, on the expiration of a period of two months from the date of the first exposure to sale, apply to the court for a decree of foreclosure.   [72]

(2) In any application under the last foregoing subsection the creditor shall lodge a statement setting out the whole amount due under the security but, without prejudice to the right of the debtor or of the proprietor to challenge that statement, it shall be sufficient for the purposes of the application for the creditor to establish to the satisfaction of the court that the amount so stated is not less than the price at which the security subjects have been exposed to sale or sold, where part of the subjects has been sold as aforesaid.   [73]

(3) Any application under subsection (1) of this section shall be served on the debtor in the standard security, the proprietor of the security subjects (if he is a person other than the debtor) and the creditor in any other heritable security affecting the security subjects as disclosed by a search of the Register of Sasines for a period of twenty years immediately preceding the last date to which the appropriate Minute Book of the said Register has been completed at the time when the application is made [¹or by an examination of the title sheet of the security subjects in the Land Register of Scotland].   [74]

(4) The court may order such intimation and inquiry as it thinks fit and may in its discretion allow the debtor or the proprietor of the security subjects a

period not exceeding three months in which to pay the whole amount due under the security and, subject to any such allowance, may—

(a) appoint the security subjects or the unsold part thereof to be re-exposed to sale at a price to be fixed by the court, in which event the creditor in the security may bid and purchase at the sale, or

(b) grant a decree of foreclosure in conformity with the provisions of the next following subsection. [75]

(5) A decree of foreclosure shall contain a declaration that, on the extract of the decree being duly recorded, [²any right to redeem the security] has been extinguished and that the creditor has right to the security subjects or the unsold part thereof, described by means of a particular description or by reference to a description thereof as in Schedule D to the Conveyancing (Scotland) Act 1924 or in Schedule G to the Titles to Land Consolidation (Scotland) Act 1868, including a reference to any conditions or clauses affecting the subjects or the unsold part thereof [³or in accordance with section 15 of the Land Registration (Scotland) Act 1979], at the price at which the said subjects were last exposed to sale under deduction of the price received for any part thereof sold, and shall also contain a warrant for recording the extract of the decree in the Register of Sasines. [76]

(6) Upon an extract of the decree of foreclosure being duly recorded, the following provisions of this subsection shall have effect in relation to the security subjects to which the decree relates—

(a) [⁴any right to redeem the security] shall be extinguished, and the creditor shall have right to, and be vested in, the subjects as if he had received an irredeemable disposition thereof duly recorded from the proprietor of the subjects at the date of the recording of the extract of the decree;

(b) the subjects shall be disburdened of the standard security and all securities and diligences postponed thereto;

(c) the creditor who has obtained the decree shall have the like right as the debtor to redeem any security prior to, or *pari passu* with, his own security. [77]

(7) Notwithstanding the due recording of an extract of a decree of foreclosure, any personal obligation of the debtor under the standard security shall remain in full force and effect so far as not extinguished by the price at which the security subjects have been acquired and the price for which any part thereof has been sold. [78]

(8) Where the security subjects or any part thereof have been acquired by a creditor in the security by virtue of a decree of foreclosure under the provisions of this section, the title thereto of the creditor shall not be challengeable on the ground of any irregularity in the proceedings for foreclosure or on calling-up or default which preceded it; but nothing in the provisions of this subsection shall affect the competency of any claim for damages in respect of such proceedings against the creditor. [79]

Notes.—1 Words in sub-s (3) added by the Land Registration (Scotland) Act 1979 (c 33), s 29(1), Sch 2, para 4.

2 Words in sub-s (5) substituted by the Redemption of Standard Securities (Scotland) Act 1971 (c 45), s 1(f).

3 Words in sub-s (5) added by the Land Registration (Scotland) Act 1979, s 29(1), Sch 2, para 4.

4 Words in sub-s (6) substituted by the Redemption of Standard Securities (Scotland) Act 1971, s 1(f).

29. Procedure

(1) The court for the purposes of this Part of this Act, and for the operation of section 11 of the Heritable Securities (Scotland) Act 1894 (application by *pari passu* creditor to sell), in relation to a standard security, shall be the sheriff having jurisdiction over any part of the security subjects, and the sheriff shall be deemed to have such jurisdiction whatever the value of the subjects. [80]

(2) Any application, or counter-application to the court under this Part of this Act shall be by way of summary application. [81]

(3) An interlocutor of the sheriff disposing of any cause under this Part of this Act shall be final, except as to question of title. [82]

30. Interpretation of Part II

(1) In this Part of this Act, unless the context otherwise requires, the following expressions have the meanings hereby respectively assigned to them, that is to say—

'creditor' and 'debtor' shall include any successor in title, assignee or representative of a creditor or debtor;

'debt' and 'creditor' and 'debtor', in relation to a standard security, have the meanings assigned to them by section 9(8) of this Act;

'duly recorded' means recorded in the appropriate division of the General Register of Sasines;

'exposure to sale' means exposure to sale by public roup, and exposed or re-exposed to sale shall be construed accordingly;

'heritable security' has the meaning assigned to it by the said section 9(8);

'interest in land' has the meaning assigned to it by the said section 9(8);

'Register of Sasines' means the appropriate division of the General Register of Sasines;

'the standard conditions' are the conditions (whether varied or not) referred to in section 11(2) of this Act;

'whole amount due' has the meaning assigned to it by section 18(4) of this Act. [83]

(2) For the purpose of construing this Part of this Act in relation to the creation of a security over a registered lease and to any subsequent transactions connected with that security, the following expressions shall have the meanings hereby respectively assigned to them, that is to say—

'conveyance' or 'disposition' means assignation;

'convey' or 'dispone' means assign;

'infeft' means having a recorded title;

'proprietor' means lessee;

'security subjects' means a registered lease subject to a security.   [84]

31. Saving

Nothing in the provisions of this Part of this Act shall affect the validity of any heritable security within the meaning of this Part which has been duly recorded before the commencement of this Act, and any such security may be dealt with, and shall be as capable of being enforced, as if this Part had not been passed.   [85]

32. Application of enactments

The provisions of any enactment relating to a bond and disposition or assignation in security shall apply to a standard security, except in so far as such provisions are inconsistent with the provisions of this Part of this Act, but, without prejudice to the generality of that exception, the enactments specified in Schedule 8 to this Act shall not so apply.   [86]

Sections 9 and 10   SCHEDULE 2

FORMS OF STANDARD SECURITY

FORM A

[To be used where the personal obligation is included in the deed]

I, A.B. (*designation*), hereby undertake to pay to C.D. (*designation*), the sum of £   (*or* a maximum sum of £   ) (*or* all sums due and that may become due by me to the said C.D. in respect of   (*here specify the matter for which the undertaking is granted*)) with interest from   (*or* from the respective times of advance) at   per centum per annum (*or otherwise as the case may be*) (annually, half-yearly, *or otherwise as the case may be*) on   in each year commencing on   ; For which I grant a standard security in favour of the said C.D. over ALL and WHOLE (*here describe the security subjects as indicated in Note 1 hereto*): The standard conditions specified in Schedule 3 to the Conveyancing and Feudal Reform (Scotland) Act 1970, and any lawful variation thereof operative for the time being, shall apply: And I grant warrandice: And I consent to registration for execution.

[To be attested]   [87]

FORM B

[To be used where the personal obligation is constituted in a separate instrument or instruments]

I, A.B. (*designation*) hereby in security of (*here specify the nature of the debt or obligation in respect of which the security is given and the instrument(s) by which it is constituted in such manner as will identify these instruments*) grant a standard security in favour of C.D. (*designation*) over ALL and WHOLE (*here describe the security subjects as indicated in Note 1 hereto*): The standard conditions specified in Schedule 3 to the Conveyancing and Feudal Reform (Scotland) Act 1970,

and any lawful variation thereof operative for the time being, shall apply: And
I grant warrandice.

[To be attested]

[88]

NOTES TO SCHEDULE 2

[1]*Note 1.*—The security subjects shall be described by means of a particular
description or by reference to a description thereof as in Schedule D to the
Conveyancing (Scotland) Act 1924 or as in Schedule G to the Titles to Land
Consolidation (Scotland) Act 1868. Where the security subjects consist of an
interest in land, other than ownership of the land, amend the description
appropriately, *eg a ground annual of £   constituted by a contract of
ground annual* (or other deed by which the ground annual was constituted)
(giving the names of the parties thereto or of the grantor and grantee), *recorded
in the Register for   on   payable out of
the subjects therein described lying in the county of
(for   in   the   burgh   of   and   county   of
                    ),* adding if necessary, *but only to the extent of
                    ;* or *a lease* (*or tack*) (giving the names of the parties
thereto) *of   the   subjects   therein   described   lying   in   the   county   of
                              (or in the burgh of
and county of   ) recorded in the Register for
                    on   adding if necessary, but only to
the extent of*

[89]

Note.—1 Note 1 of Sch 2 excluded by the Land Registration (Scotland) Act
1979 (c 33), s 15(1).

---

[1]*Note 2.*—Where the grantor has not a recorded title to the security subjects,
insert after the description thereof a clause of deduction of title as follows:—
Which subjects (*or ground annual* or *lease* (*or tack*) or, as the case may be) *were
last vested* (*or are part of the subjects last vested*) in E.F. *whose title thereto was
recorded in the Register for   (or the said Register of Sasines)*
on   (or, if the last infeftment has already been mentioned, say *in the said E.F. as aforesaid), and from whom I acquired right by* (here
specify shortly the writ or writs by which that right was so acquired).   [90]

Note.—1 Note 2 of Sch 2 excluded by the Land Registration (Scotland) Act
1979 (c 33), s 15(3).

Note 3.—Where the grantor of a standard security has granted a conveyance *ex
facie* absolute of the security subjects, or any part thereof, that conveyance
shall be referred to in accordance with Note 5 to this Schedule. In any such
case:—(a) where the grantor has been infeft in the security subjects, no clause
of deduction of title is required in the standard security, [1](b) where the grantor
has not previously been infeft in the security subjects but has right thereto by
virtue of an unrecorded title insert in the standard security after the descrip-

tion of the security subjects a clause of deduction of title as follows.—*Which subjects* (or *ground annual* or *lease* (or *tack*) or, as the case may be) *were formerly vested in* (or *are part of the subjects formerly vested in*) (give name of person last infeft in the subjects before the grantor acquired right thereto) *whose title thereto was recorded in the Register for* (or *the said Register of Sasines*) on (or if such infeftment has already been mentioned say *in the said* as *aforesaid*) *and from whom I acquired right by* (here specify shortly the writ or writs by which that right was so acquired). [91]

Note.—1 Note 3(b) of Sch 2 excluded by the Land Registration (Scotland) Act 1979 (c 33), s 15(3).

Note 4.—Where it is desired to vary any of the standard conditions contained in Schedule 3 to this Act, such variations shall be effected either by an instrument or instruments other than the standard security, and any such instrument shall not require to be recorded in the Register of Sasines or by inserting in the standard security after the description of the security subjects (and after the clause of deduction of title, if any) *And I agree that the standard conditions shall be varied to the effect that* (here insert particulars of the variations desired).

(As regards future variations, see section 16 of, and Form E and Notes 5 and 6 in Schedule 4 to this Act.) [92]

Note 5.—Where the security subjects are burdened by any other standard security or heritable security, or by any security by way of *ex facie* absolute conveyance which ranks prior to the standard security which is being granted, insert immediately before the clause of warrandice the following:—*But the security hereby granted is subject to* (here specify any deed by which such preferable rights were created and any deed modifying or altering such rights), and amend the clause of warrandice to read *And, subject as aforesaid, I grant warrandice.* Where the standard security is to rank prior or postponed to, *pari passu* with, any other existing heritable security or any other standard security, a ranking clause may be inserted in appropriate terms immediately prior to the warrandice clause, and the warrandice clause shall, where necessary, be qualified accordingly. [93]

Note 6.—Where a standard security is granted in Form A for a fluctuating or uncertain amount, provisions for ascertaining the amount due at any time may be inserted immediately prior to the clause of granting of the security, and the registration clause shall, where necessary, be amended accordingly. [94]

Note 7.—In the case of a standard security for a non-monetary obligation, the forms in this Schedule shall be adapted as appropriate. [95]

Section 11 SCHEDULE 3

THE STANDARD CONDITIONS

1. Maintenance and repair

It shall be an obligation on the debtor—

(a) to maintain the security subjects in good and sufficient repair to the reasonable satisfaction of the creditor;

(b) to permit, after seven clear days' notice in writing, the creditor or his agent to enter upon the security subjects at all reasonable times to examine the condition thereof;

(c) to make all necessary repairs and make good all defects in pursuance of his obligation under head (a) of this condition within such reasonable period as the creditor may require by notice in writing. [96]

2. *Completion of buildings, etc and prohibition of alterations, etc*

It shall be an obligation on the debtor—

(a) to complete, as soon as may be practicable, any unfinished buildings and works forming part of the security subjects to the reasonable satisfaction of the creditor;

(b) not to demolish, alter or add to any buildings or works forming part of the security subjects, except in accordance with the terms of a prior written consent of the creditor and in compliance with any consent, licence or approval required by law;

(c) to exhibit to the creditor at his request evidence of that consent, licence or approval. [97]

3. *Observance of conditions in title, payment of duties, charges, etc, and general compliance with requirements of law relating to security subjects*

It shall be an obligation on the debtor—

(a) to observe any condition or perform any obligation in respect of the security subjects lawfully binding on him in relation to the security subjects;

(b) to make due and punctual payment of any ground burden, teind, stipend, or standard charge, and any rates, taxes and other public burdens, and any other payments exigible in respect of the security subjects;

(c) to comply with any requirements imposed upon him in relation to the security subjects by virtue of any enactment. [98]

4. *Planning notices, etc*

It shall be an obligation on the debtor—

(a) where he has received any notice or order, issued or made by virtue of the Town and Country Planning (Scotland) Acts 1947 to 1969 or any amendment thereof, or any proposal so made for the making or issuing of any such notice or order, or any other notice or document affecting or likely to affect the security subjects, to give to the creditor, within fourteen days of the receipt of that notice, order or proposal, full particulars thereof;

(b) to take, as soon as practicable, all reasonable or necessary steps to comply with such a notice or order or, as the case may be, duly to object thereto;

(c) in the event of the creditor so requiring, to object or to join with the creditor in objecting to any such notice or order or in making representations against any proposal therefor. [99]

5. Insurance

It shall be an obligation on the debtor—

(a) to insure the security subjects or, at the option of the creditor, to permit the creditor to insure the security subjects in the names of the creditor and the debtor to the extent of the market value thereof against the risk of fire and such other risks as the creditor may reasonably require;

(b) to deposit any policy of insurance effected by the debtor for the aforesaid purpose with the creditor;

(c) to pay any premium due in respect of any such policy and, where the creditor so requests, to exhibit a receipt therefor not later than the fourteenth day after the renewal date of the policy;

(d) to intimate to the creditor, within fourteen days of the occurrence, any occurrrence which may give rise to a claim under the policy and to authorise the creditor to negotiate the settlement of the claim;

(e) without prejudice to any obligation to the contrary enforceable against him, to comply with any reasonable requirement of the creditor as to the application of any sum received in respect of such a claim;

(f) to refrain from any act or omission which would invalidate the policy.

[100]

6. Restriction on letting

It shall be an obligation on the debtor not to let, or agree to let, the security subjects, or any part thereof, without the prior consent in writing of the creditor, and 'to let' in this condition includes to sub-let. [101]

7. General power of creditor to perform obligations, etc, on failure of debtor and power to charge debtor

(1) The creditor shall be entitled to perform any obligation imposed by the standard conditions on the debtor, which the debtor has failed to perform.

(2) Where it is necessary for the performance of any obligation as aforesaid, the creditor may, after giving seven clear days' notice in writing to the debtor, enter upon the security subjects at all reasonable times.

(3) All expenses and charges (including any interest thereon), reasonably incurred by the creditor in the exercise of a right conferred by this condition, shall be recoverable from the debtor and shall be deemed to be secured by the security subjects under the standard security, and the rate of any such interest shall be the rate in force at the relevant time in respect of advances secured by the security, or, where no such rate is prescribed, shall be the bank rate in force at the relevant time. [102]

8. Calling-up

The creditor shall be entitled, subject to the terms of the security and to any requirement of law, to call-up a standard security in the manner prescribed by section 19 of this Act. [103]

9. *Default*

(1) The debtor shall be held to be in default in any of the following circumstances, that is to say—

- (a) where a calling-up notice in respect of the security has been served and has not been complied with;
- (b) where there has been a failure to comply with any other requirement arising out of the security;
- (c) where the proprietor of the security subjects has become insolvent.

[1](2) For the purposes of this condition, the proprietor shall be taken to be insolvent if—

- (a) he has become notour bankrupt, or he has executed a trust deed for behoof of, or has made a composition contract or arrangement with, his creditors;
- (b) he has died and a judicial factor has been appointed under section [11A of the Judicial Factors (Scotland) Act 1889[2]] to divide his insolvent estate among his creditors, [3or his estate falls to be administered in accordance with an order under section 421 of the Insolvency Act 1986];
- (c) where the proprietor is a company, a winding-up order has been made with respect to it, or a resolution for voluntary winding-up (other than a members' voluntary winding-up) has been passed with respect to it, or a receiver or manager of its undertaking has been duly appointed, or possession has been taken, by or on behalf of the holders of any debentures secured by a floating charge, of any property of the company comprised in or subject to the charge. [104]

Notes.—1 Standard condition 9(2) applied by the Sex Discrimination Act 1975 (c 65), s 53(4), Sch 3, para 3(5)(b); the Race Relations Act 1976 (c 74), s 43(4), Sch 1, para 3(5)(b); and the National Heritage Act 1980 (c 17), s 1(4), Sch 1, para 3(4)(b).

2 Words in sub-para (2)(b) substituted by the Bankruptcy (Scotland) Act 1985 (c 66), s 75(1), Sch 7, para 8.

3 Words in sub-para (2)(b) substituted by the Insolvency Act 1985 (c 65), s 235, Sch 8, para 18, and the Insolvency Act 1986 (c 45), s 439(2), Sch 14.

---

10. *Rights of creditor on default*

(1) Where the debtor is in default, the creditor may, without prejudice to his exercising any other remedy arising from the contract to which the standard security relates, exercise, in accordance with the provisions of Part II of this Act and of any other enactment applying to standard securities, such of the remedies specified in the following sub-paragraphs of this standard condition as he may consider appropriate.

(2) He may proceed to sell the security subjects or any part thereof.

(3) He may enter into possession of the security subjects and may receive or recover feu-duties, ground annuals or, as the case may be, the rents of those subjects or any part thereof.

(4) Where he has entered into possession as aforesaid, he may let the security subjects or any part thereof.

(5) Where he has entered into possession as aforesaid there shall be transferred to him all the rights of the debtor in relation to the granting of leases or rights of occupancy over the security subjects and to the management and maintenance of those subjects.

(6) He may effect all such repairs and may make good such defects as are necessary to maintain the security subjects in good and sufficient repair, and may effect such reconstruction, alteration and improvement in the subjects as would be expected of a prudent proprietor to maintain the market value of the subjects, and for the aforesaid purposes may enter on the subjects at all reasonable times.

(7) He may apply to the court for a decree of foreclosure.   [105]

11. *Exercise of right of redemption*

(1) The debtor shall be entitled to exercise his [¹right (if any) to redeem the security on giving notice] of his intention so to do, being a notice in writing (hereinafter referred to as a 'notice of redemption').

(2) Nothing in the provisions of [¹this Act] shall preclude a creditor from waiving the necessity for a notice of redemption, or from agreeing to a period of notice of less than [¹that to which he is entitled].

(3)(a) A notice of redemption may be delivered to the creditor or sent by registered post or recorded delivery to him at his last known address, and an acknowledgment signed by the creditor or his agent or a certificate of postage by the person giving the notice accompanied by the postal receipt shall be sufficient evidence of such notice having been given.

(b) If the address of the creditor is not known, or if the packet containing the notice of redemption is returned to the sender with intimation that it could not be delivered, a notice of redemption may be sent to the Extractor of the Court of Session and an acknowledgment of receipt by him shall be sufficient evidence of such notice having been given.

(c) A notice of redemption sent by post shall be held to have been given on the day next after the day of posting.

(4) When a notice of redemption states that a specified amount will be repaid, and it is subsequently ascertained that the whole amount due to be repaid is more or less than the amount specified in the notice, the notice shall nevertheless be effective as a notice of repayment of the amount due as subsequently ascertained.

(5) [¹Where the debtor has exercised a right to redeem, and has made payment] of the whole amount due, or [¹has performed] the whole obligations of the debtor under the contract to which the security relates, the creditor shall grant a discharge in the terms prescribed in section 17 of this Act.   [106]

Note.—1 Words in sub-paras (1), (2) and (5) substituted by the Redemption of Standard Securities (Scotland) Act 1971 (c 45), s 1(g).

12. The debtor shall be personally liable to the creditor for the whole expenses of the preparation and execution of the standard security and any variation, restriction and discharge thereof and, where any of those deeds are recorded, the recording thereof, and all expenses reasonably incurred by the creditor in calling-up the security and realising or attempting to realise the security subjects, or any part thereof, and exercising any other powers conferred upon him by the security. [107]

Interpretation

In this Schedule, where the debtor is not the proprietor of the security subjects, 'debtor' means 'proprietor', except
(a) in standard conditions 9(1), 10(1) and 12, and
(b) in standard condition 11, where 'debtor' includes the proprietor.
[107A]

Sections 14, 15, 16 and 17   SCHEDULE 4

FORMS OF DEEDS OF ASSIGNATION, RESTRICTION, AND OTHERS

FORM A

ASSIGNATION OF STANDARD SECURITY

Separate

I, A.B. (*designation*), in consideration of £   hereby assign to C.D. (*designation*) a standard security for £   (*or* a maximum sum of £   , to the extent of £   being the amount now due thereunder; *in other cases describe as indicated in Note 2 to this Schedule*) by E.F. in my favour (*or* in favour of G.H.) recorded in the register for   on   (*adding if necessary*, but only to the extent of £   of principal); With interest from
[To be attested]   [108]

FORM B

[To be endorsed on the standard security]

As above save that instead of the words 'a standard security for £   ' (or otherwise, as the case may be) insert 'the foregoing standard security'. *Where the security is for a fluctuating amount whether subject to a maximum or not, add* 'to the extent of £   being the amount now due thereunder.'   [109]

FORM C

RESTRICTION OF STANDARD SECURITY

I, A.B. (*designation*), in consideration of (*specify consideration, if any*) hereby disburden of a standard security for £   (*or* a maximum sum of £   ; *in other cases, describe as indicated in Note 2 to this Schedule*) by C.D. in my favour (*or* in favour of E.F.) recorded in the Register for

on   (*adding if necessary*, but only
to the extent of £   of principal) ALL and WHOLE (*describe the subjects
disburdened in the same way as directed in Note 1 to Schedule 2 to this Act in the
case of a description of security subjects*).

[To be attested]   [110]

FORM D

COMBINED PARTIAL DISCHARGE AND DEED OF RESTRICTION OF STANDARD SECURITY

I, A.B. (*designation*) in consideration of £   paid by C.D. (*designation*) (*or, as the case may be*), hereby discharge a standard security for
£   (*or a maximum sum of £   ; in other cases, describe as
indicated in Note 2 to this Schedule*) by the said C.D. (*or by E.F.*) in my favour
(*or in favour of G.H.*) recorded in the Register for   on
                             but only to the extent of £   of principal; And
I disburden of the said standard security (*adding if necessary*, but only to the
extent of £   of principal) ALL and WHOLE (*describe the subjects
disburdened in the same way as directed in Note 1 to Schedule 2 to this Act in the
case of a description of security subjects*).

[To be attested]   [111]

FORM E

VARIATION OF STANDARD SECURITY

[To be endorsed on the standard security]

I, A.B. (*designation*), agree that the foregoing standard security granted by me
(*or by C.D.*) in favour of E.F. recorded in the Register for
                             on   (*if there have been previous
variations insert* 'as varied') shall with effect from   be
varied so that (*here insert particulars of the variation agreed*); And I, E.F.
(*designation*) (*or if the creditor is not the person in whose favour the standard security
was granted say* G.H. (*designation*) the creditor now in right of the said
standard security) consent to the variation hereby effected.

[To be attested]   [112]

FORM F

DISCHARGE OF STANDARD SECURITY

Separate

I, A.B. (*designation*), in consideration of £   (*where the security is in
respect of a maximum sum or of all sums due or to become due or is in respect of a
personal obligation constituted in an instrument or instruments other than the
standard security add* being the whole amount secured by the standard security
aftermentioned) paid by C.D. (*designation*) (or, *as the case may be*) hereby
discharge a standard security for £   (or a maximum sum of
£   *in other cases describe as indicated in Note 2 to this Schedule*) by the

said C.D. (or by E.F.) in my favour (*or* in favour of G.H.) recorded in the
Register for   on   (*adding if necessary*, but only to the extent of £   of principal).

[To be attested]

[To be endorsed on the standard security]

As above save that instead of the words 'a standard security for £   (*or a*
maximum sum of £   *in other cases describe as indicated in Note 2 to
this Schedule*)' *insert* 'the foregoing standard security'.   [113]

NOTES TO SCHEDULE 4

General

Note 1.—Where the grantor of an assignation, discharge or deed of restriction
of a standard security, or the creditor consenting to a variation of a standard
security, is not the original creditor and has not a recorded title, insert at the
end of the deed a clause of deduction of title as follows: *Which standard security*
(adding, if necessary, *to the extent aforesaid* or, as the case may be) *was last
vested in the said* (give name of original creditor) *as aforesaid* (or where the last
recorded title to the standard security was in favour of a person other than the
original creditor say *in J.K. whose title thereto was recorded in the said Register of
Sasines on*   ) *and from whom I acquired right by* (here
specify shortly the writ or writs by which right was so acquired).

Where the grantor of an assignation, discharge or deed of restriction of a
standard security, or the creditor consenting to a variation of a standard
security, although not the original creditor, has a recorded title, no specification of the title of the grantor or creditor is required.   [114]

Note 2.—In an assignation, discharge or deed of restriction, (1) a standard
security in respect of an uncertain amount may be described by specifying
shortly the nature of the debt or obligation (eg, all sums due or to become due)
for which the security was granted, adding in the case of an assignation, *to the
extent of £   being the amount now due thereunder* and (2) a standard
security in respect of a personal obligation constituted in an instrument or
instruments other than the standard security itself may be described by
specifying shortly the nature of the debt or obligation and referring to the
other instrument or instruments by which it is constituted in such manner as
will be sufficient identification thereof.   [115]

Note 3.—If the original infeftment upon a standard security has been taken
otherwise than by recording the security in the Register of Sasines, insert
immediately after the word 'recorded' the words *along with notice of title
thereon* (adding, if such notice is not in favour of the original creditor, the name
of the person in whose favour it is drawn).   [116]

Note 4.—If part of the security subjects has already been disburdened, there
may be inserted in an assignation, after the specification of the standard

security assigned, a reference to the previous partial discharge or deed of restriction. [117]

Note 5.—The variation docket Form E of this Schedule shall be used only when the personal obligation or other matter to which the variation relates was contained in the standard security, or in a variation thereof which has been duly recorded. Variations in a personal obligation or other matter constituted in an instrument or instruments which have not been so recorded may be altered by an instrument in appropriate terms which shall not be required to be recorded in the Register of Sasines. [118]

Note 6.—Where the grantor of a variation docket does not have a recorded title to the security subjects, insert at the end of the variation and immediately before the consent by the creditor a clause of deduction of title as follows: *the security subjects to which the said standard security relates being last vested in* (give the name of the person in whom the security subjects were last vested) *whose title thereto was recorded in the said Register of Sasines on*
and from whom I acquired right by (here specify the writ or writs by which such right was so acquired). [119]

Section 18   SCHEDULE 5

PROCEDURES AS TO REDEMPTION

FORM A

NOTICE OF REDEMPTION OF STANDARD SECURITY

To A.B. (*address*)
TAKE NOTICE that on   (*state date of repayment*) C.D. (*designation*), will repay the sum of £   (*or* the whole amount due) secured by a standard security by the said C.D. (*or* by E.F.) in your favour (*or* in favour of G.H.) recorded in the Register for   on
. Dated this   day of
(*To be signed by the debtor, or proprietor, or by his agent, who will add his designation and the words* Agent of the said C.D.)
In the case of a standard security for a non-monetary obligation this Form shall be adapted accordingly. [120]

FORM B

I, A.B., above named, hereby acknowledge receipt of the Notice of Redemption of which the foregoing is a copy. Dated this   · day of
(*To be signed by the creditor, or by his agent, who will add his designation and the words* Agent of the said A.B.) [121]

FORM C

Notice of Redemption, of which the foregoing is a copy, was posted (*or*

otherwise, as the case may be) to A.B. above named on the
                              day of

*(To be signed by the debtor, or proprietor, or by his agent, who will add his
designation and the words* Agent of the said C.D. *and if posted the postal
                              receipt to be attached.)*   [122]

FORM D

No. 1

CERTIFICATE OF CONSIGNATION ON REDEMPTION OF STANDARD SECURITY WHERE DISCHARGE CANNOT BE OBTAINED

I, A.B. (*designation*) (solicitor) certify that consignation of the whole amount
due under the standard security aftermentioned was made as after stated and
was necessitated by reason of a discharge being unobtainable after due notice
of redemption had been given.
STANDARD SECURITY for £   (*or a maximum of £   ;
in other cases describe as indicated in Note 2 to Schedule 4 to this Act*) by C.D. in
favour of E.F. recorded in the Register of Sasines for   on
AMOUNT CONSIGNED £   , being £   of principal,
£   of interest and £   in respect of ascertained expenses.
BANK IN WHICH CONSIGNED (*specify bank or branch of bank, with
address, in which above amount consigned*) conform to deposit receipt dated
              in name of the person appearing to have the best right
thereto (*specifying his name and designation if known*) (*or if he is only a partial
creditor say* to the extent of £   ).
                              [To be attested]   [123]

No. 2

CERTIFICATE OF DECLARATOR OF PERFORMANCE OF DEBTOR'S OBLIGATIONS UNDER STANDARD SECURITY WHERE DISCHARGE CANNOT BE OBTAINED

I, A.B. (*designation*) (solicitor) certify that a decree of declarator of performance of the obligations of the debtor under the standard security aftermentioned was pronounced as after stated and was necessitated by reason of a
discharge being unobtainable after due notice of redemption had been given.
STANDARD SECURITY by C.D. in favour of E.F. recorded in the Register
for   on
DECREE OF DECLARATOR by the Sheriff of   at
              in the application of the said C.D. (*or J.K. (desig-
nation*), who is now the debtor (*or the proprietor of the interest in land
contained*) in the said standard security).
                              [To be attested]   [124]

Sections 19 and 21   SCHEDULE 6

PROCEDURES AS TO CALLING-UP AND DEFAULT

FORM A

NOTICE OF CALLING-UP OF STANDARD SECURITY

To A.B. (*address*)

TAKE NOTICE that C.D. (*designation*) requires payment of the principal sum of £   with interest thereon at the rate of   per centum per annum from the   day of
(*adding if necessary*, subject to such adjustment of the principal sum and the amount of interest as may subsequently be determined) secured by a standard security by you (*or* by E.F.) in favour of the said C.D. (*or* of G.H. to which the said C.D. has now right) recorded in the Register for
on   ; And that failing full payment of the said sum and interest thereon (*adding if necessary*, subject to any adjustment as aforesaid), and expenses within two months after the date of service of this demand, the subjects of the security may be sold.

Dated this   day of
(*To be signed by the creditor, or by his agent, who will add his designation and the words* Agent of the said C.D.)

In the case of a standard security for a non-monetary obligation this Form shall be adapted accordingly.   [125]

FORM B

NOTICE OF DEFAULT UNDER STANDARD SECURITY

To A.B. (*address*)

TAKE NOTICE that C.D. (*designation*), the creditor in a standard security by you (*or* by E.F.) in favour of the said C.D. (*or* of G.H. to which the said C.D. has now right) recorded in the Register for   on
                    requires fulfilment of the obligation(s) specified in the Schedule hereto in respect of which there is default; And that failing such fulfilment within one month after the date of service of this notice, the powers competent to the said C.D. on default may be exercised.

Dated this   day of
(*To be signed by the creditor, or by his agent, who will add his designation and the words* Agent of the said C.D.)

Schedule of Obligation(s) in respect of which there is default.

To (*specify in detail the obligation(s) in respect of which there is default*).   [126]

FORM C

I, A.B., above named, hereby acknowledge receipt of the foregoing Notice of (Calling-up), (Default) of which the foregoing is a copy of the notice *adding where appropriate* 'and I agree to the period of notice being dispensed with (*or* shortened to   ).'

Dated this   day of

(To be signed by the person on whom notice is served, or by his agent, who will add his designation and the words Agent of the said A.B.) [127]

FORM D

Notice of (Calling-up) (Default), of which the foregoing is a copy, was posted (*or otherwise, as the case may be*) to A.B. above named on the day of
(To be signed by the creditor, or by his agent, who will add his designation and the words Agent of the said C.D. *and if posted the postal receipt to be attached.)* [128]

Sections 22 and 24   SCHEDULE 7

CONTENTS OF CERTIFICATE STATING A DEFAULT

1.   A certificate which is lodged in court by the creditor for the purposes of section 22 or 24 of this Act shall contain the information required by the following provisions of this Schedule.
2.   A certificate shall state—
    (i) the name and address of the creditor and shall specify the standard security in respect of which the default is alleged to have occurred by reference to the original creditor and debtor therein and to the particulars of its registration;
    (ii) the nature of the default with full details thereof.
3.   The certificate shall be signed by the creditor or his solicitor, and a certificate which does not comply with the foregoing requirements of this Schedule shall not be received in evidence for the purposes of the said section 22 or 24. [129]

Index

References are to paragraph numbers; numbers in square brackets refer to material in the Appendix.